New Perspectives on the Right

Series editor
Richard Hayton

The study of conservative politics, broadly defined, is of enduring scholarly interest and importance, and is also of great significance beyond the academy. In spite of this, for a variety of reasons the study of conservatism and conservative politics was traditionally regarded as something of a poor relation in comparison to the intellectual interest in 'the Left'. In the British context this changed with the emergence of Thatcherism, which prompted a greater critical focus on the Conservative Party and its ideology, and a revitalisation of Conservative historiography. *New Perspectives on the Right* aims to build on this legacy by establishing a series identity for work in this field. It will publish the best and most innovative titles drawn from the fields of sociology, history, cultural studies and political science and hopes to stimulate debate and interest across disciplinary boundaries. *New Perspectives* is not limited in its historical coverage or geographical scope, but is united by its concern to critically interrogate and better understand the history, development, intellectual basis and impact of the Right. Nor is the series restricted by its methodological approach: it will encourage original research from a plurality of perspectives. Consequently, the series will act as a voice and forum for work by scholars engaging with the politics of the right in new and imaginative ways.

Reconstructing conservatism?

MANCHESTER
1824

Manchester University Press

Reconstructing conservatism?

The Conservative Party
in opposition, 1997–2010

Richard Hayton

Manchester University Press

Published by Manchester University Press
Altrincham Street, Manchester M1 7JA, UK
www.manchesteruniversitypress.co.uk

British Library Cataloguing-in-Publication Data is available

Library of Congress Cataloging-in-Publication Data is available

ISBN 978 1 7849 9389 4 *paperback*

First published by Manchester University Press in hardback 2012

This edition first published 2016

The publisher has no responsibility for the persistence or accuracy of URLs for any external or third-party internet websites referred to in this book, and does not guarantee that any content on such websites is, or will remain, accurate or appropriate.

Printed by Lightning Source

Contents

List of tables and figures

Acknowledgements

The origins of this book lie in doctoral research I undertook in the Department of Politics at the University of Sheffield between 2004 and 2008. This would not have been possible without the generous award of a University Studentship, for which I am most grateful. I also owe a debt of gratitude to friends and colleagues in the department who made it such a supportive place to pursue postgraduate study. In particular I would like to thank Andrew Taylor, Andrew Gamble and Mike Kenny for their wise counsel and intellectual guidance over a number of years. Others who commented on parts or all of the manuscript, or endured more conversations about its contents than they deserved, include Adam White, Bona Muzaka, Colin Hay, Matt Bishop, Sean Carey and Tim Heppell. At Manchester University Press I would like to thank my Commissioning Editor Tony Mason and the anonymous reviewers for their helpful input. My thanks are also due to the interviewees who generously gave their time and shared with me their thoughts on the state of the Conservative politics, both on and off the record. I know that my family will be delighted to hear that this book is finally finished, and I am thankful for all their support over many years. Finally, an enormous thank you to Louise, not only for her critical eye over much of this work, but most importantly for all her love, and for being the linchpin of our team.

Richard Hayton
Sheffield, May 2011

Abbreviations

CSR	'Common Sense Revolution'
ECPG	Economic Competitiveness Policy Group
EEC	European Economic Community
EMU	Economic and Monetary Union
EPP	European People's Party
ERM	Exchange Rate Mechanism
EU	European Union
EvfEl	English votes for English laws
GDP	gross domestic product
IMF	International Monetary Fund
MEP	Member of the European Parliament
MP	Member of Parliament
NHS	National Health Service
OBR	Office for Budget Responsibility
OMOV	'one member, one vote'
ONS	Office for National Statistics
PCP	Parliamentary Conservative Party
PFI	private finance initiative
QMV	qualified majority voting
SEA	Single European Act
SRA	strategic–relational approach
TRC	Tax Reform Commission
UKIP	United Kingdom Independence Party
VAT	value added tax

Part I

Theory and context

1

Introduction: the Conservative Party and electoral failure

Introduction

The arrival of David Cameron in Downing Street in May 2010 marked a critical moment in Conservative Party politics. Although under his leadership the Conservatives had failed to secure an overall Commons majority, Cameron had successfully brought to an end the longest period of opposition in his party's history since the infamous 1922 Carlton Club meeting. For all political parties, power is of vital importance; as the events of 1922 demonstrated it is the Conservative Party's *raison d'être*. Consequently by succeeding where William Hague, Iain Duncan Smith and Michael Howard failed, in developing an effective opposition strategy and entering Number 10, David Cameron had fulfilled the most elemental criteria against which the party judges its leaders: he was a winner.

This book is concerned with the actions, perceptions and strategies of the Conservative Party elite leadership in opposition, between 1997 and 2010. At the heart of this research lies a simply stated question. Why did it take the Conservative Party so long to recover power? After landslide defeat in 1997, why was it so slow to adapt, reposition itself and rebuild its support? This becomes all the more puzzling when the adaptive record of the party is considered. It is the most successful electoral organisation in democratic European history, having governed (either independently or in coalition) for 91 of the 111 years of the 'long Conservative century' between 1886 and 1997 (Seldon and Snowdon, 2001: 27). Such was its dominance the party became known, and regarded itself, as 'the natural party of government'. Yet, having suffered a crushing defeat in 1997, the Conservatives made little discernible progress in 2001 (and on some measures retreated further) and managed only a marginal advance in 2005. After three leaders and eight years of opposition, the Conservatives still returned fewer MPs than Labour at their nadir in 1983. Further to this, 1997–2010 is particularly unusual when compared to the other lengthy spells of opposition the party endured in the twentieth century. After the 1906 Liberal landslide the Conservatives were out of office for nearly a decade, but had recovered sufficiently to restore parity with the Liberals in the two general elections of 1910 (Coetzee, 2005: 103–6). Similarly after Labour's landslide victory in 1945, the Conservatives recovered to cut the government majority to just five in 1950, and returned to office in 1951.

The 1997 defeat followed eighteen years of Conservative government – an unprecedented period of electoral success built on Thatcherite statecraft. This book argues that an appreciation of the ideological legacy of Thatcherism is important for understanding the party in the years of opposition that followed: paradoxically, this legacy is an important part of the explanation of the failure of Conservative statecraft that ensued. As such, this book argues that ideology played a central role in framing and shaping the strategic debates that took place in the party in the 1997–2010 period, and that we therefore need to take sufficient account of this in our analysis. This chapter develops this argument through an overview of previous work on Conservative politics, suggesting that the historical literature underplayed the role of ideology, whilst Marxist-inspired political analysis structurally favoured it, risking the exclusion of agency from our understanding of events. By bringing these two traditions together we can offer a more refined account which avoids privileging structure or agency in our explanations. The book argues that this is important, as context can both enable and constrain political action, so to better understand the process of political change we need to focus on the dialectical relationship between actors and their environment.

An important part of the explanation of Conservative electoral failure in this period was the revitalisation of the Labour Party under Tony Blair's leadership. By repositioning his party and changing its image Blair redrew the political map, leaving it barely recognisable compared to that of the 1980s. As one of the key architects of New Labour argued, 'without Labour as a demonic enemy, conservatism lacks bearing and purpose' (Gould, 1999: xii). However, whilst these external factors were undoubtedly important, they are not the focus of this book, which is concerned primarily with the internal dynamics of Conservative politics during this time.

The choice of research emphasis therefore inevitably influences the explanation that results from it. Research into internal party organisation and dynamics will point to the effect these have on party performance. Studies of New Labour will consider how it impacted upon the political landscape. This is unsurprising (it would be odd if it were not the case), but is worth highlighting. Nor need this be problematic, as long as it is clear where the focus of each particular study lies, and if we recognise that each necessarily represents a partial and to some extent value-laden interpretation. No explanation can hope to account for every possible variable to the exact degree. Indeed, the value of different research projects is often situated in the particular angle or emphasis that they take.

The focus of this book is the leadership of the Conservative Party between 1997 and 2010, and how the key strategic actors (namely the successive leaders of the party and other senior politicians) understood, and sought to address, the party's electoral failure. Through documentary analysis and elite interviews, it looks to expose competing interpretations of this problem, and explain how these were translated into party strategy. As previously noted, a key premise of this research is that the legacy of Thatcherite conservatism constituted an important aspect of this process. By exploring several notable sites of ideological dispute for Conservatives (Europe, national identity, moral issues and economic policy) the book seeks to uncover how party leaders were both ideologically influenced, and how they sought to manage competing ideological pressures. As such, this research is concerned in large part with internal party dynamics: it considers how party strategy was devised and implemented, and whether (and why) sub-optimal electoral strategies were pursued. External, contextual factors – most obviously the electorate – are of course important, but the focus is not on these independently, but on how the key strategic actors interpreted and understood them, and sought to orientate strategy towards them.

This approach locates the research within a body of academic work which has documented the history and strategy of the Conservative Party. However, as this chapter explains, this existing literature struggles to provide a satisfying answer to the puzzle of how such a successful electoral organisation, feted for its adaptive capacity, apparently lost its traditional strengths. In part, this is because there is not much of it. With the exception of the various sustained analyses of Thatcherism (perhaps in a reflection of the ideological leanings that preponderate in the academy) academic attention has historically tended towards Labour rather than the Conservatives. This propensity was understandably amplified in the 1990s by the rise of New Labour and the commensurate collapse of the Conservative Party as a governing force, although this academic trend has been somewhat rebalanced by the upswing in interest prompted by the election of David Cameron. This difficulty is compounded because for many years the primary task of students of the Conservative Party, whether working in a historical or political science tradition, was to explain its enduring success. Studies that did consider its periodic spells of opposition were, in the main, preoccupied with demonstrating how these were used to refresh Conservative ideas and organisation in preparation once again for government (for example, Ball and Seldon, 2005; Seldon and Snowdon, 2001).

This chapter provides an overview of the literature on the Conservative Party, with particular emphasis on how it has understood, and sought to account for, its electoral success and failure. It is grouped into two broad categories: a historical tradition which has emphasised the role of pragmatic elite leadership, and a Marxist-inspired analytical tradition which has emphasised the institutionalised sources of Conservative power. This characterisation is something of an academic conceit for, as we shall see, there is substantial crossover between these two clusters. However, it is useful as a means to highlight both the strengths and limitations of the literature with regard to understanding contemporary Conservative politics. Following this, the emerging body of work on the Conservatives under Cameron is considered. The remainder of the chapter then outlines the analytical approach utilised and the structure of the rest of the book.

The historical tradition

As Addison notes, despite the Conservative Party's status as the oldest surviving political party in Britain, for much of the twentieth century it was a neglected area of historical study: it was, quite simply, 'out of fashion' (1999: 289). This began to change in the 1970s when a number of historians, led by Robert Blake, subjected the Conservatives to serious academic study. There now exists a distinguished scholarly tradition, which has recorded Conservative Party history, with definitive works by Robert Blake (1970, 1998) and John Ramsden (1995, 1996, 1998) at the forefront. Substantial contributions have also been made by Stuart Ball (1998), John Charmley (1996), Alan Clark (1998), Andrew Davies (1996), Brendan Evans and Andrew Taylor (1996), Anthony Seldon (1996), and Seldon and Ball (1994). This chapter identifies important themes in this tradition which also which recur in studies of the contemporary era.[1]

Emblematic of this body of work is the title of Davies' *We, The Nation: The Conservative Party and the Pursuit of Power* (1996). The recurring theme is a fascination with the political success of the Conservative Party: its quest for power, and its aptitude for modifying itself in pursuit of that objective. As Addison comments, the Conservatives 'have long been renowned for their ability to adapt to new conditions while retaining something of their old identity' (1999: 289). This capacity for reform and reinvention is viewed with awe, not least because it has often revealed itself in unpropitious circumstances. In a typical account, for example that by Seldon and Snowdon, this takes on a cyclical character: after a lengthy period of government (they point to those that ended in 1905, 1945 and 1964) and facing an increasingly hostile climate, the party would be propelled into opposition. Once there, however, the Conservatives typically installed a new leader, renewed their popular appeal, and the party's 'organisation, membership, morale and funding all recovered'. At the heart of this was adaptability: 'the party's reconciliation to political, economic and social change often helped its return to power' (Seldon and Snowdon, 2001: 27).

Flexibility in the face of change was thus trumpeted as the key to Conservative electoral success, derived in substantial part from the party's willingness to change its leadership (Clark, 1998: 491). As the title of Ramsden's (1998) single-volume history would have it, the Conservatives had *An Appetite for Power*. In this respect loyalty to the party and the resultant public unity was their 'secret weapon', the periodic absence of which led to defeat. Allegiance to the leadership was not unconditional, however, and on occasion was withheld from unsuccessful leaders. Reflecting on his own time at the helm Iain Duncan Smith wryly observed that: 'It's still the secret weapon of the Conservative Party, the trouble is it's just got so very secret, nobody can find it anymore!' (private interview, 2006). Conservative leaders embody the party and its course, and failure is not treated kindly. As John Bercow comments, the Conservative Party 'wants and expects to be led' (private interview, 2008).

Allied to this proclivity was the widespread idea, popular amongst Conservatives themselves, that theirs was a non-ideological party. Ramsden typifies Conservative history when he argues that where the party faced a choice between power and doctrinal goals, it generally favoured power (cited in Addison, 1999: 296). A weakness of Ramsden's work, Addison argues, is that the role of ideology 'deserves more systematic treatment' than he provides (1999: 295). However, in most Conservative history ideology only plays a secondary role and, where it is acknowledged, it is subservient to adaptability. From this perspective, conservatism, if it is indeed an 'ideology', must itself be flexible. The primary function of ideology is as a tool, often used in opposition, to refresh and revive the Conservatives' appeal. For Barnes (1994) the fact that the Conservatives, unlike their opponents, were 'non-ideological' was the source of their adaptable nature and consequent success.

The difficulty for contemporary work in this tradition is in explaining prolonged Conservative electoral failure. As it measures leadership against the criteria of electoral success, the conclusion has to be that from the mid 1990s until the election as leader of David Cameron, the party was condemned by devastatingly poor leadership. In this respect, the Major premiership has been lambasted by a number of Conservatives who have compared it unfavourably with Thatcher's (Ridley, 1992; Tebbit, 2005). The agency-centred analysis of the historical tradition means that Hague, Duncan Smith and Howard must also be blameworthy. For example, for Collings and Seldon, Hague's leadership represented the 'most futile period in Opposition in the last one hundred years. It was an utterly bleak period that could have been largely avoided with a steadier hand and a clearer strategic direction' (2001: 624). If anything, the party's efforts between 2001 and 2005 were, given the more favourable circumstances of Labour's waning popularity, even less impressive. Having conceded that Hague had 'little room for manoeuvre', Seldon and Snowdon grant no such allowance to his successors:

> The finger of blame can be pointed far more clearly at Duncan Smith, and above all Howard. Had Duncan Smith stuck to his centrist beliefs, and had the personality to impose his will on the party, real progress would have been made. But the real culprit is Howard, who managed to be so tactically and strategically inept. Blair and New Labour were no longer the forces in 2003–5 they had been. Howard's singular achievement was to let them off the hook, and hand them victory. (Seldon and Snowdon, 2005c: 741)

Howard's contribution to Conservative Party fortunes may yet be reassessed by historians, given that it was the precursor to the return to office under Cameron. However, a more general problem for such agency-focused historical analyses is that the mechanism previously utilised to ensure Conservative success, namely the willingness to eject ineffective leaders, was in regular use between 1997 and 2005. In a little over eight years the party changed its leader on four occasions, but its general election performance remained historically poor. Only under Cameron was a substantial upward and sustained shift in the opinion polls recorded, and even this took time to achieve: only from autumn 2008 were the Conservatives consistently ahead in most opinion polls (Green, 2010: 672). This approach also risks overlooking the fact that in certain respects and against some measures Hague, Duncan Smith and Howard were successful: Hague in reforming the party organisation and reducing internal tensions over Europe, Duncan Smith in renewing policy, and Howard in uniting the party.

In 2005, Seldon argued that 'considering the poor choices the party has made since 1997, it must now muster the courage to elect the leader with the best chance of winning the next election' (Seldon, 2005). This raises the obvious questions of why the party failed to do so in 1997, 2001 and 2003, and why doing so should require courage, rather than commonsense or self-interest. This book argues that an important part of the answer was the influence of ideology. From a political analyst's perspective, Heppell has persuasively demonstrated that ideology has been a key determinant of voting behaviour in elections to the Conservative leadership (Heppell, 2008; Heppell and Hill, 2008). Consequently for Heppell the contrast between 2005 and the preceding leadership elections was clear – with the election of Cameron 'the era of ideology was ending and Conservatives were re-engaging with the merits of pragmatism in the pursuit of power' (Heppell, 2008: 193).

However, for agency-centred historiographers, the ideational dimension is less easily accommodated. One way out of this difficulty is to claim, as the late Ian Gilmour did, that since Thatcher the Conservative Party has not really been Conservative (or indeed small-c conservative) at all, but has fallen victim to alien dogma (Chapter 2). Mark Garnett's contemporary history sits broadly within this perspective. Garnett's work represents a valuable contribution in no small part because of its sensitivity to and appreciation of the role of political ideas, and in this respect draws inspiration from the 'ideological turn' witnessed in relation to studies of the Conservative Party in the 1980s. However, whilst he does not go as far to claim that pre-Thatcher the Conservatives were un-ideological, he does imply that there was something particularly virulent and pernicious about the neo-liberalism which took hold in the party in the 1970s and 1980s (Garnett, 2003, 2004; Denham and Garnett, 2001, 2002; Gilmour and Garnett, 1997).

The move towards greater consideration of Conservative ideology was a response to the limitations of the historical tradition in accounting for the rise and nature of Thatcherism. In Turner's view, the result has been two sets of literature running in parallel – one emphasising the structural and societal changes that drove the emergence of the New Right in the United Kingdom and elsewhere, and an agency-focused historical interpretation. The latter 'concentrates on the disappointment felt in the party and in the electorate at the ineptitude of Labour government and the failure of Heath's Conservative Party to win elections, to oppose effectively after it had lost them, or to tackle the non-parliamentary resistance of the over mighty trade unions' (Turner, 1999: 286). In other words, this literature explains the emergence of Thatcher and her policy programme by reference to Heath's ineffective (or even incompetent) leadership, rather than as part of a broader ideological or political shift. For observers in the historical tradition, these events were essentially contingent and agency-driven. However, the upsurge in interest from political analysts in Thatcherism prompted a search for a more encompassing interpretation, as discussed below.

Thatcherism and the political–analytical tradition

The transformative effect of Thatcherism reached even into the realm of Conservative Party studies. Previously, Turner suggests, this field had suffered somewhat 'from an excess of "engagement" among its historians', who tended to be 'active sympathisers' if not actual party activists (1999: 276).[2] Thatcherism (itself a term first coined by the Left) instigated rigorous academic study of the party by some of its fiercest ideological antagonists. As the historical tradition had been concerned with accounting for long-term Conservative electoral success, analysts of Thatcherism sought to explain its capture of economic, political and ideological debate. Pioneering work by Stuart Hall and Martin Jacques (1983) employed Gramscian Marxism to characterise Thatcherism as a hegemonic project. This 'authoritarian populism', Hall argued, was a dangerous combination of 'the resonant themes of organic Toryism', such as the nation, authority and the family, with the 'aggressive themes of a revived neo-liberalism', primarily anti-statist competitive individualism (Hall, 1983: 29).

For Andrew Gamble, Thatcherism was an attempt to restore the conditions for Conservative hegemony. He argued that, as a political project, Thatcherism had three key objectives: the restoration of the Conservative Party to electoral dominance; the revival of 'market liberalism as the dominant public philosophy'; and the rejuvenation of state authority combined with a freeing-up of the market economy (Gamble, 1994a: 4). Jessop *et al.* (1988) also viewed Thatcherism as a hegemonic project: for them it was an attempt to 'reconstitute the electoral base' of the Conservative Party which was in long-term structural decline (1988: 86). They argued that Thatcher sought to reorder both the economy (in the interests of international capital) and ideological discourse to sustain such a shift.

Evans and Taylor highlighted the curious similarity of the critiques of Thatcherism offered by 'One Nation' Conservatives such as Gilmour (1992), and those from the Marxist-left such as Jessop, Gamble and Hall, who share the opinion that Thatcherism was a clear ideological 'project' which divided the nation. Such critiques, they argue, are 'underpinned by their main mistaken judgement, that Thatcherism was a dogmatic ideological project which represented a departure from the party's traditions' (Evans and Taylor, 1996: 230). A more accurate interpretation, they suggest, is to see Thatcherism as simply the latest episode in the history of a party that has long been ideologically conscious in its resistance to statism and socialism (1996: 240).

Evans and Taylor are right to stress the continuities of Thatcherism with Conservative Party history in terms of both its desire for electoral success, and its ideological unease with high levels of state intervention. However, it is possible to analyse Thatcherism as a 'project' whilst also recognising that it is part of a broadly defined Conservative tradition. There was a particularity to Thatcherism, as an interpretation of and response to the context of the late 1970s. The concern with that context, and the character of the response to it, are both derived from long-standing Conservative tradition. However, that response manifested itself as a more coherent and strategic political project than had previously been seen under a Conservative government. Gamble was therefore correct when he suggested that Thatcherism is best understood as a political project, the primary objective of which was the reversal of British national decline (1994a: 4).

These Marxist-inspired analyses share an interest (absent, as Turner noted, from much of the agency-focused historical literature) in locating Conservative electoral success in the wider social, economic and political context. Consequently, they tend to exhibit a greater theoretical self-awareness and reflectivity. Like the historical analyses, they seek to account for the party's adaptive capacity, but they focus less on internal party machinations and attempt to situate this in relation to society as a whole. In this way they are, broadly, much more structuralist than the historical tradition: party change is prompted mainly by external structural crises of the economy, state and society. Only through a consideration of these factors can the emergence and success of Thatcherism be understood.

We can therefore conceptualise various competing narratives of Thatcherism, each of which is embedded in a wider tradition. There is no essentialist account of Thatcherism: rather a variety of interpretations exist (Bevir and Rhodes, 1998: 97–111). However, we can identify a shift in the way the Conservative Party was studied in the light of Thatcherism, bringing political science concerns to bear on the historical tradition. It would be wrong also to dismiss this turn as merely 'structuralist' because many of these accounts consider agential factors and highlight the contingent nature of Thatcher's electoral success. The Gramscian leanings of some also provide a welcome sensitivity to the importance of ideas. However, the concern of this mode of analysis is largely with explaining how ideology is used to provoke, explain, or sustain wider socio-economic shifts. It is useful, therefore, to characterise the dominant turn of the literature on Thatcherism as one of movement towards more structurally inclined modes of explanation, in contrast to the agency-focused historical narratives that preceded them. In many ways this was a welcome corrective, but brought with it the tendency to underplay the vital role of strategic actors and leadership.

This concern prompted the most influential single contribution to the debate about Thatcherism, Jim Bulpitt's statecraft thesis. Bulpitt reasserted the importance of leadership strategy for understanding Conservative Party politics. His approach 'stresses the need to examine the activities of party leaders in terms of their statecraft – namely the art of winning elections and, above all, achieving a neces-sary degree of governing competence in office' (1986: 19). Less emphasis is placed on the ideological particularity of Thatcherism: its distinctiveness lies in its statecraft (Bevir and Rhodes, 1998: 101–2). In short, Bulpitt viewed the historical concern of Conservative Party statecraft as the preservation of an autonomous, centralised government with sole control over issues of 'high politics' (1986: 21–2).

The statecraft approach has much to commend it, and has been successfully applied by Buller (2000). It can be seen as an attempt to balance structure and agency, but has a number of limitations. It is somewhat imprecise, with a rather narrow conception of leadership motives, and has a tendency to underplay the important role of political ideas. This stems from Bulpitt's juxtaposition of statecraft against modes of analysis that favour either ideology or policy (1986: 19). Ideology effectively remains a means to an end and subservient to the statecraft imperative. Perhaps the most beneficial lesson we can take from considering the statecraft approach (aside from the importance of leadership itself) is that political leaders have multiple objectives against which to measure their achievements, but central to these is political success in terms of holding power.

Bulpitt's work is best appreciated as a valuable corrective to the tendency, pre-valent at the time it was published, to emphasise the particularity and novelty of Thatcherism. This was not only a feature of some Marxist analyses but was common amongst Conservative critics who denounced the new creed as foreign to conser-vatism (Gilmour, 1992). It is within this debate about Thatcherism that state-craft is most useful. It also highlights the value of explicitly incorporating both conduct and context into our analysis, that the strategic–relational approach (SRA) utilised in this research brings to the fore. However, before the SRA is outlined, it is worth considering the academic work that has focused on the Conservative Party in opposition since 1997.

Contemporary analyses

The 1997–2005 period suffered a general neglect in Conservative Party studies.[3] With the fall of communism, Marxist political analysis waned. Aligned with a general decline of interest in the Conservatives following their ejection from office, the relatively sparse literature examining the party in the aftermath of the 1997 election defeat lent more heavily on the historical tradition. As discussed above, much of this is agential in its approach and the focus of its analysis was consequently on the inadequacy of Conservative Party leadership strategies, tactics and personnel. How-ever, a more subtle reading suggests that there has been something of an amalgama-tion of the two streams of work identified above, and that a political–analytical hue can be identified in much of the contemporary work.

Seldon and Snowdon used their historical perspective to draw parallels between the Conservative predicament in 1997 and that faced by the party in the mid nineteenth century, after the repeal of the Corn Laws (2005b: 244). Paradoxically, a period of immense electoral success (1979–97) saw the Conservative Party lose its hunger for power and its adaptability: 'the two keys' which accounted for its hegemony. In this respect, they argued that Mrs Thatcher is personally liable: whilst she achieved 'much of lasting benefit for Britain', she also damaged the party by making it 'more of a right-wing, ideological force than it had traditionally been' (2005b: 245). In their explanation of Conservative failure, Seldon and Snowdon seek to combine internal factors such as 'ill-considered' organisational reform (2005b: 251) and confused policy-making and marketing (2005b: 252–5, 262) with external factors such as Labour's reputation for competence and effective opposition from the Liberal Democrats (2005b: 256, 263). However, beyond a stinging critique of strategic decision-making by Hague, Duncan Smith and Howard, they struggle to link these together into a convincing explanation as to why such strategic errors were repeatedly made.

Both popular and academic interest in Conservative politics received a substantial boost from Cameron's election as leader in 2005, and the mini-boom in academic output that followed had as its primary focus the 'Cameron effect', namely the extent to which his leadership has transformed the party.[4] A valuable study by Dorey, Garnett and Denham (2011) covers the 1997–2010 period in its entirety, although their analysis of policy development and modernisation concentrates on the Cameron leadership.

As well as the academic studies, the Conservatives' troubles have been the subject of much journalistic comment. Bale (2010) has noted the importance of the media as an arena for party political activity: the modern media acts as a complex conduit of ideas and information between politicians, activists, journalists, voters and (at least occasionally) academics. Media reports are consequently a valuable resource drawn upon throughout this book, both to trace particular events and as a barometer of the party's success or failure in winning round journalistic and public opinion. Book-length studies by journalists such as Simon Walters (2001) and Peter Snowdon (2010) draw upon their insider access as part of the 'Westminster village' and blur the line between journalism and contemporary history. Perhaps inevitably such works focus on the personalities of those involved and the conflicts between them, which limits their analytical purchase and appreciation of wider contextual factors. They are nonetheless valuable resources precisely because they provide a detailed record of day-to-day political activity and behind-the-scenes disputes.

Perhaps the most comprehensively analysed aspect of Conservative Party politics over the past two decades has been the various leadership elections. As well as a range of journal articles (for example Alderman, 1998; Heppell and Hill, 2008a, 2009, 2010), two book-length studies on this topic have been published (Denham and O'Hara, 2008; Heppell, 2008a). As a review by Tim Bale noted, both of these volumes 'are in a long and fine tradition of writing on British politics that eschews self-styled scientific schemas for a more common-sense, historical approach' (2009:

365). Such a characterisation could be applied, not altogether unfairly, to nearly all the contemporary analyses mentioned in this section. However most, whilst not necessarily wearing their theoretical standpoint as a badge of honour, to a greater or lesser extent draw upon the political analytical tradition identified above. Whilst differences of degree of course remain, there has been an effective merging of these two academic currents in this field of study. This can be seen in the work of Bale himself: notably in his assessment of modernisation under Cameron (2008) and in his superb book-length study of the post-Thatcher era (2010).

Bale's volume has set the standard as the key text charting the history of the Conservative Party from Thatcher to Cameron. By bringing a historical institutionalist perspective to a detailed ordered narrative Bale has produced an invaluable book which provides an unrivalled depth of coverage of the events under scrutiny. Through its different structure and approach this book complements Bale's work rather than acts as an alternative to it. Where Bale favours a chronological approach this book is thematic, centred on a number of key dilemmas in contemporary Conservative politics (this also differentiates this volume from that by Dorey, Garnett and Denham, 2011). This allows key ideas and issues to be considered across the period as a whole, aiding an appreciation of how key intellectual and ideological debates both inform and influence how politicians understand their locale and choose to act, and frame political debates more broadly.

Structure of the book

This research concentrates on the 1997–2010 period, for several reasons. Most obviously this encompasses the relevant period of Conservative opposition in its entirety, allowing leadership strategy to be examined from electoral defeat in May 1997 to regaining office in May 2010. The book considers how the party responded to defeat, and seeks to explain why it struggled to return to a position from which it could effectively challenge for power, and how it eventually did so. As such, a key task of the book is to contextualise and explain the emergence and nature of contemporary conservatism under the direction of David Cameron. It does this in two ways. Firstly, by tracing the debates over strategy amongst the party elite, and scrutinising the actions of the leadership, it situates Cameron and his 'modernising' approach in relation to that of his three immediate predecessors: Michael Howard, Iain Duncan Smith and William Hague. This holistic view aids the identification of strategic trends and conflicts, and an appreciation of the Conservatives' evolving response to New Labour's statecraft. In this respect the book also benefits from a series of interviews with leading Conservative politicians who were either involved directly in, or were closely associated with, the development of party strategy during this period. Secondly, the book highlights and considers in depth four particular dilemmas for contemporary conservatism, each chosen as they present Conservatives with a significant ideological challenge.

The structure of the book reflects these objectives. Chapter 2 provides contextual background to the study through an examination of the work of three key Conservative thinkers (John Gray, Ian Gilmour and David Willetts) that is used to consider the intellectual response of conservatism to the Thatcherite legacy. This ideological uncertainty over the direction of Conservative politics after Thatcher is an important frame of the debates in the party post-1997. This chapter also provides a brief overview of the electoral problem facing the Conservative Party in 1997.

Chapter 3 provides an overview of the leadership strategies pursued by the Conservatives in two full terms of opposition, between 1997 and 2005. It analyses the Conservative reaction to a landslide defeat in 1997, and considers how the competing interpretations of defeat influenced the strategies pursued by the party leadership. This assessment includes an examination of electoral strategy across the period, particularly the two general election campaigns of 2001 and 2005. The chapter concludes that the strategies pursued by Hague, Duncan Smith and Howard were sub-optimal: they underachieved even within the inauspicious context that they faced. This forms the backdrop to both the discussion of Cameron later in the book, and the examination of efforts to reconstruct conservatism in relation to the key dilemmas of European integration (Chapter 4); national identity and the English question (Chapter 5); social liberalism versus social authoritarianism (Chapter 6); and the problems posed by a neo-liberal political economy (Chapter 7). These four case-study chapters explore in detail how the party leadership sought to manages these challenges, as well as considering what they suggest about the current state of Conservative politics. The concluding chapter (Chapter 8) draws together the findings of the research, and considers the implications in relation to the prospects for the Conservative-led coalition government.

The organisation of the book along these lines is also influenced by the theoretical standpoint that guided the research. As a broadly defined organising perspective, the book draws on the SRA, which highlights the way in which political actors make strategic choices informed by their interpretation of the context they face. The structure of the book consequently reflects this through the inclusion of contextual chapters before those which examine the strategy and actions of the leadership in greater detail. The way in which the SRA informed the research is outlined below.

Utilising the SRA in political analysis

The SRA highlights the dialectical nature of the interplay between structure and agency by concentrating on the interaction between the two in the 'real world' rather than in the realm of abstract theory that the two terms imply. To assist in this objective the SRA utilises the concepts of *strategic action*, which is that taken by conscious, reflective strategic actors, and the *strategically selective context* in which it is formulated and takes place (Hay, 2002a: 126–34). As such, the key contribution of the SRA is to do away with the structure–agency dichotomy, and to shift our analysis instead into the field of strategy – that is, behaviour orientated towards context. It directs us to see the Conservative Party both as a strategic actor and as an institution, constraining and enabling actors within it. For example, the party provides the leader with institutionalised resources, such as a public platform, supporters and a campaigning organisation, but also acts as a constraint, as a leader must retain the confidence of their parliamentary colleagues and (to a lesser extent) party members. The SRA is, in a sense, a heuristic device for exploring how the Conservative Party uses strategy in pursuit of its goals, and how that strategy affects, and is affected by, the strategic context. By placing strategic leadership at the centre of our analysis, the SRA is well suited to this research, which focuses on the strategy of the Conservative Party as an organisation with the objective of gaining and holding political office, and on the role of leaders within it in directing party strategy.

The SRA thus directs the focus of our analysis into a number of different arenas, towards which leadership strategy is orientated. Most notably these are the parliamentary party, the wider party (membership), the electorate and ideology. An appreciation of this multi-layered context is needed to understand Conservative Party strategy in the 1997–2010 period. Strategic decisions which may appear 'irrational' if measured against only a restricted contextual variable – for example, the pursuit of the median voter position – can be better understood when placed in this wider framework. Rather than trying to ascribe particular causal weighting to various factors, however, the SRA concentrates on the process of formulating, implementing and understanding strategy. Thus, later in the book the focus is on noteworthy dilemmas for the leadership, and traces strategy regarding these over time. In short, we should not see 'strategic success' as agential victory over structure, or strategic failure as agents being 'defeated' by structures. Apparent failure in one area might indicate the higher priority ascribed to other dimensions: for example at certain times, party unity may take precedence over developing an inclusive electoral appeal.

This is not to claim that previous work on the Conservative Party has ignored either the role of strategic actors or of the strategically selective context. As previously discussed, much of the literature closely examines the actions of leading figures in the party, and by doing so provides a detailed history. The research presented here is not a rejection of the elite-historian tradition, but by being theoretically reflective aims to build upon it. For example where agency-focused accounts do consider 'structure', it tends to be when it restricts what actors can do or inhibits their strategic objectives. What the SRA aims to do, however, by focusing on the structure–agency relationship, is to highlight how structure not only curtails action, but enables, shapes and is transformed by it. By considering this over a significant length of time, we also reveal the importance of path-dependency as the context is altered over time. Thus, we can see how the handling of an issue by one party leader shapes how it is dealt with by their successors. The SRA thus helps us to *anticipate* how strategy might be shaped by context, assisting our effort to explain why something happened as it did, as well as how it happened.

The analytical work on Thatcherism, much of it derived from a Marxist tradition, highlighted the structured nature of Conservative hegemony. However, by stressing the institutionalised sources of electoral dominance, it risked presenting a somewhat static view of history insufficiently sensitive to historical contingency. For example, Gamble very usefully identifies the pillars of Conservative hegemony as 'state, union, property, and empire' (1995: 8), and the decline of each of these played a part in the Conservative Party's fall in the mid 1990s. However, explaining events since 1997 needs to go beyond this: whilst further electoral failure in 2001 and 2005 might be accounted for by the continuing absence of these pillars, revival under David Cameron cannot.[5] The context is changing and responsive, so even where it might appear inauspicious it is not fixed but is susceptible to strategic action. Outcomes are not predetermined, so even in difficult circumstances a range of strategic options present themselves. Again, this highlights the benefit of considering a lengthy spell of opposition. Faced with an unfavourable context in 1997, should the Conservatives have acted differently, for example by pursuing a more consistent effort to change party image over a two-term strategy, even if this risked (further) short-term unpopularity?

As the previous section explored, the SRA is useful for capturing the importance of ideology. That ideology has performed an important role in Conservative Party politics over the past thirty years is a widely recognised fact, most clearly illustrated by divisions over European integration, but also in shaping party strategy more generally. Disagreement over strategy not only betrays ideological disparities in terms of the direction in which different actors would *like* to see the party move, but also ideologically informed variation in terms of how the context (and competing strategic choices) is understood. This is illustrated by the surprisingly widespread view amongst Conservative politicians that a huge swathe of the electorate (often referred to as the 'forgotten' or 'silent' majority) would flock back to the party if only it were more vigorously right-wing.[6]

Finally, it is worth briefly mentioning the 'performative dimension' of political action (Hay, 2009). The way that politicians publicly perform (particularly through the media) is a vital part of contemporary politics, a fact better appreciated by politicians than academic analysts. Here, the terminology of the SRA is particularly apt, as politicians are indeed actors on a public stage, even if their view of the audience (the electorate) is somewhat blurred or even erroneous. Politicians assume a variety of positions on the stage in an effort to address different parts of the audience, although they can never be absolutely sure that their messages will be transmitted in the way they would like. The period under examination here is a case in point: William Hague used his superlative performances at Prime Minister's Questions to rally his backbenchers and secure his position as leader at a time when they had little else to cheer about. Iain Duncan Smith, by contrast, was armed with arguably a much better strategy for Conservative electoral revival, but as a relatively weak Commons and media performer was unable to convince his own colleagues, let alone the public, of the merit of his approach. In short, a good strategy, well suited for the strategically selective context is not enough: it needs to be executed effectively.

Conclusion

The fundamental purpose of political parties is to win elections and implement their agenda in office. In the twentieth century no party appeared to validate this more strikingly than the Conservatives, and scholars dedicated themselves to explaining this success. However, between 1997 and 2010 the party endured one of its longest spells in opposition, raising questions about the causes of failure and, rather more intriguingly, the slow pace of change to rectify it. In this respect the existing literature has some limitations. In particular, the agency-centred historical tradition leads to explanations based on the shortcomings of individual leaders, lacking sufficient appreciation of vital contextual factors. Conversely, whilst the political–analytical tradition has many strengths, its spotlight on explaining Conservative hegemony risks limiting its effectiveness in accounting for its subsequent collapse.

In short, this review suggested the need for a more nuanced theoretically informed approach, drawing on the strengths of both the historical and political science literature. Statecraft has much to commend it in this regard. Leadership is at the core of what any political party does, how it communicates with the electorate, how it interprets reality and how it defines its strategy. As the agency-focused nature of its historiography shows, this is particularly so in the case of the Conservative Party. As Taylor has noted, 'the importance of the leader and the style of leadership for the Conservative Party cannot, therefore, be underestimated' (2008: xiii). Statecraft is limited, however, by its focus on governing and the Thatcher era.

Since Bulpitt's (1986) article was published, a wider debate in political science over the nature and relationship of structure and agency has gathered apace. This has been an important element of the movement towards more theoretically informed political analysis. One more generalised theoretical approach that seeks to overcome the dualism of structure and agency is the SRA. Surprisingly, this is not an approach that has been explicitly applied to party politics, for which it is well suited. By directing the focus of analytical attention to strategic action it offers a potentially fruitful new avenue for studies in this field, and appears particularly apt in the case of the Conservative Party, where elite leadership has played a central role throughout the party's history. Applied with the notion of the strategically selective context, the SRA provides the framework for an analytical perspective which highlights the interplay between strategic action and the environment in which it takes place, and the importance of how that environment is interpreted and understood by political actors.

Analysing Conservative defeat in the 2001 election, Norris and Lovenduski argued that politicians 'may fail to learn from electoral defeat due to selective perception' (2004: 85). Evidence they presented from the 2001 British Representation Study demonstrated that the Conservatives were further from the median voter than either Labour or the Liberal Democrats: an outcome which they attributed to a failure by Conservative politicians to accurately gauge public sentiment on key issues. This book argues that to understand and explain this persistent failure by Conservative politicians to reconstruct conservatism in an electorally appealing form after the 1992 election and locate it closer to prevailing policy moods it is necessary to take sufficient account of the ideological dimension. The ideological viewpoints of individual actors may help explain the selective perception identified by Norris and Lovenduski, while ideology also forms part of the context within which strategic decisions are made. By unpacking this process in relation to key areas of ideological contestation for Conservatives in the early twenty-first century, this book provides a nuanced understanding of the politics of opposition between 1997 and 2010 and provides a portrait of conservatism as the party entered into coalition and returned to office.

Notes

1 See Addison (1999) and Turner (1999) for reviews of much of this historical literature.
2 The Conservative peer Lord Blake being foremost among them (Turner, 1999: 276; Blake, 1970).
3 Some exceptions to this are the edited collection by Garnett and Lynch (2003) that provides the most comprehensive academic overview of the 1997–2001 period. Reviews of each parliament are also provided by chapters in the various general election series texts, for example Butler and Kavanagh (2002); Cooper (2001); and Cowley and Green (2005). Focusing on the Hague years, Kelly (2001) has analysed his ill-fated electoral strategy, and Harris (2005) provides a detailed examination of the politics of nationhood under his leadership. Hayton and Heppell (2010) offer one of the few sustained analyses of the Iain Duncan Smith era; while Dorey (2004) unpacks the Conservative policy agenda in the 2001–5 parliament. Taylor (2005) surveys the 1997–2005 period to expose the failure of the Conservatives to develop a coherent narrative under the leadership of Hague, Duncan Smith or Howard.
4 Key works in this respect include an assessment of Cameron and ideological and policy consensus with New Labour by Kerr (2007); electoral strategy and the pursuit of the 'centre ground' by Quinn (2008); and the constraints of the Thatcherite inheritance by Evans (2010). Policy positioning under Cameron has also been assessed, for example on the environment (Carter, 2009); the economy (Dorey, 2009); the constitution (Flinders, 2009) and family policy (Hayton, 2010b; Kirby, 2009). The edited collection by Lee and Beech (2009) provides a comprehensive analysis of Cameron's first three years as leader

of the opposition, with chapters dedicated to the Conservatives' approach to most major areas of public policy.

5 See Hay and Wincott (1998) for an analysis of the 'latent structuralism' (1998: 952) of historical institutionalism.

6 Just such a view was expressed by Lord Tebbit (private interview, 2007).

2

Thatcher's legacy: late-twentieth-century conservatism in context

It was a totally no win situation.
(Lord Parkinson, private interview, 2006)

Introduction

In 1997 the Conservative Party faced dual crises: an ideological crisis of the purpose of conservatism, and an electoral crisis of the politics of support. This chapter explores the context faced by the new leader of the opposition through an examination of both of these dimensions. Whilst these can be distinguished for analytical purposes, the two are inextricably linked. The chapter argues that these problems were mutually reinforcing and that, unsure of its own purpose and direction, the Conservative Party struggled to find or articulate a convincing narrative to the electorate. This uncertainty derived in substantial part from the intellectual debate about conservatism after Thatcher. This is explored in this chapter by reference to three key conservative intellectuals: Ian Gilmour, David Willetts and John Gray.

The chapter argues that each of these writers is emblematic of a differing response within conservatism to the post-Thatcher political settlement. The following intellectual trends are identified: anti-Thatcherite (Gilmour); neo-Thatcherite (Willetts); and post-Thatcherite (Gray). These differing perspectives provided a backdrop to the debate amongst Conservative politicians over the party's intellectual and strategic direction following the 1997 election defeat. However, these intraparty deliberations were framed largely within the neo-Thatcherite viewpoint, which acted as a limitation on their scope for reform and modernisation. This reflected the enduring hold of Thatcherism on the Conservative Party. How this played out in strategic decision-making in relation to key policy areas between 1997 and 2010 is explored in later chapters.

All three authors present both a normative dimension (of what conservatism should be) and a pragmatic dimension, in terms of how it might be articulated. Gilmour regarded Thatcherism as an anathema to conservatism, a variant of doctrinal neo-liberalism alien to the British Conservative way; Willetts, by contrast, saw Thatcherism as merely another chapter in a consistent and developing conservative tradition. Gray argued that conservatism was 'undone' by Thatcherism and was effectively dead, whereas Gilmour argued that to be electorally successful the party needed to return to the 'One Nation' tradition. In an early precursor to Cameron's vision of 'the big society', from the early 1990s Willett argued for a Conservative vision for communities based on voluntary association, which he regarded as compatible with a free market position. However, before these perspectives are surveyed in greater detail, the next section considers how the Conservatives' electoral base was challenged by the rise of New Labour and provides a brief overview of the electoral problem the Conservatives faced in 1997.

The electoral problem

This section outlines the electoral problem the Conservative Party faced throughout the mid to late 1990s. These circumstances have been well documented so they do not need to be recounted at great length here. However, the increasingly difficult electoral context for the Conservatives in this period can be illustrated through an analysis of a number of key events, most notably the Exchange Rate Mechanism (ERM) *débâcle* of September 1992. Underlying this it is argued that a more fundamental reshaping of the context the party faced occurred, as the form of the political landscape post-Thatcher was revealed. The Thatcherite project was successful in forging a new economic consensus: the Labour Party was forced to accept the end of Keynesian demand management, and the doctrine of free markets gained intellectual ascendancy over that of the mixed economy. However, whilst by the end of the Thatcher era the British people were no longer for Keynes, they were still for Beveridge (Marquand, 1991: 16). In other words, while they had become convinced of the need for a free market economy, they still wished to retain the protection offered by the welfare state (see also Crewe, 1993: 18–25). Political competition between the major parties consequently turned into 'a struggle over management rather than over purpose and direction' (Marquand, 1991: 16–17). This was a contest the Conservatives were best placed to win at the 1992 general election. However, the odds in this battle over competence would change dramatically after 'Black Wednesday'. The continued public demand for welfare – despite (or perhaps because of) a decade of Thatcherism – was a key factor in the strategic context that the Conservatives would struggle to respond to over the next decade and a half. Whilst the Labour Party forged a narrative of the 'Third Way' that professed to balance free market economics with this demand, the Conservatives struggled to reconcile the logic of Thatcherism with the fundamentally incompatible ideas of Beveridge. This was a fundamental difficulty for the party as it tried to revitalise and reposition itself after the 1997 election (Chapter 3).

The result of the 1992 general election came as a surprise to many as it contradicted the prevailing trend of the opinion polls (King, 1993: 244), and the Conservatives won a fourth successive victory in spite of the ongoing economic recession. This victory emanated from even greater distrust of Labour's ability to manage the economy, which could not win over an electorate more capitalist in its orientation due to policies such as council house sales, privatisation and de-unionisation (Garrett, 1994: 121).

Leadership effects were also important at the 1992 election. John Major's greatest asset was perhaps the fact that he was neither Margaret Thatcher nor Neil Kinnock. Major's public rating was significantly better than Kinnock's and had a positive effect on the Conservatives' standing compared to that under Thatcher (Crewe and King, 1994: 125–47). Major had effectively diffused public anger over the poll tax by appointing Michael Heseltine to devise a replacement, and divisions over Europe had apparently been healed by Major's deft handling of the Maastricht Treaty negotiations, successfully completed in December 1991. Indeed, Europe scarcely featured in the 1992 election as both parties accepted the broad framework negotiated by Major, with the minor exception of the opt-out from the social chapter that Labour wished to sign (King, 1993: 230). Conservative unity over Europe proved ephemeral, however, and divisions concealed before the election soon re-emerged over the incorporation of the Treaty into law. Major's 'triumph' at Maastricht was soon forgotten in the Conservative Party when it became apparent that the treaty would restrict further the government's ability to stimulate an economic recovery within the constraints of the ERM (Thompson, 1996: 188–9). By enshrining in law a commitment to European Monetary Union (EMU) (albeit with an opt-out from the final stage), the possibility of fiscal loosening to offset the effects of the high interest-rates required to maintain sterling's position within the ERM was effectively closed off.

Major was thus partly responsible for setting the trap which sprung on 'Black Wednesday', 16 September 1992. The farcical series of events that day have been subject to much academic and public debate and need not detain us here. Suffice to say that the government's inability to defend sterling's value within the bounds it itself had set less than two years previously (despite spending £11 billion in the attempt) constituted a political crisis of gargantuan proportions. Three key consequences for the Conservative Party followed, each of which affected its popularity. Firstly the Conservatives' reputation for competent economic management was shattered, the corollary of which was a decline in their opinion poll standing. Secondly, divisions in the party over the issue of Europe were vividly reopened. Thirdly, the crisis helped create the political space that would come to be occupied by New Labour.

The 1992 election, as Morgan argues, took place 'in a mood of public doubt, against a background of uncertainty about both the economy and policy towards Europe' (Morgan, 2001: 513). In April 1992 the electorate decisively backed the Conservatives as the party best able to handle this uncertainty: within six months the prevailing opinion had been comprehensively reversed. The point of this reversal – when these issues reached crisis point – can Morgan, suggests, be pinpointed with remarkable precision, to 16 September 1992, when they 'exploded' (2001: 513).

The crisis certainly did hit the Conservatives in the polls. According to Ipsos-MORI polling data, between April and September 1992, the Conservatives' poll rating fluctuated around 42 per cent, the level achieved in the general election. At their lowest they were placed at 38 per cent, and at their highest 46 per cent. This period did see a change in Labour's position however, which improved from the 34 per cent received in the general election to approximate parity with the Conservatives. Following 'Black Wednesday', the Conservatives' poll rating began to slide, while Labour's strengthened further. By November, the Conservatives had sunk to the low-30s in all polls, Gallup placing them on 29 per cent to Labour's 52 per cent. This position deteriorated further throughout 1993 and 1994. In 1994, forty-four national opinion polls were conducted: only once did the Conservatives scrape to 30 per cent support. A Gallup opinion poll conducted for the *Daily Telegraph* in January 1995 gave Labour an astonishing 43.5-point lead: 62 per cent to the Conservatives' 18.5 per cent. So, whilst the slide in Conservative support can be dated to September 1992, other factors were clearly at work which worsened the position over the following few years. The opinion poll slump precipitated by 'Black Wednesday' was intensified by the by-election and local election humiliations of 1993, and by the election of Tony Blair as leader of the Labour Party in 1994. This slump in Conservative support persisted up to and beyond the 1997 general election, and is most clearly illustrated graphically (Figure 2.1).

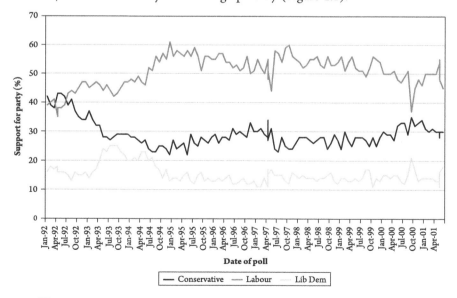

Figure 2.1 Conservative, Labour and Liberal Democrat Support, 1992–2001.
Source: Data from IpsosMORI, www.ipsos-mori.com/.

Table 2.1 Best party at managing the economy

Date(s) of poll	Conservative	Labour	Liberal Democrat	None/ Don't know
30 March 1992	36	31	11	21
15–20 September 1993	23	25	13	38
19–23 May 1994	25	33	12	29
21–24 July 1995	22	33	4	40
22–25 March 1996	24	33	6	35
21–24 February 1997	34	30	5	30
8 April 1997	33	26	5	34

Source: Data on best party on key issues from IpsosMORI, www.ipsos-mori.com/.

Opinion poll data also demonstrates how ERM *débâcle* damaged the Conservatives' reputation as the party best able to manage the economy (Table 2.1). At the time of the 1992 election, 36 per cent of those polled regarded the Conservatives as the most effective economic managers, compared to 31 per cent who thought that Labour would do a better job. By 1993, Labour had established a 2-point lead on this issue, a lead that they maintained and increased until July 1996. Interestingly, this lead actually disappeared in early 1997: polls in February and April gave the Conservatives a 4-point and a 7-point lead, respectively, on the management of the economy. These figures vindicate John Major's decision to delay the 1997 election for as long as possible, and reflect the improving state of the economy at that time. When placed alongside the 1997 election result, they also indicate that the public's perception of the parties' respective abilities to manage the economy is only one variable informing voter choice.

The Conservatives' problems were not merely related to the economy, but reflected their more generalised loss of an image of governing competence. The loss of this image began with the ERM crisis, but was by no means restricted to it. A series of further problems, notably the difficulties in ratifying Maastricht, the botched privatisation of the railways and the mining industry, allegations of sleaze and a challenge to Major's leadership of the party, all furthered the impression that the government was 'in office but not in power' (Lamont, quoted in Morgan, 2001: 513). The general decline in the public image of the Conservative Party is illustrated in Table 2.2. On virtually all measures, the public's view of the party worsens significantly in the first year after the party's re-election in 1992. The percentage of respondents agreeing that the Conservative Party keeps its promises, understands the problems facing Britain, represents all classes, has a good team of leaders, sensible policies and a professional approach all drop sharply in this period, and similar views persist until the following general election in 1997.

Table 2.2 Conservative Party image, 1992–97

Percentages of respondents agreeing that the Conservative Party . . .	April 1992	April 1993	April 1997
Keeps its promises	20	5	5
Understands the problems facing Britain	38	18	20
Represents all classes	20	9	10
Looks after the interests of people like us	21	8	9
Is moderate	19	12	11
Is extreme	16	10	10
Is concerned about the people in real need	18	10	8
Has a good team of leaders	35	13	10
Will promise anything to win votes	41	47	40
Is out of touch with ordinary people	51	57	50
Has sensible policies	31	12	14
Is professional in its approach	42	16	10
Is divided	14	30	13
No opinion	2	10	44

Source: Data on Conservative party image from IpsosMORI, www.ipsos-mori.com/.

The Conservative government had been re-elected on probation in 1992, and rapidly lost any semblance of a positive public image and its reputation for governing competence. The ERM *débâcle* contributed to this loss, but was by no means the only contributing factor. It was this general loss, combined with the emergence of a viable alternative government in the form of New Labour, which led to the Conservatives' crushing defeat in 1997. As Sanders *et al.* (2001: 789) note:

> New Labour's political triumph after 1994 under Tony Blair and Gordon Brown was to convince voters that Labour was now the party of fiscal responsibility and competent macroeconomic management. Their success in this regard severely impaired the Conservatives' ability to benefit electorally from the rising sense of economic optimism among voters that the Chancellor delivered in the 18 months or so prior to the 1997 election.

The ERM crisis came to symbolise in the public mind the loss of governing competence by the Conservatives. As such, it was important in creating the political and electoral space that came to be occupied by New Labour. More subtly, by brutally exposing the apparent powerlessness of governments to control the economy in the face of global economic forces, the crisis facilitated the discourse of globalisation that came to characterise New Labour's economic policy. The repositioning of the Labour Party purportedly in response to the changing global economic context hit the Conservatives in the 1997 election, as did the ongoing social transformation wrought by popular capitalism. Nevertheless, as Cowley (1997: 48) argues, more banal political factors were also at work:

> The transformation of the Conservative Party from dominant party to English-based rump has its roots in three perceptions of the Party: that it was incompetent; that it was disunited; and that it was sleazy. All three perceptions had some validity, but all were exaggerations . . . However, perception is more important than reality and as a result by May 1997 the British public had decided that it was time for a change.

Regardless of whether or not it was an exaggeration, the sleazy, incompetent, disunited image of the Conservative Party in the mid 1990s was hugely damaging for the party at the 1997 election. Responding to the changing social and economic context, the challenge of New Labour and recasting the image of the party formed a formidable task for the party leadership upon entering opposition in 1997.

The ideational dimension

The Conservatives in the 1990s were also confronted with a deeper intellectual problem, namely ideological confusion about the nature and purpose of contemporary conservatism. While the malaise in John Major's government typified the difficulties British conservatism faced, they were not the main cause of it. This uncertainty was one of the unintended consequences of Thatcherism and continued well into the twenty-first century. The New Right provided conservatism with a clear purpose and direction in response to the crisis of the 1970s. However, it also undermined the efforts of some Conservatives to reinvigorate conservatism in the 1990s. Since the 1980s, the ideational context for both conservatism and the Conservative Party has been defined by Thatcherism. The Thatcherite legacy has shaped and constrained Conservative political thinking, communication, policy-making and statecraft. The party struggled to reconcile itself with Thatcher's regicide, which overshadowed her successor's tenure even after he had won his own mandate at a general election. It also impaired attempts to modernise the party in opposition, inhibiting the Conservatives' famed ability to adapt in order to prosper electorally – the 'statecraft' of which Bulpitt regarded Thatcherism as the latest instalment. The 'art of winning elections and achieving some necessary degree of governing competence' (Bulpitt, 1986: 21) was, Michael Portillo suggested, undermined by the party's fixation with Thatcherism:

> During the period of tremendous success for the Conservatives, during the early-1980s particularly, very large numbers of people came into parliament for the first time. They were typically then young, white, middle-class men from the southeast of England . . . They are Thatcherites, but in this very limited and perverse sense, that they have frozen Thatcherism in time, forgetting that one of the key ingredients of Thatcherism was that it was revolutionary, it was cutting-edge, it was new. Thatcherism now of course is retro, it is twenty years past its sell-by date . . . So these rather boneheaded

old Thatcherites occupy a lot of the positions in the party, and that's another reason that has stopped the party changing. (Portillo, private interview, 2006)

Yet the effect of Thatcherism on the configuration of the political context runs much deeper than the politics of personality within the Conservative Party. If the Conservative Party was paralysed by Thatcherism, the Labour Party was – eventually – galvanised by it. The creation of New Labour can be traced directly to Thatcherism (Heffernan, 2000). As Hay noted soon after the 1997 election, the end of the Conservative Party's electoral hegemony 'may be seen as a direct consequence of New Labour's acceptance of the neo-liberal political and economic paradigm that is the sole vision animating contemporary British politics' (1997: 372). On this reading, Britain had become a 'one-vision polity' based on a 'neo-liberal post-Thatcher settlement' (Hay, 1997: 373) that swept away the post-war consensus and the last vestiges of social democracy with it. The Conservative Party, therefore, was a victim of its own success – in helping to forge this consensus it robbed itself of its primary purpose and electoral appeal: its opposition to socialism.

How conservatism reacted to this post-Thatcher settlement is considered here through the work of Ian Gilmour, David Willetts and John Gray, who represent three important intellectual trends in Conservative thought. Gilmour embodied an anti-Thatcherite position. A leading critic of the Thatcher governments of which he was for a time part, he consistently maintained that Thatcherite neo-liberalism was fundamentally at odds with the British Conservative tradition. Willetts represents a neo-Thatcherite position. He justifies Thatcherism in the context of the 1980s, but argues that it forms just one instalment in a consistent Conservative tradition. Of the three, Gray shifted his position most significantly. He rose to prominence in the 1980s as a political thinker in the Hayekian mould, but then became more heavily critical of the flawed rationalism of the New Right (Gamble, 1999: 117). Gray represents a post-Thatcherite position. Whilst his stance is far from that of most contemporary Conservative politicians and intellectuals, it is derived from a right-of-centre rather than a left-of-centre perspective, and is inherently conservative in its anti-rationalism. This typology of post-Thatcher conservatism is useful as it highlights three broad intellectual trends and provides a framework for considering how they differ and where they overlap. It also helps us to understand the ideational context within which Conservative politicians made their strategic decisions, and the limitations placed on the party by the neo-Thatcherite viewpoint.

Anti-Thatcherites: the One Nation 'wets'

Gilmour regarded Thatcherism as inherently un-conservative, as it involved the application of alien New Right monetarist 'dogma' that took precedence over the pragmatic statecraft traditionally associated with Conservative governments. From this perspective, the dogmatic nature of Thatcher and her followers caused them to stick to their ideological guns even when the results became disastrously apparent. By the time of the 1981 budget, Gilmour claims, 'evidence had by now accumulated to prove that the monetarist slaughter had been performed in the name of a false god', but the Chancellor of the Exchequer (Geoffrey Howe) 'only moved faster in the wrong direction' (Gilmour and Garnett, 1997: 312–13). Gilmour explains the seemingly bizarre attachment to monetarism as the result of the government being 'in the grip of an ideology which blinded it to the practical realities of managing the economy' (Gamble, 1993: 121).

Gilmour's anti-Thatcherite conservatism is part of the 'One Nation' strand of Conservative thought that fears social conflict, and prioritises the preservation of order and social harmony. He echoes Burke in his anti-rationalism and reveals a traditional Conservative suspicion of intellectual reasoning. 'Harmony' he states, can only be attained 'by policies which are based on practical wisdom and judicious generosity, not on the cold abstractions of the dogma of discord' (Gilmour, 1992: 279). He seems bemused as to how the Conservative Party fell prey to what to him is such patently absurd, doctrinal thinking, and his explanation as to 'why the moderates lost' (1992: 30–44) is rather unsatisfactory. He dismisses the explanation that the crises of the 1970s left the moderates bereft of alternative ideas, preferring instead the answer that the power of Thatcher's personality rode roughshod over the opposition. The moderates (including himself) were therefore 'guilty of a grave dereliction of duty' in their failure to force the Prime Minister to back down (1992: 32).

Yet the idea that the Conservative Party would so easily fall victim to such a 'foreign' doctrine, even one conveyed through a character as powerful as Mrs Thatcher, is ultimately inadequate. Whilst Thatcher and her style of leadership were vital for Thatcherism, they did not constitute it in its entirety. Context was crucial, and was strategically selective in favour of the New Right. The U-turns and failure of the Heath government provided the political space within the Conservative Party for a different approach to economic policy to gain the ascendancy. An alternative had for some time been enunciated within the party by Enoch Powell, who Thatcher later praised as 'absolutely right about the economy' (quoted in Heffer, 1998: 928): an alternative that would later be vigorously expounded by Keith Joseph (1976a, 1979). Thatcherism also drew strength from the traditional Conservative attachment to the nation, and the patriotic concern to reverse the long-run relative decline of the British economy. The context of economic decline, or at least the perception of decline, has been widely cited as a crucial factor in the emergence and formation of Thatcherism by many writers. Amongst others, Gamble (1994a), Krieger (1986), Jenkins (1989) and Marsh (1995) have highlighted the centrality of British decline to Thatcherism. Thatcherism is best understood as an attempt to reverse this decline, and in certain respects was 'as radical an attempt as any that has been made this century' (Gamble, 1993: 127). As Kavanagh (1997: 50) notes, the politics of consensus came to be seen as the politics of decline, and consequently became the subject of Thatcherite vitriol. Un-conservative measures would be required in the pursuit of the higher Conservative objective of national recovery – not only of the economy, but of the nation's social and moral virtues.

The Winter of Discontent played a vital role in persuading voters of the accuracy of the diagnosis by the Right, rather than that of the Left, of the cause of British decline. The neo-liberal explanation of Britain's economic difficulties (particularly 'stagflation'), 'was elegant in its simplicity and in its simplicity lay its persuasive capacity' (Hay, 2002b: 199). The New Right argued that the problem was one of political overload, as irresponsible politicians attempting to 'buy' their re-election precipitated fiscal crises (Hay, 2002b: 198–202; see also King, 1975). The solution, therefore, was to reassert the primacy of economic imperatives over political ones. Monetarism was seen as the best way to impose the necessary discipline on both the government and the economy. This discourse has been compared by Hay to the (in his eyes, equally spurious) discourse of hyper-globalisation that has been used by New Labour to justify the prioritising of the interests of capital (2002b: 202–3).

Gilmour's critique of Thatcherism lacks sufficient awareness of the political and economic context to provide a powerful explanatory framework. As Gamble comments, the weakness in Gilmour's account is his inability to explain 'why Thatcherism was so successful for so long if it was so flawed from the outset . . . Why should such a malign ideological bacillus have inexplicably seized on the party and been so hard to expel?' (1993: 121–2). Mark Garnett (the co-author with Gilmour of *Whatever Happened to the Tories?*, 1997) provides a more sophisticated explanation of this apparent hijack of the party in his own later work. Garnett identifies in the twentieth-century Conservative Party two competing ideological strands – free market liberalism and One Nation conservatism. According to this account, the free market tradition, whilst always present, was for most of the twentieth century the junior partner to the One Nation Conservatives. This position was reversed in the years following Thatcher's election as leader in 1975, as she and her ideological bedfellows exploited the panic about decline to mount a takeover of the Conservative Party. This victory has been so complete that 'today's Conservative Party is a liberal organisation, with a nationalistic twist' (Garnett, 2003: 112). This forms a coherent post hoc explanation of the Thatcher effect and of the party's electoral difficulties since 1992. If conservatism equals adaptability and electoral success, and if the Conservative Party has abandoned conservatism, it will, by Gilmour and Garnett's logic, be bound to suffer electorally. However, this approach fails to track the changing strategic location of conservatism, or offer a satisfactory explanation as to why it was apparently abandoned by the party.

For Gilmour, then, Thatcherism was damaging not only for the country but for conservatism and the Conservative Party. The continued adherence to ideological dogma caused the Conservative Party in opposition to reinforce the mistakes made in government, as it failed to take the pragmatic and politically sensible course. This trend is contrasted by Gilmour to the rapid recovery made after landslide defeats in 1906 and 1945. 'On both occasions, the party soon made a dramatic recovery. After the similar defeat in 1997 no such recovery has happened. Instead the party has made almost every conceivable mistake' (Gilmour, 2005). Symptomatic of this was the 'suicidal' decision not to elect Kenneth Clarke as leader in 1997, when he was 'unquestionably the best of the candidates and indeed the only one who was unquestionably qualified for the job' (Gilmour, 2001) – a mistake repeated in 2001.

The decision not to elect Clarke – the responsibility of Conservative MPs in 1997 and 2005, and party members in 2001 – can only be explained by his views on Europe, which clashed with the prevailing ideology in the party. The problem Clarke faced, Gilmour (2001) argued, was that: 'not merely in the Parliamentary Party but in the Party in the country as well, there are many Far-Right Little Englanders who, as the old American saying goes, would rather be right than President'. The 'little-Englander' mentality derives from the Thatcherite conception of national identity. Whereas Gilmour associates himself with the inherently *British* One Nation tradition (in which the stability of the British state and the maintenance of the Union are paramount), for Thatcherites such as Conservative philosopher Shirley Letwin, politics begins with individuals and values. As Gamble (1993: 125) states:

> She [Letwin] does not identify the nation with the historic Conservative state as Gilmour does, because that would mean accepting and approving of the way in which the state has developed. There is much in the way that this state has developed in the twentieth century that Thatcherism repudiates. Preserving the Union and ensuring social peace through policies that make citizens dependent, and suppress the vigorous virtues, ends by threatening the special national character of England.

Gilmour mocks the 'Conservative Europhobes' who seem to 'regard England (not even the United Kingdom) as a latter-day Kingdom of Mercia . . . cowering behind an Offa's Dyke, in the form of the English Channel, that will keep the Europeans at bay and enable it to remain a satellite of the United States', and 'bleat in Mercian style about national sovereignty and national independence' (Gilmour, 2001). The Mercian tendency that he identifies is an integral part of the Thatcherite ideology to which many Conservatives subscribe, although most baulk at the logical conclusion of English independence to which it leads (Chapter 5). Conservative scepticism towards Europe and the single currency was, ironically, one of the party's more popular policies between 1997 and 2010, which also helps explain the unwillingness to follow Gilmour's advice and pursue a more centrist line. Thatcherism, he suggested, was never popular with the general public: Thatcher's three general election wins can be explained by the 'divided opposition, her own qualities, and the failure of Old Labour to appear a credible alternative' (Gilmour, 2001; see also 1992: 271–4). After the 1997 general election, as it became clear that 'New Labour was but old Thatcherism writ large', even a 'modestly competent opposition could have made itself popular by adopting centrist policies' (Gilmour, 2001). This apparently obvious and pragmatic course for the Conservative Party upon entering opposition in 1997 was not followed. To explain this, a more sophisticated understanding of the party's struggle to adapt to the post-Thatcherite context than that provided by Gilmour is required. Gilmour is right to acknowledge the importance of the Conservative Party as a strategic actor, but his account is not sufficiently contextualised. He implies that the party's position and electoral fortunes could have been relatively easily transformed by the actions of the leadership, irrespective of the broader context, leading to bewilderment about why they have not.

For a time, the One Nation approach that Gilmour advocated was a great electoral success, as it meshed neatly with social reality and public opinion. Thatcherism achieved a similar concordance in the 1980s, as did New Labour in the late-1990s. The Conservatives' efforts in opposition can only be understood in an adequately contextualised analysis, not simply as an autonomous agent as Gilmour implies.

Neo-Thatcherism: markets and communities?

In stark contrast to the anti-Thatcherite perspective, David Willetts locates Thatcherism within a harmonious Conservative tradition, dating from Burke and Adam Smith in the eighteenth century, via Salisbury and Spencer in the nineteenth and Oakeshott in the twentieth (Willetts, 1992: 3–17). The use of the term 'Thatcherism' suggests a coherence or strategic direction not typically associated with Conservative governments. Willetts acknowledges that it 'implies that a clique of free market ideologues managed in the mid-1970s to launch a coup and capture control of the Conservative Party' (essentially Gilmour's position) but denies that this was actually the case (1992: 47). Whereas for Gilmour free market 'dogma' was anathema to conservatism, for Willetts 'the principles of free markets aligned with a strong sense of community are fundamental conservative principles . . . very little of what she [Mrs Thatcher] said could not have been found in a typical One Nation Group pamphlet of the 1950s' (1992: 51–2). Free markets have been at the centre of conservatism 'since Edmund Burke went into politics as a follower of Adam Smith', and the tendency of 'some Conservatives' (presumably the likes of Gilmour) to downplay their role in Conservative thought is 'bad history' (Willetts, 1994: 9). As such, the distinctive features of Thatcherism can be found not in the content of its political programme but in the personal qualities of Mrs Thatcher herself, and the style and tone that she brought to politics (1992: 51–4). Crucially for Willetts, 'it was still conservatism that she was expounding' (1992: 47).

Nonetheless, in a forerunner to Cameron's rhetoric of 'the big society', Willetts conceded that 'there is more to conservatism than the free market' (1994: 9). For him, the aim of modern conservatism is to 'reconcile free markets (which deliver freedom and prosperity) with a recognition of the importance of community (which sustains our values)' (1992: 92). Further, 'conservatism is at its finest and its most distinctive precisely when it integrates a commitment to the free market into the core values and institutions which hold our country together' (1994: 9). This is a call not just for Conservatives to seek to neutralise the worst effects of the market, but to use market mechanisms to strengthen communities and social institutions. Thatcherite reforms were therefore welcomed not only as necessary for economic reasons – to 'sort' the trade unions, curb inflation and reverse decline – but by reasserting the value of the market they also offered the chance of social and political enrichment. The problem for Conservatives after Thatcher was that they became 'wary of relying as heavily on the free market as we appeared to do in the 1980s' (1994: 7). Willetts believes that Conservatives should not be afraid to make the case for free markets, which he sees as integral to the British tradition and way of life. 'The tension between markets and communities is resolved because they help to sustain each other' (1992: 186). However, he argued that Conservatives needed to highlight *how* markets and communities can do this, as much of the language of Thatcherism implied that the party was only interested in free markets and economics.

This neo-Thatcherite position is distinct from the moderate One Nation position. Nevertheless, it led to some shared recommendations as to how the Conservative Party should proceed in opposition. As Willetts (2005a) told the Social Market Foundation:

> It would be a failure of imagination for a political party to say to the British people that they could only have half of what they want – either personal freedom or a strong society. Our aim must be to not just to make the British economy stronger but British society better. Surely this long promised debate about the future of Conservatism should be about how these two great principles of a dynamic economy and social cohesion come together.

Damian Green MP similarly emphasised social cohesion and communities in his Tory Reform Group Macmillan lecture in March 2000. A One Nation Conservative government would, he suggested, 'seek to use the tools at its disposal to encourage individual responsibility and the building of communities. It would take a pragmatic attitude to public services, asking how they can be improved before it asks who should be providing them' (Green, 2000). However, Green offered a different conception of conservatism. Both Green and Willetts like to advocate the pragmatic rather than the ideological nature of their respective conservatisms – Willetts claims that to label Thatcherism as 'ideological' is simply a term of abuse – but the free market does not play such a central role in Green's One Nation conception:

> We can happily proclaim victory on the economic argument and move on. A successful modern conservatism will need not just a new style, but will also need to recognise which of its traditional purposes is most important. The main purpose of a One Nation Conservative is to create *a good society for all*. In the 1970s this was correctly identified as making the main priority the reduction of the size of the state . . . Where in the 1970s the state was largely seen as the enemy, now life is more subtle . . . our absolute

core purpose must be to deliver practical improvements. Any hint that we have a different agenda will make it impossible for us to deploy new policy ideas effectively. (Green, 2000, emphasis added)

Green's position is derived from the same intellectual tradition as Gilmour's, and consequently shares the overriding desire for social harmony. However, Green has incorporated the Thatcher governments into his narrative of conservatism: they are part of the Conservative desire to 'create a good society' by responding to the challenges of the time. As such, monetarism was not dangerous alien 'dogma' as Gilmour suggests, but a tool utilised by pragmatic Conservatives to tackle the particular problems of inflation and an overly burdensome state sector. Different tools are required to respond to the problems the country now faces, particularly in terms of improving the public services. As Green explains:

> The idea that making the state smaller, having individualism as the main spoke of everything, was clearly a necessary corrective to where Britain had got to in the mid-1970s. But, precisely because the product was relatively successful, both intellectually and practically, meant that you don't, in my view, need to continue in that direction as the main spring of Conservative policy. That is what I mean when I say that its time has gone – it is not that it was false, but I think that the true Tory belief is that any Tory government will seek to maintain a proper balance between the interests of the individual, the interests of the wider community and the interests of the state. (Private interview, 2007)

This accommodation of Thatcherism represents a convergence of the One Nation and neo-Thatcherite perspectives, as both (illustrated by Green and Willetts) justify Thatcherism as a response to the crisis of the 1970s and argue that contemporary conservatism has to move beyond it. However, a tension between the neo-Thatcherite/David Willetts' position and the Damian Green/One Nation position still exists. This revolves around the role of the state, and the capacity of the state for nurturing and protecting communities. For unswerving neo-Thatcherites, it is the state, not markets, that represents the biggest threat to communities, and as far as they acknowledge social breakdown, it is generally blamed on state-led progressive politics. This view is derived from their general abhorrence of socialism, which they equate with statism, and which was blamed for everything from accelerating economic decline to social rot (Thatcher, 1993: 6–12; see also Letwin, 1992). In simplistic neo-Thatcherite conceptions, the British left (in its desire for equality) remains wedded to statism, as the state represents people collectively. Whilst congratulating themselves on defeating socialism, the neo-Thatcherite suspicion of the state therefore remains deeply ingrained. The One Nation position propounded by Green, however, subordinates its view of the state to 'values' – so it is possible to regard centralised state planning as appropriate for the Conservative governments of the 1950s, and at the same time argue that policies to 'roll back' the state were appropriate for the 1980s (Green, 2000).

In his 2005 speech to the Social Market Foundation Willetts acknowledged this potential tension, and was at pains to acknowledge that the state may be able to play a role in strengthening communities. This represents a compromise in his position, from that of 1997 when he wrote that 'the real threat to civil society comes not from the market but from the state' (1997: 3). Better government, rather than less government, was his new mantra:

> [I]t is not just a matter of rolling back the state. Of course government can't do everything, but that doesn't mean it must do nothing. We Conservatives recognise that often the state fails but we shouldn't react with glee when it does. Instead we should believe in effective government. (Willetts, 2005a)

A potential escape from the markets–communities dilemma can also be found in institutions that are neither market- nor state-based, for example charities, voluntary bodies and 'not for profit' organisations. Willetts hopes that this third sector will be the basis for the 'new idea of community' that conservatism needs (2005b: 73), and the coalition government led by David Cameron has repeatedly expressed a similar aspiration. The key institution for Conservatives in this regard was formerly the established church, with that symbol of the nation – the monarch – at its head. Religion has continued to be at the heart of conservatism in America, where George W. Bush's 'compassionate conservatism' attempted to use the glue of religious morality to bind together a society dominated by the free market. Obligation to others is placed on the shoulders of individuals, families and communities, not on the state. But Willetts recognises that if it ever existed, a strong Christian morality no longer exists in Britain's increasingly secular society, and cannot therefore form the basis of contemporary conservatism on this side of the Atlantic (2005b: 74). Other institutions between the state and the market need to be found and nurtured. The Conservative interest in localism is one attempt to do this, and is also an area where under David Cameron they found common ground with their coalition partners, the Liberal Democrats (Kruger, 2006: 36; see also Direct Democracy, 2005). Oliver Letwin's (2003) vision of a 'Neighbourly Society' was another, as was Iain Duncan Smith's reassertion of the importance of social justice (Duncan Smith, 2002b; 2002d; see also Streeter, 2002).

Willetts makes an eloquent case for the centrality of both free markets and communities to the British conservative tradition. However, as he occasionally acknowledges, and despite his efforts to dispel it, a tension between the two still remains. The resolution of the tension that he suggests is firmly on Thatcherite ground. He claims that the 'wets', who enjoyed periods of dominance between 1958 and 1965, and between 1971 and 1975, have finally been defeated by Thatcherism. Whereas previous Conservative governments succumbed, Margaret Thatcher and John Major both held firm to their pledges to 'hold inflation down and intervene less . . . The party's dangerous flirtation with corporatism and loose money is now finally over' (1992: 49). Willetts is correct to note the 'intellectual victory' (1992: 49) of neo-liberal economic theory in the Conservative Party – this consensus now extends across the political spectrum. However whilst New Labour (at least in its early years) successfully appealed to the electorate on the basis of accepting the neo-liberal economic settlement *and* developing a better society, the Conservatives struggled to convincingly do the same. Regardless of whether or not the perception is correct, the Conservatives became associated in the public mind with free market economics and little else, a perception that became particularly damaging after the ERM *débâcle* destroyed their reputation for economic competence in 1992. *Contra* Willetts, the problem for many years was perhaps the Conservatives' overwillingness to rely on the free market, certainly in their public pronouncements.

Post-Thatcherism: conservatism undone

The third perspective identified here is post-Thatcherite, exemplified by the work of John Gray. This is distinctive from anti-Thatcherism as, unlike Gilmour, in the early 1980s Gray was one of the foremost intellectual advocates of the New Right. As such, the post-Thatcherite position is important as although (like neo-Thatcherism) it began from a sympathetic position, it developed into a distinctive critical response. Gray revels in the 'unintended consequences' of neo-liberalism, rather ironically in a manner not dissimilar to the Gramscian left. As Colls commented, Gray's paradoxes come in all sizes, but 'as a general rule, the bigger the better' (Colls, 1998: 67). One of the biggest is neo-liberalism, which in the 1970s and 1980s was 'a compelling response to otherwise intractable dilemmas', but has turned out to be 'a self-undermining political project' (Gray, 1994: 7). Neo-liberalism's success was, Gray contends, dependent on the cultural and social fabric that it inevitably undermined. 'In an irony that will delight historians in years to come, the political effect of the ephemeral intellectual hegemony of the New Right in Britain, and similar countries, has probably been to accomplish the political destruction of conservatism: it may have rendered conservative parties unelectable, perhaps for a generation' (1994: 8).

This pessimism about both neo-liberalism and the electoral prospects of the Conservative Party marked a significant shift for Gray, who was for a time a supporter of the Thatcher government. He is now better known for his critique of neo-liberalism, his environmentalism and, perhaps, his fatalism. He is disillusioned with modernity, but sceptical about humanity's ability to transform things for the better: indeed, any rationally inspired attempt to do so will almost certainly make things worse (one of his many paradoxes). Nonetheless, consistent reasoning underpins Gray's intellectual journey – his position has not shifted 'qualitatively' (Gamble, 1999: 118). Unusually for a critic of globalisation and neo-liberalism, he is an Oakeshottian pessimist, inspired in his approach and method by Hayek. As Kenny notes, 'Gray remains an intellectual standard bearer for selected aspects of the conservative philosophical tradition, which he combines with a deep commitment to the value-pluralist aspect of liberalism' (1998: 84).

Gray's early position shared some similarities with that maintained by Willetts. In his essay 'A Conservative disposition' (in *Beyond the New Right*, 1993) Gray defended the policies of the Thatcher government in extending the market, and called for this agenda to be carried further forward:

> There is much farther to go in extending market institutions into hitherto sacrosanct areas, in reducing taxation, inflation and government expenditure, and in privatising industries and services. There is a strong case for introducing market choice in many social and welfare services. In all of these areas, the achievements of the past decade will provide a sound base. (Gray, 1993: 62)

However, he saw the potential danger in this programme. If Conservative policy became solely associated with marketisation, it risked provoking public 'revulsion', the result of which would be the loss of the 'traditional Tory concerns for the health of the community' to 'egalitarians and collectivists' (1993: 63). Consequently he advocated a reassertion of traditional conservatism of the One Nation ilk. The free market, whilst vital for individual freedom, 'is only one dimension of society'. Furthermore, free markets can only operate successfully and be preserved within a strong social framework. As such, 'only a reassertion of the traditional Tory concern for compassion and community' could safeguard the achievements of the Thatcher era (1993: 63).

Soon after the publication of *Beyond the New Right* Gray became a vocal critic of the marketisation agenda that he had previously backed (see Gray, 1994, 1997, 1998). This moved him closer to Gilmour's position, but was not a complete *volte-face* on his part. Gray continued to maintain that free markets could only operate successfully within a strong social framework. However, he had come to the conclusion that the effect of neo-liberal economic policies was to weaken communities and social bonds – neo-liberalism was therefore a self-undermining and self-limiting political project (1997: 1–10). This process had been carried so far that a reassertion of the paternalist and communitarian Tory tradition (of the kind he had previously espoused) was no longer a possibility. Conservatism had been undone. The resultant political consequences are (of course) ironic. The agent of the modernisation of Britain in the 1980s, the Conservative Party, forced the modernisation of the Labour Party but struggled to modernise itself. The 'capture' of the Conservative Party by neo-liberal ideas 'all but destroyed the social base of conservatism' (1994: 47) by 'hollowing-out' Tory England, whilst the 'economic constituency that gained most from early Thatcherism has been most savaged by its longer-term effects' (1997: 3). Thatcherism encouraged voters to 'question their loyalties' through rapid economic and social change. This process initially worked in the Conservatives' favour as socially mobile former Labour voters (the fabled C2s) switched their support. However, over time it 'corroded Tory support in the middle classes' and made Conservative rule 'impossible to sustain' (1998: 32). The processes of class and party dealignment identified by psephologists can be seen as part as part of this broader trend.

This forms part of a wider anti-rationalist critique by Gray of the Enlightenment and all the major ideologies that are associated with it. None can offer satisfactory solutions to dilemmas posed by the death throes of modernity. The single global market is the 'Enlightenment's project of a universal civilization in what is likely to be its final form', a self-undermining rival to democracy, the 'natural counterpart' to which is 'the politics of insecurity' (1998: 3, 17). Radical policies are therefore required to meet the human need for security, community and personal fulfilment that used to be addressed by conservatism. Market processes, 'which neo-liberalism has emancipated' must be re-embedded in communities (1997: 10). Such a project would be 'little short of revolutionary in its implications', and is of a magnitude that 'no form of conservative thought today is willing to contemplate' (1997: 10).

Upon entering opposition in 1997, the strategic terrain for the Conservative Party as defined by Gray was most unpropitious. Armed only with a redundant ideology, it could offer no solution to the economic and social problems that their New Right policies had helped to create. New Labour under Tony Blair initially filled this void, by offering the electorate a palliative promise of measures to promote social cohesion and reduce the worst effects of neo-liberalism, such as pensioner poverty, higher crime and anti-social behaviour, while still maintaining the same free market order. Alas, New Labour's attachment to a 'neo-liberal model of modernisation' meant that the effect was to give 'Thatcherism a new lease of life' (Gray, 2004: 39–40), and after some initial enthusiasm for the Blair government, Gray quickly became disillusioned. He predicted that if the Conservative Party was able to renew itself electorally (as he acknowledged that in time it probably would), lacking a relevant intellectual tradition it would struggle to respond to these challenges. 'Tory England, which it existed to conserve, is already no more than a historical memory', which leaves the party without a purpose beyond technocratic management (1997: 10).

The academic Robert Eccleshall countered Gray's pessimistic outlook for both conservatism and the Conservative Party, suggesting that Gray 'underestimates the capacity of conservatives for self-renewal' (2000a: 275). He also contended that the fortunes of the party are not necessarily linked to the intellectual conservative tradition. 'There is little correlation between intellectual purity and electoral success because conservatism in its various forms has always been something of a patchwork' (2000a: 277). This patchwork, Eccleshall argued, has always contained competing and often contradictory strands, 'whose consistency, either internally or in relation to one another, does not necessarily match standards of intellectual rigour' (2000a: 276). The intellectual 'crisis' in conservatism is perhaps then not quite as new or as apocalyptic as Gray (and others) suggested. Rather, the dominance of Thatcherite ideas in the contemporary Conservative Party is somewhat more banal. It is simply the latest chapter in a long-running debate within the party over the extent to which free market policies should be pursued – a debate that has swung for a time in the neo-liberal direction. It does not therefore represent a major break with conservatism, which Gray wrongly presents as a cogent One Nation tradition that was rather suddenly contaminated by an alien doctrine. As such, Eccleshall argues that Gray's position is lacking sufficient awareness of the intellectual history of conservatism.

Denham and Garnett consider Gray and Eccleshall's rival theses through a case study of the politics of Sir Keith Joseph. They argue that Joseph's career 'provides persuasive evidence in support of Gray's view that contemporary British conservatism is hollowed-out' (Denham and Garnett, 2002: 57). Eccleshall's primary criticism of Gray's position is, they suggest, that he is wrong to claim that New Right ideology is incompatible with conservatism, 'saying, in effect, that British conservatism can survive in contemporary conditions provided that we can accept that it is now synonymous with nineteenth century liberalism' (2002: 60). For Denham and Garnett, the neo-liberalism of the New Right runs so contrary to their understanding of conservatism that it cannot be regarded as a competing strand within that tradition. Whilst ideologies require the capacity to change in order to renew themselves and survive, 'there must be limits' to the extent of that change (2002: 60). Yet whilst claiming that neo-liberalism is alien to conservatism, they acknowledge that it has been an important position *within the Conservative Party* for over a century: 'Since Peel, the party has been split between devotees of two different – indeed deeply antagonistic – ideologies'. This division has now – finally – been all but resolved as 'one of these has left the stage of practical politics' (2002: 73). As Garnett has argued elsewhere, this means that the contemporary Conservative Party is not conservative at all, rather it is a liberal nationalist party (Garnett, 2003: 112).

The fact that by the mid 1990s neo-liberalism was in the ascendancy in the British Conservative Party is a point that Gray, Eccleshall and Garnett can agree upon. What Gray and Garnett also highlight is how the ideological dominance of this standpoint made challenging it from within the Conservative Party very difficult. Gray's post-Thatcherite critique consequently lay outside of intraparty debate, which was conducted almost exclusively within the bounds of the neo-Thatcherite perspective.

Conclusion

Lord Parkinson commented that when William Hague became leader of the Conservative Party, he faced 'a totally no win situation' (private interview, 2006). The situation confronting the Conservatives upon entering opposition in 1997 was certainly inauspicious. This chapter has located the difficulties faced by Hague along two fronts. On the electoral dimension, Hague inherited a party that had lost its reputation for governing competence, had a poor public image, and had suffered its worst election defeat in over a century. As Chapter 3 explores, Hague needed to somehow devise a strategy that would both unite the party and begin the long process of recovering its image and repositioning in a position to once again challenge for power.

However, perhaps the most fundamental problem facing the Conservative Party at this time is illustrated by the analysis of the ideational dimension. What was the Conservative Party actually for? The future purpose and direction of conservatism was far from clear, whether considered from a neo-Thatcherite, post-Thatcherite or anti-Thatcherite perspective. Differences of opinion over the causes of defeat led to confusion and disagreement over strategy in opposition, as explored in later chapters. Constrained by the neo-Thatcherite perspective, the party lacked a vibrant intellectual debate to fuel its efforts to develop a new narrative of conservatism to appeal to a twenty-first-century electorate. Ideological differences within the party over issues such as Europe (Chapter 4), national identity (Chapter 5), moral issues (Chapter 6) and the economy (Chapter 7) would shape the debate about how the party should move forward, and impact upon efforts to modernise party image and strategy.

The wilderness years: leadership strategy in opposition, 1997–2005

Leadership is hugely important. If the leader is giving you momentum there's a clear sense of direction and you tend to be following, you are moving. It is when you are static that people are standing around looking at each other and thinking 'where the hell are we going?' (Gary Streeter MP, private interview, 2008)

Introduction

In outlining the electoral and ideological crises that faced the Conservative Party on entering opposition in 1997, Chapter 2 argued that intellectual uncertainty over the direction and purpose of conservatism contributed to the difficulties the party experienced in terms of developing a new programme and narrative to combat New Labour's appeal. This chapter develops this argument through an examination of leadership strategy under William Hague, Iain Duncan Smith and Michael Howard. It contends that the dominance of neo-Thatcherism within the party limited its capacity for strategic re-orientation and electoral recovery: the Conservatives could not simply relocate themselves in the 'centre-ground' median voter position. The chapter consequently suggests that the strategies pursued by these three party leaders within these ideological bounds were sub-optimal: they underachieved even in the inauspicious electoral context they faced.

Chapter 1 showed that the 1997–2005 period has generally been characterised as one of abject strategic failure on the part of the Conservative Party leadership, which only began to be reversed in any serious and coherent way by the election of David Cameron. While this chapter argues that leadership strategy across this eight-year period was characterised by uncertainty and inconsistency, it also suggests that a more judicious picture must also take account of the challenging context identified in Chapter 2 and the way in which it was interpreted and understood by the key players at the time. Accordingly, this chapter develops an understanding as to why it took the party so long to recover power that acknowledges this complexity: something developed further in the thematic chapters that follow. It concludes that even given these difficulties the strategic leadership provided by William Hague,

Iain Duncan Smith, and Michael Howard was ultimately inadequate, and that they each underachieved even when circumstances are accounted for.

Strategic confusion, 1997–2001

The context faced by William Hague upon his election as leader of the Conservative Party could not be described as favourable. Tony Blair's New Labour government enjoyed an extended political honeymoon, and the Conservatives faced an unsympathetic media and public. The parliamentary party also remained divided on the issue of Europe. In spite of this Hague was enthusiastic about his task: he maintained that the Conservatives could win the 2001 election and never articulated a two-term strategy (Nadler, 2000: 289–92; Parkinson, 2003: 217–20). Whilst the need for a fundamental reappraisal of Conservative Party positioning and policies was apparent to most outside observers, no such consensus existed amongst Conservatives themselves. Disagreement over the reasons for defeat led to muddled and ineffective attempts to tackle its causes. Seldon and Snowdon suggest that, in opposition, the Conservative Party 'has traditionally avoided recrimination, has changed the leader, rejuvenated the party organisation to reconnect with its supporters, and adapted its policies to appeal again to the middle ground' (2005a: 244). Between 1997 and 2005, the Conservative Party changed its leader on four occasions, and frequently attempted to reinvigorate its organisation and refresh its policies, but largely failed to renew its appeal to voters. Seldon and Snowdon explain this failure as the result of the loss to Labour by the Conservative Party of its 'two secret weapons', its hunger for office and adaptability (2005a: 244). This transition, they argue, occurred during the Thatcher and Major governments, when the Conservatives metamorphosed into an 'ideological and sectional' party, the role previously occupied by Labour. The transformation of the then opposition into the 'non-ideological party' in the shape of New Labour sealed the Conservatives' fate (Seldon and Snowdon, 2005b: 245).

However, this analysis is problematic. Firstly, it implies an overly simplistic inverse relationship between success at British general elections and the vigour of a party's ideology, despite the obvious counter examples such as Labour's landslide victory in 1945 or, indeed, the Conservatives under Thatcher. Secondly, it subscribes to the 'puzzlingly long-lived notion' that the Conservative Party before Thatcher was non-ideological (Green, 2004: 2). Whilst the party was arguably more successful at *portraying* itself as non-ideological (perhaps as a result of the tradition of pragmatism and suspicion of abstract theorising in Conservative thought), this does not mean that Conservatives lacked an ideologically informed view of the world. Moreover, the more avowedly ideological rhetoric under Thatcher did not lead to electoral disaster for the Conservatives. However, the task facing the new Conservative leader in 1997 was not to purge the party of ideology, but to reconnect the party's ideological outlook and policies with a greater mass of public opinion, a challenge that remained unmet by May 2005.

A fresh start? The Hague leadership

William Hague's success in the 1997 leadership election was due in no small part to the fact that he was 'the candidate with the least number of enemies' in the party (Lansley, 2003: 221). It is telling that this was a key factor in his election, against a candidate whom the polls suggested was much more likely to appeal to the floating voters who had deserted the Conservatives in 1997. He also benefitted greatly from the failure of the right wing of the parliamentary party to unite behind one individual, support being split between Michael Howard, Peter Lilley and John Redwood. Hague's campaign sought to present him as the candidate best able to both unify and revitalise the party, and made much of his popularity amongst the new intake of Conservative MPs (Alderman, 1998: 9). Despite his unholy alliance with right-winger John Redwood, Ken Clarke was defeated in the final run-off with Hague because of his pro-European views. The Clarke–Redwood pact was part of an effort by Clarke to seize the unity mantle from Hague, who hardened his stance on the single currency in an effort to shore up his support on the right (Alderman, 1998: 11). Redwood, however, could only deliver a small proportion of his supporters to Clarke, who also lost some of his original backers (1998: 13). Lord Parkinson recalled how when he telephoned Margaret Thatcher to inform her of this link-up she was initially disbelieving, telling him 'John Redwood would never do that, he was a member of my political office'. Once confirmed, however, it was instrumental in her decision to appear with Hague and urge MPs to support him (Parkinson, private interview, 2006).

In his history of the Conservative Party Alan Clark claimed that the preoccupation of Conservative MPs with 'the balance of probability in their retaining their seats', combined with the ruthless treatment of their leaders, accounts for the party's ability to 'sleepwalk the path to whichever tactical decision will keep it in power' (Clark, 1998: 491). The vote for Hague over Clarke can be interpreted either as the victory of ideological dogmatism over traditional Tory pragmatism or, more charitably to Conservative MPs, as another example of Conservative Party statecraft, with Clarke rejected as a divisive figure unable to provide a convincing narrative of what conservatism is for. It is difficult to avoid the conclusion that Clarke's leadership bids (in 1997, 2001 and 2005) were the late casualties of the bitter ideological wrangling over Europe that consumed the party in the early 1990s (see Gamble, 1996; and Buller, 2000). However, as Heppell and Hill convincingly demonstrate, Hague's ideological acceptability over Clarke extended beyond the issue of Europe to Hague's 'drier' economic stance and more socially conservative disposition. The end result was that 'the necessary processes of adaptation, and the reconfiguring of the Conservative narrative, would be delayed by a decade' (Heppell and Hill, 2008: 64).

As a youthful, fresh figure, Hague had the opportunity to present a different tone of conservatism. As Theresa May commented, 'what William was able to do, by being a younger person, a fresh face, with new thinking, was to start a process of thinking about change in the party' (private interview, 2006). He was as well placed as anyone to unite the party, being regarded as a 'non-ideological figure' who had avoided the factional infighting of the 1990s (Nadler, 2000: 243–6; Taylor, 2003: 230). The change of leadership thus offered some hope of 'A Fresh Start' (Hague's campaign slogan) to Conservatives. Hague scored an early success with his clarification of the party's policy towards Europe in general and the single currency in particular. His decision to rule out British membership of the Euro in the event of a Conservative general election victory for at least one parliament provoked disquiet amongst the few remaining pro-Europeans on the Conservative benches, but was overwhelmingly endorsed in a ballot of party members (Garnett, 2003: 56). This tactical success, whilst not resolving the European question for the Conservatives, despatched it into the long grass for the remainder of his term of office and beyond.

Hague's early speeches demonstrate his desire to develop a more inclusive brand of conservatism. In his first speech to the party conference as leader, he declared his wish to 'tell you about an open Conservatism, that is tolerant, that believes in freedom, is about much more than economics, that believes freedom doesn't stop at the shop counter' (Hague, 1997: 3). He went on: 'I'd like to tell you about a democratic, popular Conservatism that listens . . . that has compassion at its core . . . which is rooted in its traditions, but embraces the future' (1997: 3). However, when he attempted to describe in greater depth this new kind of conservatism, Hague returned to more traditional Conservative themes. He highlighted freedom, enterprise, education, self-reliance, obligation to others, and the nation as his core beliefs and as the core values of this variety of conservatism (1997: 7–15). By stressing the importance of 'obligation to others', Hague aimed to refute those who 'labelled conservatism as being just about individualism, or even selfishness' (1997: 12). The purpose of the speech was therefore much more about changing the language, tone and emphasis of the Conservative Party's message than about any radical reassessment of policy or content. It effectively demonstrated the duality of Hague's message, which was directed at both the party and the electorate.

Hague hoped that changes of tone and language would improve the party's image, and help distance him from the Thatcher–Major era. As Nadler noted, 'throughout his leadership campaign and first years as leader, Hague's reforming rhetoric was bold and extravagant' (2000: 206). Much of this boldness was directed towards the internal organisation of the Conservative Party, which Hague attempted to rejuvenate, promising a 'democratic revolution' in his first speech as leader (Seldon and Snowdon, 2005b: 250). Hague hoped that by reforming the party organisation he could demonstrate to the public that the Conservatives were renewing themselves for government once again. He enlisted Lord Parkinson as his first Party Chairman and gave him a brief to pilot the reform process. Parkinson recalled: 'that was how

William was going to demonstrate to the country that the party had changed . . . that we were planning to be a different party in the future' (private interview, 2006). For May, these internal reforms were Hague's most significant achievement, as they began the process of change in the party, however incrementally. She regretfully acknowledged, however, that they were not accompanied by 'much policy change in terms of the issues that we campaigned on' (private interview, 2006).

As well as the policy on the Euro, Hague put his own leadership, and his package of party reforms (labelled *The Fresh Future*) to votes by party members.[1] These ballots, and the new electoral system for subsequent party leaders contained in *The Fresh Future*, represented an unprecedented extension of democracy for the Conservatives, which would resist attempts to unpick them by the outgoing Michael Howard in 2005.[2] However, this extension of 'one member, one vote' (OMOV) can be seen as coming from a more centralised, less democratic, party management. Taking inspiration from New Labour, Hague used the facade of democracy to strengthen his own position and his control over the party (Kelly, 2003: 82–106). This was an astute strategy on Hague's part, as faced with a party out of touch with mainstream public opinion, it offered the opportunity for him, with the endorsement of party members, to stamp his own message on the Conservative Party and offer a genuine 'fresh start'.

Kelly argues, however, that far from revitalising Conservative Party organisation, Hague's reforms actually weakened it. Whilst the new structures cannot be held responsible for the 2001 election defeat, they 'clearly failed to mitigate it' (2002: 38). He goes as far to suggest that in electoral terms they arguably made things worse, 'by demoralising, and thus diminishing, the party's constituency membership' (2002: 38). This is a damning critique: Hague had sold the reforms to party members as a package aimed at enhancing intraparty democracy, and with it the membership organisation. For Lees-Marshment and Quayle, however, the rationale driving the organisational changes was not primarily democratisation, but one of political marketing. They claim that the reforms were 'part of an overall strategy to make the Conservatives more market-orientated and put them in a stronger electoral position' (2001: 206). Their analysis leads to a more positive appraisal of Hague's efforts. Whilst these failed to yield results in the opinion polls or the 2001 general election, Hague did make 'significant headway in undertaking subtle but significant changes that have the long-term potential to heighten the Tories' market orientation and electoral prospects' (2001: 206).

The key issue here is whether any extension of internal party democracy is compatible with the development of a more effective marketing strategy and organisation. For example, if such reforms had the effect of making the party leadership more responsive in policy terms to the wider membership, would this leave them less able to orientate themselves to their primary 'market', namely the electorate at large? Lees-Marshment and Quayle suggest a way out of this difficulty: 'the introduction of reforms that increase individual membership power may in practice serve to strengthen the leadership' (2001: 208). This line of reasoning suggests that by devolving power to all party members (who are more likely to support the leadership) leaders can sideline radical and/or dissenting party activists. This supports the accusation noted above, that Hague centralised power. From a political marketing perspective, however, this was a prerequisite for electoral recovery: Hague's failure was not his changes to party structure, but his inability to utilise these to market the Conservative brand effectively.

Hague's deputy, Peter Lilley, understood party strategy at the time to be about decontaminating the Conservatives' tarnished image, and engaging with the current concerns of the electorate. He argued that the party needed to identify itself with contemporary issues and challenges, rather than the problems of the 1980s. For him, the 'Listening to Britain' exercise Hague initiated was about finding out what these were: 'Once we knew that we could identify ourselves with solving those problems. That was the first part of our strategy. The second part was recognising that we were seen as being nasty and looking at how to change that aspect of the image' (private interview, 2006).

Such change was certainly required if the Conservatives were to make a substantial electoral recovery. In April 1997, IpsosMORI found that 50 per cent of the British public felt that the party was 'out of touch with ordinary people', and 40 per cent believed that it would 'promise anything to win votes'. Only 11 per cent regarded it as 'moderate' and a mere 8 per cent believed that it was 'concerned about the people in real need' (IpsosMORI, 2006). In the early days of his leadership, Hague and his team appeared to grasp the need for an image as well as a policy makeover for the party. However, attempts to portray Hague as a man of the twenty-first century were the subject of embarrassment and ridicule, and looked unprofessional alongside those of the new Prime Minister (Nadler, 2000: 211–14). Just a few months into his leadership Hague's awkward public statement in response to the death of Diana, Princess of Wales contrasted sharply with Tony Blair's ability to capture and articulate the public mood. This incident illustrated the difficulties Hague experienced in attempting to develop a rapport with the media and the electorate.

In a revealing statement after his resignation, Hague acknowledged the strategic errors that he had made: 'I got this Parliament the wrong way round. I should have spent the first year or so shoring up the base Conservative vote and then reached out later on' (quoted in Walters, 2001: 111). The context of a party shaken by defeat, with a new leader at the helm, gave Hague the opportunity to style a new more inclusive (or 'compassionate') form of conservatism with wider appeal, and use the authority gained by his election and endorsement by party members to impress this on his party. In the quote above, Hague implies there was a successful 'core-vote' strategy that could have been utilised in the first few years of opposition and then built upon. However, there was no viable core-vote strategy available, illustrated by the fact that the latter half of his leadership did not shore up the core vote. At the 2001 election, the Conservatives received 8.35 million votes, over 1.25 million fewer than in 1997. On a substantially reduced turnout, the party's share of the vote advanced by 1 per cent, but the polls suggested that a higher turnout would have worked against the Conservatives (Butler and Kavanagh, 2002: 251–64; Tyrie, 2001: 5).

The fresh future curtailed

Two key events marked the shift in strategy away from 'reaching out' to 'shoring up' the base Conservative vote. The first was the 1999 R. A. Butler Memorial lecture given by the then deputy leader Peter Lilley; the second was the Conservative victory in the elections for the European Parliament later the same year. The events surrounding Lilley's speech and how it was handled by Hague are a potent illustration of the confusion amongst the party's high command about the strategy they were attempting to pursue. The speech was cleared by Hague, and was meant to elucidate the philosophy of 'Kitchen Table Conservatism' (Walters, 2001: 116). Whilst not a repudiation of Thatcherism *per se*, it was a call for a rhetorical shift by Conservatives to a narrative that recognised the value of welfare as well as the value of free markets. Lilley recognised that being associated solely with free market doctrine was damaging the party, as it served to 'reinforce people's concern that we were planning to convert public services into profit making businesses . . . that we nurse some nefarious plans to privatise health, education and almost everything else'. The free market, he argued, has never been the sole belief of Conservatives, rather 'a sense of obligation is the most fundamental Tory value of all' (Lilley, 1999).

Lilley's call for a more prominent Conservative advocacy of the importance of public services also appeared consistent with Hague's desire to forge a new identity outlined in 'Kitchen Table Conservatives' only six months earlier. This internal party document had called for a new Conservative narrative, 'which is about much more than economics', addressing issues such as the future of the public services. It called for a series of '10,000 volt initiatives' that would demonstrate in a very public way that the party was changing, and generate media attention (Conservative Party, 1998: 4–7).

Lilley's lecture was an attempt to meet this challenge. He saw it as taking forward the findings of 'Listening to Britain', although 'you didn't actually need, or shouldn't have needed, that exercise to realise that the focus had turned to improving public services, rather than the economic and industrial problems of the 1980s' (private interview, 2006). He also saw it as seeking to counter the 'unfair caricature' that the Conservatives had little interest in the public services beyond a desire to privatise them. He was warned by Nick Wood, Hague's press secretary, that the media would not admit they had previously caricatured the party inaccurately, rather 'the best you can hope for is that they will say you have changed, and abandoned these policies'. Lilley thought that was 'fair enough' and telephoned Hague to see if he was happy with that: 'he said yes, as long as you emphasise choice'. He also cleared the speech with eleven colleagues (private interview, 2006).

The reaction to the speech suggested the Conservative Party was far from ready for the kind of shocks 'Kitchen Table Conservatism' had called for. For the party, the lecture was 'one of the most incendiary in history' (Taylor, 2005: 146). Thatcher's aides informed Hague that she had 'gone ballistic' over the speech, which ironically coincided with the twentieth-anniversary celebrations of her first general election victory in 1979 (Walters, 2001: 117). Rather than play it down, party spin doctors initially portrayed the speech as a radical new departure for the Conservatives, similar in scale and importance to Labour's abandonment of Clause IV (Walters, 2001: 116; Taylor, 2005: 145–7). Lilley was surprised by the reaction, he had 'thought it would be jolly difficult to get any coverage' and saw the speech more as 'an educational resource' to 'try and teach people in the party to talk a language that didn't lend itself to being caricatured' as the party had been in the past (private interview, 2006).

At first Hague attempted to weather the storm; after all, he had cleared the speech before it was given. However, the outrage amongst the shadow cabinet, parliamentary party and local activists proved too strong, and Lilley was sacked in June (Taylor, 2005: 146). Lilley's departure was 'more or less' a direct consequence of his lecture (Lilley, private interview, 2006). Walters suggests that Hague was 'seared' by the experience: 'Having tried, tentatively, to take one-step out of the towering shadow of Margaret Thatcher, he had been forced to go running back to mummy. He was too scared to step out of line again' (2001: 118).

The furore over the Lilley's lecture weakened Hague, and made him wary of further attempts to forge a more 'inclusive' narrative of conservatism. If the key fault line in the Conservative Party was now between liberal modernisers and traditionalist reactionaries (or 'mods and rockers' as *The Times* (1998) put it), the context facing Hague was transformed in favour of the rockers by Lilley's speech.[3] It was the key moment in his decision to side with the rockers, 'despite his own sympathy for a more "inclusive" approach' (Garnett and Lynch, 2003: 258).

This shift was reinforced by the results of the 1999 elections to the European Parliament. Campaigning on a Eurosceptic manifesto entitled *In Europe, not run by Europe*, Hague led the Conservatives to a dramatic victory in the first nationwide test of the government's popularity since the 1997 general election. Despite the threat of the breakaway 'Pro-European Conservative Party' (that failed to win a single seat) and the resurgent United Kingdom Independence Party (UKIP), the Conservatives won the greatest number of seats (36) and the highest share of the vote: Labour saw its vote share slump to 28 per cent. Hague hailed the victory as 'a major breakthrough' for his party, but more cautious voices pointed to the 23 per cent turnout and Labour's continued lead in the opinion polls (BBC News, 1999). Nonetheless, the electoral success did secure Hague's position as leader, and he used the opportunity to reshuffle his shadow cabinet and evict his deputy Peter

Lilley. It reinforced Hague's position as leader and consolidated the hold of the right on power.

The Conservative campaign had been fought on the core vote messages of 'save the pound', and 'In Europe, not run by Europe'. The manifesto claimed to be that of 'a proudly British party' and promised to 'oppose all new European directives on tax harmonisation', 'oppose any extension of qualified majority voting', to protect the British rebate, and 'resist any attempt to develop a common immigration policy for the EU' (Conservative Party, 1999: 1, 16, 27). Whilst these themes played well with Conservative Party members, they lacked the appeal to form the basis of a successful general election campaign. Theresa May saw this election as a key moment for the party, as 'we took the wrong lessons from them. Having done reasonably well in those Euro elections we decided that the way forward was to adopt a core-vote strategy, and that was a mistake'. Ultimately, she suggests that was 'a collective decision' (private interview, 2006).

However, the twin issues of Europe (Chapter 4) and immigration (Chapter 5) came to characterise the public face of the Conservative Party, not least because of the amount of media attention that they received. Europe in particular dominated the Conservatives' 2001 election campaign. Gary Streeter, who was a member of the shadow cabinet, claimed that this change of strategy was not discussed beyond Hague's close circle of advisers. However, he noted that 'the election campaign that we ran took me slightly by surprise and wasn't quite what I thought we were preparing for. It did become a little bit of a core vote strategy, playing to our core support' (private interview, 2008).

In Lord Parkinson's view, Hague had little option but to pursue the core vote: reaching out beyond that was simply not a feasible possibility, as anti-Conservative feeling remained too strong:

> I'm not sure William could have broadened the party's electoral base much beyond the core vote, to be blunt. It was only four years after this horrendous defeat, and there was a real reaction against the Conservative Party. He took over a party with the smallest parliamentary representation in living memory, with no money, totally demoralised. Whatever William had done he was never going to appeal to more than the core vote. I couldn't see any floating voters coming back to us after just four years when we'd previously been in power for eighteen . . . I think William just decided to go after the core vote because it was the only vote that was likely to come his way. (Private interview, 2006)

In one sense, it would have been perverse for the Conservatives *not* to campaign on Europe and immigration – opinion polls suggested public support for the Conservative positions, particularly compared to other policy areas such as the public services. However, the focus on these issues reinforced the negative image of the Conservative Party, and failed to provide a convincing narrative about the purpose of the party.

Two slogans were deployed by the Conservatives in an attempt to give the core-vote message some coherence. The idea of the 'British Way' was first aired in Hague's October 1998 conference speech, and was an attempt to link the party explicitly with a form of national identity whilst also appealing to the One Nation tradition. This rallying cry did not survive for long, but its spirit was transferred to the 'Common Sense Revolution' (CSR) which became the dominant theme of Hague's speeches and campaigning.[4] There was a clear parallel between the CSR and Keith Joseph's advocacy of the 'common ground' in the 1970s. Joseph contrasted the common ground, which he regarded as 'the common ground with the people and their aspirations' with the 'middle ground', which is simply an unprincipled compromise between the shifting positions of politicians (1976b: 19). He argued that attempts to stay on the middle ground, in the hope of attracting the median voter, had left the Conservative Party dangerously out of touch with the people, and led to a 'left-wing ratchet' (1976b: 19). More than twenty years later the CSR was premised on a similar belief – that the politically correct liberalism of the metropolitan elite did not represent the 'real' people, who would much prefer a dose of 'common sense'. However whilst Joseph's prescription for curing the British disease in the 1970s – primarily tackling inflation and the 'union problem' (Joseph, 1976a, 1979) – chimed with the electorate and hit upon salient issues, Hague's call for a CSR did not. In 1979 the Conservatives' agenda was assisted by the Winter of Discontent, which helped to justify Joseph's thesis and tarred the Labour government with responsibility for the apparent crisis of governability and economic decline. Twenty years later, by contrast, it was the Conservatives who were held largely responsible for the problems in the public services, which the CSR professed to solve.

Harris claims that the CSR 'was narrow yet inclusive: it was inclusive to all Britons as long as they shared traditionalist values and a traditionalist approach to, for example, Europe and the issue of asylum. The mainstream majority was in direct contrast to the liberal elite' (2005: 248). This seemingly oxymoronic conclusion sums up the failure of the CSR – it *was* narrow, as it was 'inclusive' of only a certain section of the electorate, and was far from ever constituting a mainstream majority. Although it was never presented in overtly racial language, its openness only to 'all Britons' who shared certain traditionalist views implicitly excluded ethnic groups such as those Hague had flirted with at the Notting Hill Carnival. The narrow and sectional nature of this appeal left the Conservatives bereft of an overarching narrative with any widespread appeal. The Conservatives lost the 2001 election as they lacked such a narrative, they lacked a reputation for governing competence, and because the public image of both the party and its leader were poor. The focus on core-vote issues such as Europe reinforced the negative image of the party. Public enthusiasm for the Labour government had waned after four years in office, but the Conservatives did not benefit from an electoral bounce and the pendulum failed to swing. The context of Labour's commanding majority and reputation for economic management made a Conservative victory unlikely; but the failure to make any headway was a serious one, and Hague duly resigned.

The search for narrative, 2001–5

> My view was that the scale of our slaughter suggested that we needed to do some very fundamental rethinking. (John Bercow MP, private interview, 2008)

The battle between mods and rockers was rejoined in the leadership election to succeed William Hague (Chapter 6). The defeat of the doyen of the modernisers, Michael Portillo, initially appeared to be a major blow to their cause. Portillo rapidly retreated from politics, and the mantle instead passed to the archetypal rocker Iain Duncan Smith. The party Duncan Smith inherited was arguably in a more parlous state than at the time of Hague's accession. Perhaps the only major advantage Duncan Smith enjoyed over his predecessor was a greater realisation amongst at least a few of his colleagues of the scale of the challenge they faced if they were ever be returned to power (see for example, Tyrie, 2001). However, Streeter claimed that whilst the number of his colleagues on the Conservative benches who realised 'the extent to which we needed to change' was on the rise, the increase in numbers was 'a trickle, not a flood'. In his view, 'maybe twenty or thirty people were moving' (private interview, 2008). John Bercow echoed this, suggesting that 'colleagues in the parliamentary party, and party workers in the country, still felt that there was no need for the party to change in a fundamental way' (private interview, 2008). This was important as the lack of a widespread conviction about the need for change was not only a key factor in the choice of Duncan Smith as leader, but would also impede his efforts to pursue a change agenda.

The election of Duncan Smith offered no immediate prospect of a solution to the Conservatives' popularity problems, inspiring little public or media enthusiasm. Under the new rules for electing the leader, Duncan Smith received 54 votes in the second ballot of MPs, to Clarke's 59 and Portillo's 53; before winning 60.7 per cent of the vote in the final all-party run-off against Clarke. This system was blamed for the election of Duncan Smith and the travails that followed, despite the lack of evidence to suggest that a different result would have been achieved under the old rules (Cowley and Green, 2005: 47–50).[5] Had either Clarke or Portillo emerged victorious, they would have faced the same apparent lack of legitimacy having secured (like Duncan Smith) barely one-third support in the parliamentary party. They would also have faced the same problem of how to respond to the Blairite Labour hegemony. In the context of rising economic prosperity Labour had successfully made improving the public services the electorate's key concern, and their 'Third Way' narrative suggested a new agenda somewhere between privatisation and marketisation on the one hand and traditional state-centric approaches on the other. Whilst the government's progress in improving the public services between 1997 and 2001 did not fulfil the electorate's hopes, the Conservatives had 'evolved neither a convincing narrative nor effective statecraft' in answer to this quandary (Taylor, 2005: 152).

The brief tenure of Duncan Smith also demonstrated the importance of the individual decisions and actions of leaders. A vote of confidence in his leadership was ultimately triggered by the faintly ridiculous 'Betsygate' scandal, when he was accused of impropriety over the employment of his wife in his private office (Duncan Smith was later exonerated); but other more serious avoidable mistakes were made (O'Hara, 2005: 296–7). The fiasco over the Adoption and Children Bill exposed his tactical ineptitude as a leader, and the irony of the former Maastricht rebel demanding that the party 'unite or die' was not lost on many. His weak grip on the party was apparent to the both the media and the public, particularly after his botched attempt to install Barry Legg as chief executive of Conservative Central Office (Redwood, 2004: 156). Duncan Smith lacked the charismatic public persona necessary for success in the media age, and the polls suggested that he was an electoral liability (Garnett and Lynch, 2003b: 8). Nonetheless, an embryonic Conservative narrative emerged during his leadership, and a substantive policy renewal process began.

On the quiet: progress under Duncan Smith

Despite his reputation as a traditionalist hardliner, Duncan Smith showed signs of having heeded some of the lessons of defeat. Within weeks of being elected leader, he expressed his desire to re-establish the Conservative Party as a party of ideas by launching a policy review. The early days of his leadership were overshadowed by the events of 9/11, but he used his first keynote conference address as leader to proclaim that 'public services are our greatest mission', and pledged to 'bring an open mind to the task of reforming public services' (Duncan Smith, 2001).

This speech marked the beginning of a concerted effort by the Conservatives to reposition themselves as a party of the public services, an agenda that would outlive Duncan Smith's leadership and be taken into the 2005 general election and beyond. It also marked a shift in rhetoric towards pragmatic politics, and a search for attractive policies. Members of the shadow cabinet made speeches and wrote articles on the subject of schools, hospitals and crime consistently over the following four years (in contrast to the preceding parliament). The issue of Europe received a much lower profile, although opposition to the proposed European Constitution was quickly established. However, a commitment to the public services presented a strategic dilemma to the Conservatives. How could they balance their desire for lower taxes with the new dedication to public services? (Taylor, 2005: 144–53).

The process of policy renewal made progress under Duncan Smith, and his record in this regard compares favourably to that of his predecessor (Seldon and Snowdon, 2005a: 259–62). Duncan Smith pledged to 'champion the vulnerable', with a revival of public services 'as community institutions, not branch offices of government'

(Duncan Smith, 2002b). He used his first anniversary as party leader to declare publicly his desire to defeat 'the five giants' that blight Britain's poorest communities. The targets he selected – 'failing schools, crime, substandard healthcare, child poverty, and insecurity in old age' – were less instructive than the language he chose to employ, which deliberately echoed that of the Beveridge Report (Duncan Smith, 2002d; Seldon and Snowdon, 2005a: 260–1). Similarly, his speech to the 'Compassionate Conservatism Conference' a year later declared that Labour should not be allowed a monopoly on compassion, as poverty 'is too important [an issue] to leave to any one political party' (Duncan Smith, 2003).

Duncan Smith saw this as a two-stage strategy. The first stage was 'to move away from the subjects that we are most readily identified with . . . [on to] issues that are not normally associated as priorities of the Conservative Party' (Duncan Smith, private interview, 2006). Hence the persistent focus on public services:

> When people were asked about their priorities, they normally started with health, and then went go things like education and employment, and we needed to reflect those priorities as our own. I had a sense that the public needed to instinctively begin to re-identify with the party that they felt cared about what they did, a big challenge. (Private interview, 2006)

The second phase was then to 'refocus the party even further still, into the problems of the worst-off in society' (private interview, 2006). The aim of this was not to win votes in the deprived areas of Britain, but to demonstrate 'that the Conservative Party back in government would want to govern in the best interests of Britain as a whole' rather than in the interests of a privileged elite with which it had (unfairly, in his view) become identified (Duncan Smith, private interview, 2006).

This attitude demonstrated that Duncan Smith had appreciated one of the major electoral problems that the Conservative Party faced – its public image, which Hague's CSR had reinforced as a narrow, sectional party. Duncan Smith hoped to change this not by changing policy on Europe or immigration (these were in fact firmed slightly), but by concentrating on other issues. For Duncan Smith, 'we needed at least two years working away at this before we even talked about those [Europe and immigration] again' (private interview, 2006). As such, Duncan Smith made a consistent attempt to recast conservatism in the language of 'Compassionate Conservatism', with key foci on tackling poverty and improving the public services. Arguably, only a figure from the right such as Duncan Smith could pursue such a strategy, as it drew criticism from that wing of the party (Cowley and Green, 2005: 52).

Like Hague's brief flirtation with compassionate conservatism it failed, despite the greater persistence of Duncan Smith. It failed not because it lacked intellectual coherence but because of poor leadership and party image. Conservative Party image data remained stubbornly negative under both Duncan Smith and Howard, showing little deviation from the picture bequeathed by Hague (Table 3.1).

Table 3.1 Conservative Party image, 1997–2005

Percentages of respondents agreeing that the Conservative Party . . .	April 1997	May 2001	September 2003	April 2005	Change, 2001–5 +/− %
Keeps its promises	5	5	4	3	−2
Understands the problems facing Britain	20	18	20	22	+4
Represents all classes	10	8	8	9	+1
Looks after the interests of people like us	9	11	9	11	−
Is moderate	11	12	14	12	−
Is extreme	10	12	12	14	+2
Is concerned about the people in real need	8	9	11	14	+5
Has a good team of leaders	10	7	8	8	+1
Will promise anything to win votes	40	46	35	45	−1
Is out of touch with ordinary people	50	36	32	32	−4
Has sensible policies	14	15	16	17	+2
Is too dominated by its leader	10	13	5	16	+3
Is professional in its approach	13	13	14	15	+2
Is divided	44	30	34	23	−7
No opinion	9	10	19	14	+4

Source: Data on Conservative Party image from IpsosMORI, www.ipsos-mori.com/.

Duncan Smith was hampered from the beginning by a lack of support in the parliamentary party, and he failed even to convince key members of his shadow cabinet of the merits of his approach (Seldon and Snowdon, 2005a: 260). Theresa May noted that support for the 'change' agenda amongst her shadow cabinet colleagues 'varied' (private interview, 2006). One shadow cabinet member commented that: 'I didn't dislike Iain personally but thought that his leadership was completely hopeless and there wasn't the slightest chance of us winning an election under his leadership' (private interview, 2005). Another of Duncan Smith's frontbench colleagues echoed this sentiment: 'He was a pleasant enough fellow but totally ill-suited to the task of leading the Conservative Party' (private interview, 2009). For Streeter, 'the agenda was coming right, although I'm not sure that people believed it from us at that stage, and that's important'. The central problem was Duncan Smith's personal appeal and skills: 'Iain was not electable as a Prime Minister. It was just about his personal leadership, he just wasn't up to it' (private interview, 2008). Perceptions by his colleagues of Duncan Smith's leadership limitations were important: a widespread doubt about his ability to lead made his task in pursuing an agenda to change the positioning and image of the Conservative Party all the more difficult.

Like Hague, Duncan Smith also showed signs of deviating from this agenda in the light of his failure to increase the level of Conservative Party support. John Bercow, who resigned from Duncan Smith's shadow cabinet (Chapter 6) saw his agenda for change as limited and undermined by a number of problems. He accepts that Duncan Smith started the policy renewal process, but only on 'a pretty modest scale'. He also suggested that when this did not lead to an improvement in the opinion polls, Duncan Smith changed tack when he should have held his line: 'once he failed to make progress in the polls he retreated into his shell and started to adopt the core vote approach . . . I thought that was a great pity' (Bercow, private interview, 2008).

Duncan Smith's legacy was the policy agenda adopted by Michael Howard (albeit in a pared-down form) and in helping create the political space in which Cameron would later push forward a modernisation agenda (Hayton and Heppell, 2010). As Theresa May noted, 'Iain did a lot more to change the party and to move the change agenda forward than many people actually realise' (private interview, 2006). As a result of Duncan Smith's efforts the Conservatives had a more consistent policy agenda, with a greater range of substantive policies on key issues such as health, education and crime. However, they had failed to dissipate the perception that they were 'the nasty party', and their protestations about tackling poverty and improving the public services therefore remained unconvincing. This failure derived in part from Duncan Smith's limitations as a leader and public communicator, but also from the broader neo-Thatcherite viewpoint within which he had to operate. Lacking leadership authority he was unable to orchestrate a shift in the Conservatives' positioning or public image even towards the boundaries of this discursive framework. This left the Conservatives in a bind. To revert their focus to the unholy 'Tebbit trinity' of Europe, immigration and tax would only serve to reinforce the 'nasty party' image, and confirm public suspicions of their true colours.[6] However, the Conservative message on poverty and the public services, hampered by a lack of support amongst some Conservatives themselves and the poor communication skills of their leader, had failed to convince a sceptical electorate. A change of leadership, despite fear of yet more bloodletting, became the most palatable option.

Abandoning the search: Michael Howard and a third defeat

The effort to develop a coherent narrative was abandoned by Michael Howard. His emphasis was on delivery. 'It's time for action' was the by-line of the party's 2005 manifesto, which also laid out a timetable for action for the first few months of Conservative government. Howard told colleagues that: 'Talking about small concrete measures to improve people's lives is what I'm about, not having a big idea or vision'. This frustrated some, one shadow minister commented that: 'The dye was cast then. We were not going to have a strategy' (quoted in Kavanagh and Butler, 2005: 38).

This was a strategic error by Howard. His coronation dispelled fears of further public bloodshed in yet another leadership contest, and his leadership brought unity to the party and the apparent revival of the desire for power traditionally regarded as the key to Conservative hegemony. Howard's early pronouncements as leader also suggested that he would take forward the reform agenda begun by Duncan Smith. Two months after becoming leader, he gave a major speech to the think-tank Policy Exchange outlining his vision of 'The British Dream'. In it, Howard discussed proposals for improving schools and the health service, better provision of childcare, his support for civil partnerships, and how to 'help families achieve the work–life balance that is best for them' (Howard, 2004: 14). There was no mention of immigration or asylum, and just one passing reference to the European Union. Today, he declared, 'we face new challenges. As the country's economy has strengthened and stabilised, the failings of our public services have become clear' (2004: 18). As such, this speech appeared to recognise, as Duncan Smith had done, the importance of the public services in the forthcoming election.

Howard acknowledged that a lot of policy work had been carried out under his predecessor, and regarded his own leadership as a continuation of the broad agenda Duncan Smith had set, claiming 'there was no radical shift' (Howard, private interview, 2006). However, Duncan Smith had tried to deploy a two-stage strategy: the first stage involving a greater focus on the public services and the development of new policies in this area, and a second stage aimed at changing people's image of the Conservatives through a focus on issues not traditionally associated with the party, particularly the social justice agenda. By his own acknowledgement, Howard failed to carry this forward: 'Yes, I probably didn't do enough in terms of talking about championing the vulnerable, although I subscribe to his general approach . . . we developed the policies that Iain had started to develop' (private interview, 2006). By contrast, Duncan Smith saw his strategy as neglected by his successor, but then picked up once again by David Cameron (Hayton and Heppell, 2010: 440–2). Theresa May views the Howard period in a similar way:

> I think Michael, to a very great extent, returned us to the more traditional Conservative Party areas . . . there were some areas where he did carry forward the change . . . but the wider issues of social justice, and helping the vulnerable, those sort of things were not really carried forward. (Private interview, 2006)

This shift in emphasis towards core Conservative themes can be seen throughout Howard's later speeches, and in the Conservative campaign at the 2005 election. A typical Howard speech, in the run-up to the election, declared that 'it's time to take a stand on the issues that matter' (Howard, 2005). In this speech Howard suggested that voters 'unhappy about higher taxes, uncontrolled immigration, rising crime and dirty hospitals' should 'take a stand' and 'be true to our country' by voting against the government (2005). Although public service issues such as health and education were mentioned, Howard's claims that the Conservatives would address them more successfully than Labour lacked credibility or a coherent critique. Specific pledges such as 'cleaner hospitals' addressed genuine public concerns, but did not represent a programme for significant public service reform – an agenda Labour continued to dominate. This failure is even more damning as Howard's authority – having successfully inculcated his MPs with discipline and unity – offered him the opportunity denied to Duncan Smith to pull the party behind the 'Compassionate Conservatism' narrative. Instead, Howard calculated that his own image as a Thatcherite right-winger (not dissimilar to that of his predecessor) would render such a pitch unconvincing.

Howard's message to the country at the 2005 general election was an offer of incremental, quantifiable measures tied to Howard personally (he pledged to resign if he failed to deliver). The Conservatives lost their reputation for governing competence with the ERM *débâcle* in 1992, and this accountability pledge was an attempt to restore faith in the party's ability to manage the country. The Conservatives' campaign was criticised for the prominence given to immigration policy, although this can be partly explained by the increased salience of the issue (Chapter 5). The influence of Lynton Crosby, Howard's election strategist, was also important in determining the tone of the campaign. As Michael Howard noted, while Crosby did not determine the content of policies, 'in terms of the emphasis we gave to different policies and the way that we presented them, certainly Lynton's advice was very influential' (private interview, 2006). Compared to the party's campaign of four years previously, Howard's five pledges covered a broader range of concerns. Duncan Smith's public service agenda was utilised, albeit in a grossly pared-down form. The core theme of Duncan Smith's agenda – concern for the vulnerable and the need for social justice – no longer featured. Without this, the Conservatives lacked an overarching narrative, and were left with managerialism, with Howard to be personally accountable, as the unifying theme. Without an economic crisis to destroy Labour's reputation for economic competence, it was a battle that the Conservatives could not hope to win.

Conclusion: strategic failure

The scale of the Conservative Party's woes in 1997 is well documented: after eighteen years in office, the 'natural party of government' saw its share of the vote and representation in the House of Commons collapse, in a landslide defeat the size of which few had anticipated. Four years later, 'Labour's second landslide' produced another defeat of similar statistical magnitude, arguably the worst result in the Conservative Party's history (Geddes and Tonge, 2001; Tyrie, 2001: 3). The general election of 2005 saw the government's majority more than halved, and the Conservative ranks swelled to 198, a net gain of 32 seats. This result prevented the implosion of the Conservative Party as a credible political force. The party came within 3 percentage points of equalling Labour's share of the vote, although this was largely due to a decline in support for the governing party from 40.7 per cent in 2001 to 35.2 per cent in 2005. The Conservatives actually out-polled Labour by 57,000 votes in England, although they won 93 fewer seats. However, the 32.4 per cent of the national vote received by the Conservatives represented an improvement of only 0.7 per cent on 2001, and the party's share of the vote fell in the North East; the North West; Yorkshire and Humberside; and, perhaps most surprisingly, the East Midlands (Ashcroft, 2005: 85; Kavanagh and Butler, 2005: 204–7). Michael Howard followed the precedent set by William Hague and John Major before him by resigning the day after the election.

These three consecutive defeats represent the Conservatives' worst electoral performance for over a century. This failure was the result of an unfavourable political terrain combined with poor strategic decision-making by the party leadership. The external factors of a resurgent centrist Labour Party and an electoral system biased against them made a Conservative return to power within four years of 1997 highly improbable, but the failure to make any substantive progress towards that goal represented a serious breakdown for an organisation that prides itself on being a governing party (Ball, 2005: 1).

After the 1997 election Willetts and Forsdyke suggested that the Conservatives could either move rapidly to regain the electorate's confidence, or be forced to change more slowly by a series of defeats, either way change was 'inescapable' (1999: 1). The Conservatives chose the long road to renewal after 1997 (Hayton, 2012). Constrained by the dominance of neo-Thatcherism within the party, Hague, Duncan Smith and Howard all struggled to re-orientate the Conservatives and pursue a consistent strategy towards recovery. In the early part of Hague's leadership, (unsuccessful) efforts were made to rebrand the party and to provide a sense of distance from the Thatcher–Major era. In the words of the then Party Chairman 'we tried everything', though nothing seemed to work (Ancram, private interview, 2007). This lack of a consistent or clear approach left the party with only a narrow core-vote appeal to fall back on in 2001, which only served to make the job of his successor all the more difficult. Duncan Smith made a more prolonged attempt to forge a consistent narrative, but also with little apparent positive effect in the polls. In policy terms, Duncan Smith did lay some important foundations, and in the development of his social justice agenda began the long process of re-engaging the Conservatives with issues that had received little attention from Thatcherism. However, his inability to manage his party or present it in a credible way meant that his leadership was doomed. For Seldon and Snowdon, Michael Howard 'had the easiest task, and his failure was thus the greatest' (2005b: 143). The relatively fortuitous circumstances he enjoyed, of a policy agenda, rapidly united party and an embryonic inclusive narrative, were not transformed into a coherent strategy, and were ultimately reduced to a 'mean-spirited and reactionary' election campaign (Portillo, 2005).

A classic Downsian analysis would suggest that the party should have moved rapidly to reposition itself in the 'centre-ground' position of the median voter following defeat in 1997. Such an explanation is clearly inadequate, and by unpicking the strategic calculations of key actors we can paint a more nuanced picture. In this case, the analytical division between 'mods and rockers' in the Conservative Party reflects a disagreement over electoral strategy based on differing interpretations of the political situation and the nature of the party's context. The presence of a threat to the party's 'right flank' in the form of UKIP undoubtedly informed these strategic calculations, inhibiting a Downsian repositioning. The perceived need to retain the party's core vote informed strategic decision-making, but in articulating an appeal designed to do this the party reduced its attractiveness to the wider electorate. This influenced the election campaigns of both 2001 and 2005, with the focus on immigration during the latter being a deliberate ploy to neutralise the UKIP threat.

The three leaders and eight years of opposition examined in this chapter expose a record of strategic electoral failure by the Conservative Party. During this time the Conservatives were unable to fulfil the minimum requirement for an opposition party: the presentation of a credible and coherent governing alternative. Incapacity to appreciate the reasons for defeat in 1997 led to strategic confusion and a failure to develop a consistent narrative of conservatism in this period. This chapter has demonstrated how a combination of leadership failings and ideological and contextual constraints inhibited progress towards this objective, and thus serves as important backdrop to the discussion of how this began to change under the leadership of David Cameron. The chapters that follow discuss this in greater depth in relation to four particular dilemmas for contemporary conservatism, namely European integration, national identity, social morality and neo-liberal political economy.

Notes

1 An all-party ballot was also held by Hague on his draft manifesto in October 2000. For a breakdown of the results from all of these ballots see Kelly (2003: 88).

2 After the 2005 election defeat, Howard immediately announced his attention to resign the party leadership, but not until a review had been conducted into the rules for selecting the next leader. Party activists rejected the eventuating plan to return the choice of leader back to MPs.

3 *The Times* borrowed the 'mods and rockers' analogy from the conflicting 1960s youth subcultures. The rockers were associated with heavy drinking and 1950s rock and roll, whilst the mods experimented with recreational drugs, rhythm and blues, and psychedelia. In the case of the Conservative Party, *The Times* saw the mods as liberal modernisers, and the rockers as authoritarian traditionalists. This is discussed at greater length in Chapter 6.

4 For a systematic analysis of the CSR strategy, see Harris (2005), particularly Chapters 6 and 7.

5 For example, Michael Howard and Peter Lilley are both of the view that Duncan Smith would have emerged victorious had the final decision remained with MPs (Denham and O'Hara, 2008: 69, n. 47).

6 The 'Tebbit trinity' is Andrew Rawnsley's phrase, quoted in O'Hara (2005: 324).

Part II

Themes and issues

4

The European question

Introduction

The European question has long been a difficult one for the Conservative Party, as it goes to the heart of the question of national identity. Like the issue of immigration, which is examined in Chapter 5, it challenges, and has often been seen as threatening British, and particularly English, national identity. For the Conservative Party, which has historically identified itself with 'the nation', this has caused particular problems. As Britain lost its empire and searched for a new role, so did the Conservative Party. Europe, as Harold Macmillan realised, potentially offered a post-imperial identity for both (George and Sowemimo, 1996: 244). However, not least because of de Gaulle's vetoes, Macmillan was unable to settle the debate in the Conservative Party decisively in favour of Europe. Even after Edward Heath successfully negotiated British entry to the European Economic Community (EEC), his own enthusiasm for the project was not spread through the party as a whole (George and Sowemimo, 1996: 246).

The issue of European integration is of special significance in terms of understanding post-Thatcherite Conservative politics as, on the surface at least, during the period of opposition under scrutiny it appeared to lose much of its potency, as the parliamentary party united around a broadly Eurosceptic position. This represented a dramatic shift compared to the intense divisions Europe caused in the 1980s and 1990s. Key to this was contextual change in terms of the diminishing electoral salience of the issue, and an ideational shift within the Conservative Party itself. This chapter analyses how this once noxious issue was apparently resolved, and how this process related to the wider question of the Conservative Party's strategy and electoral problems between 1997 and 2010. The chapter examines how the party hierarchy sought to manage it in relation to both party and public opinion, and considers whether the leadership deliberately sought to neutralise the issue, or whether this was an unintended consequence of, or independent from, their actions. How this impacted upon Cameron's modernisation agenda is also explored. Finally, the chapter considers the potential for the issue to regain its toxicity for the Conservatives in the future, and suggests that it retains the potential to cause significant difficulties for the party in office.

The European problem

Since the end of the Second World War, the contours of British politics have been shaped by the question of the United Kingdom's place in the world, as a former hegemonic power adjusting to a new position of reduced global status. Europe emerged as a choice for Britain, 'although the choice was born from a lack of alternatives' (Geddes, 2005b: 122). This process had profound domestic as well as geo-political implications, drawing into question understandings of British identity and the future of the UK state. This manifested itself in both a preoccupation with the politics of decline,[1] and in the debate about Britain's relationship with the American superpower and the emerging economic and political association in Europe. British relations with Europe have increasingly been seen as conflicting with the 'special relationship' with the United States, and it is unclear whether Britain will be able to continue to view itself feasibly as a bridge between the two, or whether it will be forced to opt for one over the other (Gamble, 2003: 1).

These questions are difficult ones for all political parties, and have tended to cut across traditional left–right ideological demarcations, within and between parties. For Conservatives, Britain's relation to Europe has always been regarded and understood in the context of a particular view of the state and the nation. Between 1945 and 1975, the Conservative view of the state was dominated by the 'progressive right', which accepted the welfare state and Keynesian economic strategy in the interests of maintaining social order and national unity (Smith, 1999: 187; Gamble, 1974). On to this progressive right view can be mapped the Heathite national strategy of Europeanist economic modernisation (Lynch, 1999: 28–38). This theory of the state was challenged by the New Right critique, and Heath's national strategy was opposed by a Powellite alternative (Lynch, 1999: 38–45). Following Thatcher's election as party leader in 1975, a Thatcherite theory of the state began to emerge, and came to dominate the Conservative standpoint from the late 1970s. This view 'rejected the pluralism of traditional Conservatism, taking from Enoch Powell the idea of the supreme importance of Parliament as the sovereign decision-maker, with the elected executive at its pinnacle' (Smith, 1999: 188). This perspective continues to underpin the predominant Conservative position, that European integration threatens to undermine national sovereignty and with it the integrity of the state and the legitimacy of its institutions. In this sense, the current Conservative view of the state is a traditional and rather inflexible variant of the Westminster Model (see Smith, 1999: 9–37). More conspiratorial versions of this story regard the European Union as attempting to 'break-up' the United Kingdom so that it can be subsumed within a federal 'Europe of the regions' super-state (Booker and North, 1997; Hitchens, 1999: 364–7). Yet Conservative administrations led the process of British engagement with Europe from the early 1950s that culminated with accession to the EEC in 1973 under Edward Heath, and supported continued membership (whilst in opposition under the leadership of Margaret Thatcher) in the 1975 referendum campaign. Labour, by contrast, was suspicious of attempts to join the EEC, and Wilson's decision to hold a referendum was prompted by party and cabinet divisions. Even this clear vote in favour of the 'Common Market' failed to heal Labour's internal rift, and by the early 1980s the Conservatives could rightly claim to be the 'party of Europe' as their opponents advocated withdrawal from the EEC and suffered the Social Democratic Party (SDP) breakaway in large part because of the issue (Butler, 1996: 934).

As in many other areas, it was the Thatcher governments that broke this pattern in British politics. Thatcherism profoundly altered the shape of the strategic environment faced by the Conservatives, but also had an internal effect on the party and its own understanding of that context through a transformation of its dominant ideological perspective. At the heart of this ideological shift was the economic liberalism of the New Right, but as Gamble (1996: 35) argued, it also included a turn towards more overtly (English) nationalist discourse and, to some degree, away from the idea of patriotic Britishness associated with state and empire that the Conservatives had traditionally defended. Previously, a One Nation political strategy had 'established the Conservatives as the party of nation, Empire and Union, the authentic voice of a state patriotism built around British identity and institutions'. This strategy had substantial electoral and political benefits, but by the late 1960s was undermined by decolonisation, declinism, Celtic nationalism, and an emerging multiculturalism (Lynch, 1999: 49). Powellism, Lynch suggests, was 'a Tory nationalist reaction to this ... [that] replaced imperial myths with those of national homogeneity and unfettered parliamentary sovereignty' (1999: 49), and in which the genesis of the Thatcherite politics of nationhood can be found (1999: 47).

Powell was a radical and a forward-thinking Conservative to the extent that he sought to redefine national identity in terms suited to the end of empire. However, in his endeavours to define a post-imperial destiny, Powell promulgated a myth of an ancient, unchanging England that pre-dated the imperial era. This exclusivist stance almost inevitably became a race-based argument. The idea of national *difference* is central to this story, and difference in particular from Europe. As Thatcher herself argued, 'Britain *is* different. That is why Britain is still repeatedly at odds with the other European countries' (2002: 366). Mindful of political constraints, while in office Thatcher was reluctant to translate her Powellite rhetoric and sympathies into their logical policy conclusions, but the lineage between Powellism and Thatcherism is clear.

The Thatcher years were instrumental in creating the circumstances which led to intense Conservative disunity over Europe, notably over the ratification of the Maastricht Treaty in the early 1990s. The stricter view of sovereignty promulgated by Powellism and Thatcherism was central to this, as a zero-sum conception that saw any move towards sharing or 'pooling' sovereignty as a loss, even if it could be justified on 'pragmatic' statecraft grounds as being in the national interest. Gamble attributes the rise of Euroscepticism in the Conservative Party directly to Thatcher herself. Her leadership, he argues, led to the denial of the possibility (maintained by the Conservative Party leadership previously) that 'Britain could be both European and Atlanticist' (2003: 176). Having signed the integrationist Single European Act (SEA) in 1986, Thatcher performed a *volte-face* in her 1988 Bruges speech, which articulated a pungent Euroscepticism. Being voiced by an incumbent Prime Minister this signalled that Conservative opposition to Europe was no longer restricted to the backbenches. It also inaugurated the party management problems that Thatcher's successor would face, particularly during the ratification of the Maastricht Treaty.

The attachment to neo-liberalism is also important for understanding Thatcherite attitudes towards European integration. As Thatcher noted in her Bruges speech, her government had not 'rolled back the frontiers of the state in Britain, only to see them re-imposed at a European level with a European super-state exercising a new dominance from Brussels' (Thatcher, 1988). A party's outlook towards European integration can thus be understood as a function of its (domestic) political position, particularly its view on the appropriate role of the state in the management of the economy. Marks and Wilson used cleavage theory to analyse party responses to European integration, and concluded that the issue 'is assimilated into pre-existing ideologies of party leaders, activists and constituencies that reflect long-standing commitments on fundamental domestic issues' (2000: 433). Neo-liberals consequently support European integration to the extent that it contributes to the weakening of market restraints. However, they oppose political integration as they fear it would create a new source of authority for regulating markets (2000: 455). Thatcher's support for the SEA was therefore consistent with a neo-liberal strategy, which saw a comparative advantage in a deregulated, low-tax economy within a single market area. Qualified majority voting (QMV), for example, regarded by some as one of the most significant erosions of British sovereignty, was supported by Thatcher as a necessary means to this end (Gamble, 2003: 176; Marks and Wilson, 2000: 455).

In their survey of European conservative parties, Marks and Wilson found that most supported EMU 'as the final step' in the creation of a liberalised single market. However, as they also note, neo-liberalism 'exists alongside a national orientation' in most conservative parties (2000: 455). For Conservatives, nationalism thus supplies the 'unambiguous bottom line for European integration', namely that 'the national state should not share with European institutions its legitimate sovereign right to govern persons living in its territory' (Marks and Wilson, 2000: 455). In Britain, the single currency (unlike the single market which a majority were willing to accept) was viewed by most Conservatives as an infringement of that right, much more so than the completion of the single market. The symbolic significance of abolishing pound sterling was a step too far for Conservative Eurosceptics, who argued fiercely against it on political grounds (they feared it would lead to a federal Europe) rather than in purely economic terms (e.g. Lamont, 1999).

Whilst it is a very useful stylisation of how views on European integration are informed by concerns at other levels of governance, Marks and Wilson's generalised model can only go so far in explaining the distinctive positions of different conservative parties. In the case of the British Conservative Party, the prevalent position on European integration has also been affected by a neo-liberal view of globalisation, which Baker, Gamble and Seawright (2002) have characterised as 'hyperglobalism'. This variant of neo-liberalism has led some Conservatives to oppose membership of the European Union completely. Conservative MP Douglas Carswell, for example, argues that British participation 'has been a political and economic disaster' and believes that 'if we do not leave sooner rather than later it will be a catastrophe' (2006: 1). For hyperglobalists, 'the national policy-making constraints of globalisation are welcomed because they rule out the kind of social democratic and socialist measures which are viewed as incompatible with British national identity, forcing the government to set the people free whatever its ideological predilections' (Baker, Gamble and Seawright, 2002: 409). The competition state is therefore compelled to pursue a free market policy of minimal state intervention in order to maintain national economic prosperity in the globalised economy. This not only 'sets the people free', but entails a Hayekian form of spontaneous order, of which the nation is the natural product.

The hyperglobalist and Eurosceptical strand of British conservatism that Baker, Gamble and Seawright identify thus rejects the rationally planned European Union as a threat to the nation, and as an infringement of their (limited) view of freedom that will inhibit competitiveness and undermine the economic gains of Thatcherism. For advocates of this position, the European Union threatens to undermine the neo-liberal project at home (e.g. Portillo, 1998). Articulated through a discourse of globalisation, the Thatcherite mantras of 'no alternative' and 'no turning back' ascended 'to a global plain' (Geddes, 2004: 195). Although a few prominent Europhiles in John Major's government, notably Michael Heseltine and Kenneth Clarke, continued to view EMU as an essentially economic question and prevented Major from hardening government policy beyond the position of 'wait and see', by the time of the 1997 election the Conservative Party was generally Eurosceptic in outlook. In an effort to pacify this sentiment Major conceded that a referendum would be held on Euro membership in the event that the government recommended entry.

A 1994 survey of the Parliamentary Conservative Party (PCP) found the majority of Conservative MPs to be clearly Eurosceptic: 50 per cent favoured the passing of an act of parliament to 'establish explicitly the ultimate supremacy of Parliament over EU legislation'; 60 per cent thought that the Commission should lose the ability to initiate legislation; and 85 per cent thought that Britain should use its veto to prevent the introduction of QMV for foreign and defence policy. Further, in the opinion of 79 per cent, the way to achieve greater democratic accountability over the European Union was not through reform or democratisation of European-level institutions, but by 'strengthening the scrutiny by national parliaments of the EU legislative process'. A repeat of the survey in 1998 found these figures to have increased to 69 per cent; 61 per cent; 90 per cent; and 84 per cent, respectively (Baker, Gamble and Seawright, 2002: 417).

This degree of Euroscepticism played a decisive role in the 1997 leadership election, as the seemingly better qualified, more experienced, more popular but Europhile Kenneth Clarke was passed over in favour of William Hague, who was understood to be less pro-European (despite Clarke's unholy alliance with arch-Eurosceptic John Redwood). A mock advertisement for the job of Conservative leader published in *The Economist* in March 1997 stated that candidates '[m]ust be of Eurosceptical disposition, but not so Eurosceptical as to split the party', and Hague met these criteria in a way that Clarke could not (*The Economist*, 13 March 1997, quoted in Harris, 2005: 100). Similarly in 2001, attitudes to European integration played an important part in the election as leader of the former Maastricht rebel Iain Duncan Smith, who won by a clear margin (again over Ken Clarke) in a ballot of party members (Chapter 3). The following sections analyse Conservative positions on European integration between 1997 and 2010, and consider whether an understanding of this is essential for an understanding of the Conservatives' travails in opposition.

William Hague: managing the European question, 1997–2001

On becoming Conservative Party leader, Europe presented William Hague with challenges on both the ideational and electoral dimensions. In electoral terms, the Conservatives had been badly affected by their image as a disunited party, and Europe was central to this picture. At the time of the 1997 election, MORI surveys found that 44 per cent of respondents saw the Conservatives as divided (Table 3.1, p. 53). Cowley comments that, 'by the middle of 1996, the percentage of people who thought that the Conservatives were united had fallen into single figures. The public saw the Conservatives as riven' (Cowley, 1997: 40–1). In fact, the 1992 parliament had not been an unusually rebellious one on the Conservative benches: in relative terms the level of dissent was similar for other recent parliaments (Cowley, 1997: 41). As Cowley notes, contrary to public perception 'cohesion remained the norm, dissent the exception', and there was 'no collapse in Party discipline' (1997: 42). Europe, however, particularly the ratification of the Maastricht Treaty, was a highly visible exception, over which more than 60 per cent of Conservative back-bench dissent activity during the 1992 parliament occurred (Cowley, 1997: 42). Hague therefore needed to settle party policy on European integration, particularly on the most pressing and divisive issue of a European single currency, as a matter of urgent party management.

Europe presented a difficult challenge to the Conservatives in party management terms in part because of its ideational aspect: unwillingness to compromise from strongly held positions had served to highlight the ideological fissures in the party under Major, and threatened to do the same under Hague. Conservative divisions over Europe also reflected the malaise over the purpose and direction of conservatism discussed in Chapter 2. Thatcherism had a transformative effect on conservatism, and by the early 1990s arch-Thatcherites such as Shirley Letwin were convinced that the primary purpose of the Conservative Party had to be to defend Britain and the 'British way' of politics from the threat posed by European integration. Letwin argued:

> The unfortunate truth is that although 'we are all capitalists now', the battle fought by the Thatcher government has to be fought all over again, but on a new terrain, with a new vocabulary, and new weapons. And what is at issue is even more fundamental than the issue in 1979 – it is the independence of Britain, it is the supremacy of British law and self government in Britain. (1996: 176)

Thatcherite malice to the enemy within (the trade unions and socialism) was thus not dissipated with their self-proclaimed victory, but transferred to the even more threatening enemy without, the European Union. Letwin's position was not shared by all Conservatives, but it does illustrate the intellectual shift wrought by Thatcherism.

Whereas 'One Nation' or anti-Thatcherite Conservatives such as Ian Gilmour argued that Britain's best hope of maintaining global influence was through the European Union and warned that to 'cling to formal sovereignty' risked 'becoming an American satellite' (Gilmour and Garnett, 1997: 378), by 1997 this no longer represented anything other than a small minority view within the Conservative Party. David Willetts agreed with Letwin to the extent that any Conservative 'committed to the integrity of the United Kingdom' will recognise 'that ultimately the issues involved here are far more than economic'. Concerns over European integration, he claims, 'rest on the recognition that there is indeed more to Conservatism than simple economic liberalism' (Willetts, 1996: 83). Hague's former Party Chairman, Michael Ancram, stated clearly that in his view: 'The State and European integration are mutually incompatible . . . the only Europe compatible with the protection of our sovereignty and the smaller state is a European partnership of sovereign nations' (Ancram, 2007: 14). The neo-Thatcherite view that Europe represents a fundamental threat to British sovereignty has thus established a hegemonic position within British Conservative discourse.

For Hague and his successors, the effect of this ideological transformation of the party under Thatcher and Major was to restrict the scope of viable party management strategies for the leadership on the issue of Europe. Hague needed to devise an approach that could exist within this realignment of Conservative thinking, whilst not either reinforcing the public impression that the Conservatives were either 'extreme' or 'obsessed' with Europe, and also without splitting the party. The most urgent issue facing Hague in this regard was the party's policy on membership of the single currency. The formula Hague struck upon was that the Conservatives would oppose entry during the current parliament or in the next. The party could thus campaign against membership without actually ruling it out 'on principle' or 'forever'. This was the basis of Hague's call to 'save the pound' during the 2001 election campaign, although this was effectively neutralised by Labour's pledge to hold a referendum before British entry. Hague established this line in October 1997, and suffered two shadow cabinet resignations (Ian Taylor and David Curry) as a result (Harris, 2005: 150).

In the autumn of 1998 Hague held a ballot of party members to seek approval for this policy, which was overwhelmingly endorsed, with 84 per cent of returned papers in favour (Harris, 2005: 165; Garnett, 2003: 56). For Bale, Hague adopted this line as: 'he wanted, firstly, to maintain Tory distinctiveness in a manner which seemed to play well with public opinion and, secondly, to use the internal referendum on the issue to give the impression of an authority he sadly lacked' (Bale, 2006: 388). This is perhaps a little harsh on Hague. To have maintained the 'wait and see' line of his predecessor would have been nigh on impossible in the face of deepening Euroscepticism in his ranks, and the position of not joining 'for the foreseeable future', which he used in the first couple of months of his leadership, suffered from an intense vagueness to the extent of appearing almost meaningless. The all-party ballot was also a success in that it brought a degree of legitimacy to the policy (which held firm for four years) and was a tactical victory of sorts over its vocal critics such as Heseltine and Clarke. For some, such as Hague's chief policy advisor Daniel Finkelstein and his Party Chairman Michael Ancram, it 'was significant because it enabled the Conservative Party to finally stop talking about Europe' (Harris, 2005: 166). Ancram commented that Hague 'wanted to put the issue effectively to bed . . . so that's why we had a referendum in the party on it' (Ancram, interviewed in Harris, 2005: 166).

Hague's policy also had the advantage that it was generally in line with public opinion: polls continued to show public scepticism over joining the Euro (ICM, 2001). It did not succeed, however, in radically changing the image of the Conservatives as a disunited party. By the 2001 election 30 per cent of the public still regarded the Conservatives as divided, down 14 points since April 1997 (Table 3.1, p. 53).

'Harder but quieter': European policy, 2001–5

Bale characterises Conservative Party positioning on Europe between 1997 and 2005 as becoming 'harder but quieter' (2006: 388–91). Following Hague's clamorous calls to 'save the pound', a much quieter line was rapidly established under his successor, Iain Duncan Smith. One of his first moves as leader was to harden Conservative policy, to rule out membership of the single currency permanently. As Bale comments, this 'was intended not just to "close" the issue within the party but also to prevent it dominating the Tory campaign in the 2005 general election in the way it had done four years earlier' (2006: 388). Duncan Smith succeeded in this regard: the party said very little on Europe under his leadership. This was a deliberate effort to move away from core-vote issues, which may, ironically, have weakened his position as leader. Theresa May commented that, 'there were a lot of people who voted for Iain because they thought he would be sound on Europe and would put Europe centre-stage. And he didn't: one of the first things he did was to park Europe as an issue' (private interview, 2006). However, as May went on to acknowledge, this was only one factor in Duncan Smith losing the confidence of the parliamentary party:

> It was a mixture of things. I think it was partly a reaction against the way that he was trying to take the party. I think it was partly the feeling that he hadn't done what they thought he would do, i.e. return to a 'core vote', right wing, be an anti-Europe leader. Partly, some of the personal issues about his leadership; and partly the fact that there were others who had an interest in becoming leader, and were therefore agitating, or getting others to agitate on their behalf. (May, private interview, 2006)

The decision by Duncan Smith to deliberately focus on issues other than Europe was a rational interpretation of the strategic context he faced. The 2001 election had demonstrated that a campaign focused on Europe was not a winning formula, whilst it also risked inflating the profile of UKIP (Bale, 2006: 388). The issue also had a low level of electoral salience (Figure 4.1). According to IpsosMORI (2010) opinion poll data, at the time of Duncan Smith's election as party leader in September 2001, only 9 per cent of voters regarded European integration as an important issue. Since then, it has remained a relatively low-salience issue, although brief spikes of public interest occurred in June 2003 (when Gordon Brown announced the assessment of the economic tests for joining the Euro); in May and June 2004 (at the time of the European elections and Labour's concession of a referendum on the proposed European constitution); and in June 2005 (when the debate about the renegotiation of Britain's rebate hit the headlines).

By comparison, 43 per cent of those polled in September 2001 regarded health as an important issue, 30 per cent named education and 60 per cent cited defence (an abnormally high figure in response to 9/11) (IpsosMORI, 2010). Duncan Smith therefore saw Europe as a low salience issue on which the Conservative position was relatively well known, and chose instead to focus on the priorities identified by the public. As he commented:

> Well I didn't think there was any point in talking about it [Europe] really, because I didn't think there could be anyone in Britain who didn't know what our view was . . . I cleared-up the position over the single currency, and in actual fact we didn't discuss it again for the whole time I was there. The constitution came to the fore in the second year, but we dealt with that with our referendum policy . . . So we stayed off Europe for a while. (Private interview, 2006)

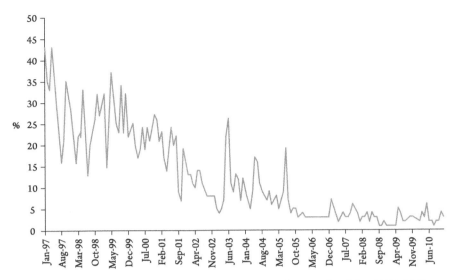

Figure 4.1 The salience of European integration to the British public, 1997–2010.
Questions: What would you say is the most important issue facing Britain today? What
do you see as other important issues facing Britain today? (Respondents are unprompted,
answers are combined). *Source*: IpsosMORI (2010).

Ann Widdecombe concurred with the rationale of this policy, commenting that:
'the one big plus of having Iain Duncan Smith was that it shut everybody up
about Europe, because everybody knew where he stood' (private interview, 2007).
Chapter 3 highlighted the deliberate strategy pursued by Duncan Smith to reposition the Conservatives as a party of the public services, and develop a new Conservative narrative based around 'championing the vulnerable' and social justice.
The 'harder but quieter' European policy was integral to this strategy. This failed
not because it lacked coherence, but because of poor leadership and party image
problems. Chapter 3 also noted how Duncan Smith's agenda was only partially
carried forward by Michael Howard, who abandoned the search for a narrative
based around the language of 'compassionate Conservatism', but did retain elements
of the broader policy approach. Howard maintained the relative silence on Europe
established by his predecessor. Although not a former Maastricht rebel like Duncan
Smith, Howard's Euroscepticism was widely acknowledged. In his own words, his
position was clear: 'I'm not in favour of ceding more powers to the European Union;
on the contrary I'm in favour of bringing powers back from the European Union'
(private interview, 2006).

However, Howard's decision not to make European integration a prominent issue
was not informed by the same strategic logic that underpinned Duncan Smith's
avoidance of the subject. As Cowley and Green comment, Duncan Smith was

'determined to escape the criticism levelled at Hague in 2001 for running a single-issue campaign on Europe' (Cowley and Green, 2005: 51). In this sense, the position adopted by Duncan Smith on Europe, and his success in enforcing it, was dependent, although it had failed electorally, on the legacy left by Hague. The mistake of focusing on Europe in 2001 was widely recognised, even amongst Conservative MPs, increasing willing compliance with Duncan Smith's tactic of minimising the issue. The Labour government was also happy not drawing attention to what for them was not a strong suit. When the proposed European constitution came on the agenda in 2002, it was dealt with in the Conservative Party by a promise of a referendum (as noted by Duncan Smith above). By taking a firm position to oppose the single currency permanently, and to oppose (and offer a referendum on) any future constitutional treaty, Duncan Smith also aligned himself with mainstream opinion with the PCP, 'the number of pro-European Conservative MPs having diminished yet further at the 2001 election' (Cowley and Green, 2005: 51). Armed with his own impeccable Eurosceptic credentials, there could be little doubt amongst Conservative MPs that Duncan Smith would honour these commitments.

Howard was therefore happy to maintain Duncan Smith's 'harder but quieter' position on Europe, as it was a success in party management terms, gave the party space to discuss other issues and created some distance from the discredited 2001 election campaign. However, retention of this element of Duncan Smith's approach should not be allowed to disguise the overall shift in strategy directed by his successor. Duncan Smith had attempted both to change the image of the Conservative Party and to forge a new narrative of conservatism by concentrating more attention on issues of public concern which were viewed as Conservative weaknesses, and focusing much less on traditional Conservative messages on tax, immigration and Europe. Under Howard, tax and immigration policies acquired renewed prominence, and immigration in particular came to dominate the Conservatives' 2005 election campaign. Although the issue was different, the mistake of allowing one issue to dominate was the same as that made by Hague in 2001 (Bale, 2006: 388). Howard's policy on Europe cannot be seen as part of a coherent broader approach in the way that Duncan Smith's can. Rather it was derived from tactical and party management convenience; and a less developed understanding of, and response to, the 2001 defeat.

For Howard, to draw parallels between his 2005 campaign and that led by William Hague's in 2001 is unfair. He sees the two as very different, as in 2001 the issue of Europe and the Euro had been neutralised by Labour's pledge of a referendum, whereas this was not the case with immigration:

> It [immigration] wasn't at all like Europe in the 2001 election. The problem about Europe at the 2001 election, where we concentrated a great deal on the Euro, was that everyone knew that they were going to have a referendum on the Euro, so they thought understandably that that wasn't really a reason for voting Conservative in a general election. If they didn't like the Euro they could perfectly happily vote Labour

and vote 'no' to the Euro. There wasn't going to be a referendum on immigration, so I think it was completely different. (Private interview, 2006)

In this sense, Howard's understanding of the reasons for defeat in 2001 seems to be based around the idea of tactical failure, rather than the more fundamental critique informing Duncan Smith's attempts to recast conservatism, and with it the image of the Conservative Party, in a 'compassionate' light. Howard therefore either failed to grasp, or simply disagreed with, Duncan Smith's assessment of the 2001–5 context the Conservatives faced. One possible explanation for this could be that Howard saw the Conservative Party's image problems, and electoral failure in 1997 and 2001, as being specifically related to Europe, rather than a broader problem encapsulated by Theresa May's comment that the Conservatives were seen as 'the nasty party'. More likely, however, is that Howard noted the lack of progress in the opinion polls under his predecessor, and made a tactical assessment of what he thought he could achieve in a probable eighteen months before the next general election. Howard did make some attempts to 'reach out' in the early days of his leadership, for example his 'The British Dream' speech to Policy Exchange (Howard, 2004). These were abandoned as the election neared, and it is possible that had he remained as leader Duncan Smith would similarly have been pressured to retreat on to traditional Conservative issue strengths.

When asked what his key priorities on becoming leader were, Howard replied: 'Impose discipline on the party. Work towards achieving a clear message. And attempting to convince the electorate that we were a credible alternative to the government' (private interview, 2006). His approach to policy on Europe can be understood in these terms. Raising the issue's prominence risked exacerbating division and indiscipline in the party, and obscuring Howard's message. As such, it would have done little to enhance the Conservatives' credibility as a government in waiting. It therefore made sense to downplay the issue.

Cameron's Conservatives and Europe, 2005–10

Europe remained a relatively low-salience issue during David Cameron's time as leader of the opposition (Figure 4.1, p. 70). Following the precedent set by Duncan Smith and Howard, Cameron did not make European integration a central campaigning theme for the Conservatives in opposition. However, the subject did play a notable role in Conservative Party politics in relation to two issues: firstly membership of the European People's Party (EPP) in the European Parliament; and secondly the ratification of the Lisbon Treaty.

In a move that attracted criticism from some of his natural supporters Cameron first pledged to withdraw Conservative MEPs from the EPP and form a new group as part of his 2005 leadership election campaign. This was a barefaced attempt to secure the backing of Eurosceptic MPs, and helped Cameron garner sufficient support to defeat the right-wing Eurosceptic candidates Liam Fox and David Davis (Lynch and Whitaker, 2008: 34). This pledge was eventually fulfilled in June 2009, when the Shadow Foreign Secretary William Hague announced that the Conservatives had reached an agreement with Eurosceptic parties from seven other EU member states to establish an anti-federalist group in the European Parliament. The long delay in realising his commitment to leave the EPP can be explained by the difficulty in finding a sufficient number of credible mainstream allies in the European Parliament to form a new group, and fierce opposition to the policy from some Conservative MEPs (Lynch and Whitaker, 2008: 35). Indeed, shortly after the formation of the new group the party's longest-serving MEP and former leader in the European Parliament, Edward McMillan-Scott, rebelled against it and was expelled from the party. McMillan-Scott stood for (and won) the position of vice-president of the European Parliament, in defiance of the party whip and against the official candidate of the newly formed Conservative and Reformist Group (ECR). This incident illustrated unease amongst some Conservative MEPs about the change and embarrassed the party leadership, but the dissent did not become more widespread.

Withdrawal from the EPP confirmed what had already become clear in the 1997–2005 period, that the Conservatives were now an almost exclusively Eurosceptic party. It also offered potential reassurance of that fact to those Conservative voters who regarded the issue as important, and who might otherwise have been tempted to vote for UKIP. The strong performance of UKIP in the 2009 European Parliament election served as a reminder to the Conservatives that right-wing Eurosceptics had other options available when deciding how to vote. Whilst the Conservatives won the most seats (26) at that election, their share of the vote was a far from emphatic 27.7 per cent. With 13 seats and 16.5 per cent of the vote, UKIP were able to secure second place ahead of Labour and the Liberal Democrats (Hayton, 2010a). This result highlighted the challenge Cameron faced in attempting to develop a strategy with the capacity to appeal to a sufficiently broad spectrum of the electorate to deliver success in a general election, without losing the votes of what might otherwise have been regarded as traditional Conservative supporters.

The Lisbon Treaty emerged out of the ruins of the EU Constitutional Treaty, which was abandoned after it was rejected by French and Dutch voters in referendums held in May and June 2005, shortly after the UK general election. Pressure from the Conservatives under Michael Howard had led Prime Minister Tony Blair to commit the British government to holding a referendum before ratifying the proposed EU Constitution, and it consequently did not play a major part in the 2005 election campaign. After the replacement Lisbon Treaty was signed by Europe's leaders in December 2007 the Labour government declined to offer a referendum on ratification. The Conservatives opposed the new treaty and once again called for a referendum, arguing that it was in essence the failed constitutional proposals under a new banner (Lynch, 2009: 190). Cameron thus continued the trend established by Hague and continued by Duncan Smith and Howard of calling for a plebiscite on any significant extension of EU competencies. After the Lisbon Treaty came into force in late 2009 Cameron declined to promise a retrospective referendum should the Conservatives return to office, although the 2010 manifesto accused Labour of 'a betrayal of this country's democratic traditions' for failing to hold one at the time. The manifesto also pledged to legislate to create a 'referendum lock', in an effort to force any future government to consult the people before endorsing any future European treaty (Conservative Party, 2010: 113).

The approach Cameron adopted on European integration was consequently broadly consistent with the pattern established by his three predecessors. As Philip Lynch points out the 'Cameron effect' on the Conservative approach to European matters was rather less pronounced than on many other policy areas: the modernisation project to change the language and image of the party seemed to largely neglect this area (2009: 205). Criticising Cameron's failure to extend his reform agenda into this area, Michael Portillo accused him of turning 'from Jekyll to Hyde, foaming like a Tory reactionary of the old school'. Euroscepticism was therefore the 'one survivor' of modernisation, not least because many of the leading modernisers emerged from the party's Eurosceptic right wing (Portillo, 2006). So, for Portillo, Cameron's failure to confront his party's Euroscepticism is a strategic error in that it runs counter to his overall approach, and is a tactical error, as by 'blundering into this terrain he will resurrect the party's reputation for being divided and self-obsessed' (2006). However, as Portillo himself acknowledged, Euroscepticism performed a useful function for Cameron as a link to the elements of the party unconvinced by his broader approach. So the maintenance of the firm Eurosceptic line he inherited would appear to be a sound judgement by Cameron that helped him carry party opinion into other areas where it may have been reluctant to venture.

Analysis: Conservative positioning and the salience of European integration

Intertwined with ideational factors such as the ideological positions of Conservative MPs are electoral concerns and calculations, notably relating to the salience of key issues. The salience of European integration declined notably between 1997 and 2010, upholding the logic of the Conservative leadership's efforts from 2001 onwards to downplay the issue. Oppermann argues that this transformation into a low-salience issue was the successful outcome of deliberate New Labour strategy. He suggests that as the Blair government's approach to Europe was not in concordance with the 'deeply entrenched Euroscepticism' of the British public, New Labour had a strong electoral incentive to attempt to reduce, or at least contain, its public salience (Oppermann, 2008: 157). Oppermann notes that, 'between 1997 and 2006, the approval ratings of New Labour's European policies lagged behind those of the

Conservative Party's policies in 7 out of 10 years'. Furthermore, at both the 2001 and 2005 general elections, voters who regarded the issue as important were more likely to favour the Conservatives' policies (2008: 162). Labour responded to this electoral threat through a mix of different strategies, notably by deferring major European policy decisions; by pledging referendums on such decisions; by attempting to depoliticise such decisions so they appeared technical rather than political (for example the five economic tests with respect to joining the Euro); and by downplaying the apparent differences between government policies and those of the Conservative opposition (Oppermann, 2008). This effort to neutralise the issue contrasted markedly with Labour's strategy in the six years before Tony Blair became leader, when the party 'repositioned itself as a distinctly pro-European alternative to the increasingly Eurosceptic Conservative government' (Oppermann, 2008: 171).

Labour's failure to make a serious effort to re-orientate public opinion in a more pro-integrationist direction can be regarded as a major shortcoming of their time in office, and a significant missed opportunity. For instance Peter Mandelson has noted that 'Britain's leaders have done a good job of selling globalisation . . . But they have done less well explaining the role of the EU in helping Britain defend its interests in a globalised world' (Mandelson, 2007: 1). For some, it reflects New Labour's predilection for an Anglo-Saxon (or Anglo-American) neo-liberal economic model, in preference to a more social democratic 'European' capitalism. Jessop, for example, argues that the government 'deliberately, persistently, and wilfully' drove forward 'the neo-liberal transformation of Britain' (Jessop, 2007: 282). Indeed, the British government under Blair was 'far keener to export lessons of US enterprise culture and welfare-to-work to the European Union' than they were to facilitate a transfer of ideas in the other direction (2007: 287). Numerous other authors see New Labour in similar terms: Bauman saw the lasting legacy of the Blair years to be the consolidation and 'institutionalisation' of Thatcherism (Bauman, 2007: 60); and Fullbrook (2007: 160) declared that neo-liberalism 'is the ideology of our time' and characterised the Blair governments. From such perspectives, New Labour's adjustment of its stance on European policy issues, and its efforts to neutralise them, can be understood as part of a wider ideological shift, as the transformative effect of Thatcherism on British politics continued to be felt.[2] Whatever the motivations, the outcome does however, appear clear: the public salience of European integration declined dramatically (Figure 4.1, p. 70), thereby augmenting the space available for the government to pursue a European policy at odds with public sentiment at minimal electoral cost.

However, as Figure 4.1 shows, the salience of European integration did not follow a smooth downward trajectory: spikes of public interest occurred at the time of related high-profile political episodes, for example the assessment of the economic tests for joining the Euro in 1997 and 2003, and the 1999 European elections (Oppermann, 2008: 165–6). Oppermann divides the Blair premiership into 'two distinct phases', either side of the 2001 general election. The first phase is marked by a high level of electoral salience for the issue of European integration: on average, 24.5 per cent of poll respondents regarded it as an important issue, and at 'the 2001 general elections, the importance attached to European issues was second only to health policy' (Oppermann, 2008: 164). By contrast, during the second phase, Europe 'was considered to be among the most important political issues of the day by an average of only 8.6% of respondents' (2008: 165). For Oppermann, this drop can be partly ascribed to Labour's strategies, as noted above. However, a factor he overlooks, which may also have contributed to this fall, is the Conservatives' changing approach to European policy. Notably, the steep decline in the public salience of the issue only occurs *after* the 2001 general election, when the Conservatives under Iain Duncan Smith deliberately chose to downplay the matter. This could be interpreted in one of two ways: either the Conservatives were responding to Labour's (successful) strategy to defer and defuse the issue; or public concern with European integration fell as it was the subject of less political conflict, as the Conservatives went quiet on the subject.

Using data from the British Election Panel Survey (BEPS), Geoffrey Evans' (1998) analysis of Euroscepticism and Conservative electoral support found that the British public became more Eurosceptic during John Major's premiership. By 1996, on an issue-proximity model, the Conservative Party 'was even closer to aggregate public opinion, when compared with its main competitors, than it had been at the time of the 1992 election' (1998: 573). This failed, however, to translate into increased electoral support. The problem was threefold: firstly voters displayed confusion over the Conservatives position; secondly the appearance of disunity put voters off; and thirdly they tended to be swayed by other issues.

For Evans, by failing to pursue a consistent Eurosceptic line the Conservatives under Major squandered 'the potential electoral benefit provided by popular Euroscepticism' (1998: 590). The ambiguous nature of the government's attitude to European integration under Major actually caused voters to inaccurately place the Conservative position on an issue-proximity scale, to the extent that, by 1996, voters perceived themselves to be closer to the positions of Labour and the Liberal Democrats. Pro-European voters tended to view the Conservatives as anti-European, while Eurosceptics took the opposite view (Evans, 1998: 581–2). No such confusion arose with regard to the other major parties. As Evans argues, the palpable reason for this was surely the clear public divisions in the Conservative Party over the issue of Europe at the time. Disunity therefore had a double-whammy impact, not only on the public image of the party (see Chapter 3), but also on the credibility of the party on the one important issue which should have been a Conservative electoral trump card.

In the light of this, William Hague's strategy on Europe might be regarded as eminently sensible. Hague hoped that a consistent Eurosceptic position would reverse the damage inflicted on the party by the image of disunity whilst, as Evans highlighted above, it also offered potential electoral dividends. Moreover, on becoming leader he inherited a situation where his party was far behind Labour on all major issues with the exception of Europe. As a comparison of Tables 4.1 and 4.2 illustrates, by the time of the 2001 election he had failed to make significant inroads into this situation. In April 1997, six issues were cited as 'important' by at least 20 per cent of the electorate. They were health (63 per cent), education (54 per cent), Europe (43 per cent), unemployment (28 per cent) crime (27 per cent) and the economy (22 per cent) (MORI, 2008a). Labour had large leads on three of these (health, education and unemployment); the Conservatives had a small lead on the economy, whilst on crime and Europe both had similar levels of public approval.

The major change between 1997 and 2001 (Table 4.2) was the emergence of a large Labour lead on the economy. Labour retained clear leads on health, education and unemployment, leaving Hague with two issues, crime and Europe, on which his party was in touching distance of the government. Combined with the

Table 4.1 Best party on key issues, April 1997

	Conservatives %	Labour %	None/ Don't know %	Labour lead %
Crime	28	29	36	+1
Economy	33	26	34	−7
Education	21	40	24	+19
Europe	25	24	42	−1
Health	15	47	28	+32
Unemployment	18	42	34	+30

Source: Data on best party on key issues (MORI, 2008c, 2008d, 2008e, 2008f, 2008g, 2008h).

Table 4.2 Best party on key issues, February 2001

	Conservatives %	Labour %	None/ Don't know %	Labour lead %
Crime	26	30	38	+4
Economy	18	44	34	+26
Education	17	44	30	+27
Europe	26	27	40	+1
Health	14	42	35	+28
Unemployment	12	48	37	+36

Source: Data on best party on key issues (MORI, 2008c, 2008d, 2008e, 2008f, 2008g, 2008h).

continued electoral salience of European integration (see Figure 4.1, p. 70), his decision to campaign heavily on Europe at the 2001 elections, when he warned the British public that they had just 'two weeks to save the pound' (Jones, 2001: 1) appears rational.

So why did Hague's strategy fail? The conventional wisdom is that this was a core-vote strategy that failed dramatically, as illustrated by the outcome of the 2001 election result. Leach rehearses the standard critique of Hague's leadership:

> Hague's obsession with Europe meant that Labour's general record and Conservative alternatives never received detailed scrutiny. His tough line with dissent meant that the party was perceived as 'dogmatic', and 'extreme' rather than united, particularly among those voters who recalled that all the main developments in the UK's relationship with Europe had been undertaken by previous Conservative governments. The party was effectively denying its own past. (Leach, 2002: 207)

An alternative view, however, could be that Hague's strategy was a relative success. It secured Hague a notable victory at the 1999 European elections, thereby securing his position as leader (Chapter 3). And it may have been the optimal vote-maximisation strategy available to him: in other words, another leader or another strategy may have actually resulted in the Conservatives doing even worse. As Harris comments, 'the future of the Conservative Party on May 2nd 1997 was by no means guaranteed: the parliamentary party was literally tearing itself apart over the issue of Europe, party membership was rapidly dwindling and it was on the brink of bankruptcy' (Harris, 2005: 105). In this context, to have stabilised the party so that it did not implode and lose further ground electorally, and to have brought a semblance of unity on the most divisive issue for the Conservative Party since tariff reform, is no mean achievement. As Lord Parkinson commented, 'The big thing was to hold the party together . . . I don't think there was a strategy William could have devised that would have increased his vote beyond what he got, quite frankly'. In his view, a different leader could have achieved no more (private interview, 2006). By contrast Andrew Cooper, Hague's former Director of Strategy (1997–99) saw little benefit to the 'core-vote' strategy with Europe as its centrepiece, so consequently saw little risk in pursuing an alternative, broader agenda (Cooper, 2001).

The Hague years were also important in shaping the context for his successors. Hague's overtly Eurosceptic policies and rhetoric, enforced with strict parliamentary discipline and sanctioned by the party ballot, marked the completion of the process of legitimising opposition to European integration signalled by Thatcher's Bruges address. Duncan Smith would have been unable to harden and quieten the Conservative Party's approach to European integration so rapidly or with such ease had it not been for his predecessor's actions. The relative intraparty unity Cameron enjoyed on Europe between 2005 and 2010 would also not have occurred in the absence of measures taken by Duncan Smith and Howard to downgrade the issue's importance. Yet by toughening the party's Eurosceptic stance, they also acted as a limitation on his modernisation agenda. The 1997–2010 period can therefore be seen as an important phase in the transition by the Conservatives into a firmly Eurosceptic party. As discussed, this ideological shift in the party is one (major) element of the Thatcherite transformation of British conservatism, but as this chapter has demonstrated it was a dialectic process affected and institutionalised by key political actors.

Conclusion

This chapter began by exploring why European integration has long been a difficult issue for Conservatives in Britain. For several decades, Europe was *the* defining issue in Conservative Party politics, and was central to any understanding of it. Damian Green suggested that during Cameron's period as leader of the opposition this was no longer the case:

> For most of the 1980s and 1990s, to the enormous damage of the Conservative Party, Europe was an issue that defined you. It didn't matter what you thought about anything else, if you stood on one or other side of the Europe debate that defined you as right-wing or left-wing. Well actually now that's not true, it was never completely true, and it's now much less important an issue for the party as it was then. (Private interview, 2007)

Europe was talismanic of the Thatcher legacy, and was emblematic of the party's difficulties in the 1990s, when the Conservatives came to be seen as fractious, divided and ideologically obsessive. Yet the chapter ends with the suggestion that 1997–2010 saw a transformation of Conservative politics in relation to Europe. Compared to the feuding of the Thatcher and Major eras, it was certainly not the source of significant party management problems for the leadership. However, at the end of this period the question to what extent this simply reflected the fact that the party was in opposition, and therefore to what degree divisions would reopen with the party's return to government remained unanswered. The chapter has argued that this period saw the near-universal acceptance of a vigorous Euroscepticism within the Conservative Party. Not faced with the responsibilities of office, this was something the party leadership could readily accept and indeed encourage, as it was in tune with the instincts of the leaders themselves and delivered party management benefits. This Eurosceptic consensus was not even challenged by Cameron's modernisation strategy after 2005, which was accommodated to it. However, the pragmatic need for the UK government to have a productive working relationship with the European Union and fellow member countries remains very strong. The challenge for the Conservative Party in office will therefore be to balance the reality of British membership of the European Union and the resultant day-to-day issues that will inevitably arise with the prevalent Eurosceptic instincts of their party.

Notes

1 On the politics of decline and 'declinism' as an ideology see Tomlinson (2000). For an overview of the impact of the debate about decline on British politics, see English and Kenny (2000), particularly the chapters on theories of decline (Gamble, 2000b) and party ideologies and decline (Eccleshall, 2000b). On Thatcherism and decline, see Gamble (1994a, 1994b) and Krieger (1986).

2 Human agency has of course been central to this, and the Labour government has been widely criticised for failing to counter neo-liberalism more vigorously since 1997 (see, for example, Hall, 1998, 2007; Jessop, 2007; Wilson and Macaulay, 2007).

5

National identity and the English question

The Conservative Party is the nationalist party *par excellence*. A Conservative Party which cannot present itself to the country as a national party suffers under a severe handicap. (Enoch Powell, quoted in Lynch, 1999: xi)

Introduction

The question of national identity, epitomised by the issue of European integration, has long been problematic for the Conservatives (Chapter 4). This chapter also explores the question of identity, through an examination of Conservative Party policy and discourse in two further areas: immigration and devolution. Chapter 4 showed how with only a handful of dissenters, the Conservative Party settled on a Thatcherite Eurosceptic position. It also argued that 1997–2010 saw Euroscepticism embedded by the party leadership as the defining feature of Conservative policy in relation to national identity. However, the end of bitter internal feuding over Europe did not mean the end of challenges to Conservative conceptions of national identity.[1]

In the United Kingdom the debate about both devolution and race/immigration issues is intimately related to the 'English question' – that is, the emergence of a stronger and more visible sense of Englishness and its political, cultural and constitutional implications. This chapter argues that devolution challenged the traditional Conservative view of the British state by fundamentally altering its structure, leading some Conservatives to question the historic role of their party as the defender of the Union. Higher levels of immigration pushed the issue up the political agenda and increased its electoral salience, and the way in which Conservatives sought to respond to this reveals a significant dilemma: whether to seek to exploit the issue via policy and rhetoric, or develop a more inclusive image.

This chapter argues that the debate over national identity remained a key arena of ideological contestation within the Conservative Party between 1997 and 2010. The dominance of neo-Thatcherism in the form of Euroscepticism was not, perhaps as might have been anticipated, accompanied by a similarly caustic English nationalism. On the contrary, the chapter argues that in spite of the challenge of devolution and a concentration of electoral support in England, the Conservative leadership largely sought to resist the clarion call issued by some sympathisers to champion breaking the Union. Conservative caution in this respect derived from both the endurance of a traditional attachment to unionism (something closely associated with the One Nation tradition, but also claimed by Thatcher) and disagreement over the electoral costs and benefits of a radical repositioning as an English party. It also reflected a broader cultural issue: uncertainty over where Britishness ended and Englishness began, and the question of whether the two could ever be effectively disentangled. This was, as the chapter explores, a particularly difficult issue for the Conservative Party, which had traditionally placed nationhood at the centre of its identity and electoral appeal.

The chapter surveys these issues thematically. Firstly it considers the intraparty debate over how to respond to devolution between 1997 and 2010. Secondly it examines Conservative policy and rhetoric in relation to immigration across the same period. In the light of these two areas, the final section considers the implications of the Conservatives' reluctant drift towards becoming an English party. Wary of embracing outright little-Englander populism, the Conservatives also struggled to articulate a convincing narrative of Britishness. The chapter concludes that the Conservatives were without a dominant, coherent view of national identity during this period in opposition, and this was reflected in a sometimes inconsistent electoral and policy approach in the areas analysed. As in relation to other policy areas, the party leadership did not determine a clear answer to the dilemma of whether to pursue a 'core-vote' strategy in the politics of nationhood, or seek to develop a more inclusive brand of conservatism.

Devolution: from opposition to acceptance

The Conservative Party traditionally identified itself as the party of the Union – indeed, it is still officially known as the Conservative and Unionist Party. Gamble identified the Union as one of the four pillars of Conservative political hegemony in the twentieth century (1995: 13–16). Along with defence of the Empire, the constitution, and property, defence of the Union was a key feature of the Conservative Party's identity and electoral appeal. However, by the mid 1990s each of these pillars had been undermined, to the extent that conservatism could be said to be in 'crisis' (Gamble, 1995: 13).

Conservative commitment to the Union was weakened by the political situation in Northern Ireland in the 1970s which led to a breakdown in relations with the Ulster Unionists, who opposed the 1973 Sunningdale Agreement. This breach was further entrenched in the 1980s and 1990s as the Conservative government pursued a strategy of disengagement from the province which culminated in the 1994 Downing Street Declaration. As Gamble (1995: 15) noted:

> The key passage in the Declaration was the statement that the British Government had no selfish or strategic interest in Northern Ireland, and that if ever the Ulster

people wished to separate from the United Kingdom, the British Government would not oppose it . . . The message of the Declaration was not lost on the Unionists. They had to recognize that there was now no party at Westminster which was committed in principle and in all circumstances to the maintenance of the Union.

Conservative commitment to the Union with Northern Ireland no longer rested on the presumption that the Union was an inherently good thing which should be defended on principle, but merely on the grounds that it remained the democratic will of the people. This had implications for the Conservative approach to devolution in other parts of the United Kingdom.

At the 1997 general election, the promise of constitutional reform was a key feature of Labour's manifesto. The central plank of this was devolution to Scotland and Wales, subject to public approval by referendum. The Conservatives campaigned vigorously against this, John Major warning that the country had just '72 hours to save the Union', claiming that Labour's proposals would mean 'the break-up of the United Kingdom as we know it' (quoted in Jones, 1997). This was a consistent theme of Major's, who likewise at the 1992 general election had called on voters to 'wake up' to the dangers of devolution (quoted in Jones, 1997).

Similarly under William Hague, the Conservatives fought against devolution in the referendum campaigns in Scotland and Wales. Harris claims 'the Union played an important part in Hague's understanding of British national identity' and that this opposition stemmed from his belief that 'it would inevitably spark the process of the disintegration of the Union' (2005: 129). However, once the referendums had been held, and despite the very close result in Wales, the Conservatives quickly moved to accept the new arrangements.[2] In his first major speech on the constitution as party leader, Hague acknowledged the dilemma he faced: should Conservatives seek to reform, reverse or advance the changes Labour was making? And what were the implications for the Conservative Party? As Hague asked, 'What happens to the defenders of the status quo when the status quo itself disappears?' (1998b: 2). Rapid constitutional change is, he acknowledged 'bewildering for many Conservatives', not least because 'the public is at best bemused and at worst uninterested' (1998b: 2). This public apathy was partly the Conservatives' own fault, as 'the merits of our existing constitutional arrangements were so self-evident, we believed, that it was hardly worth making the intellectual case for them' (1998b: 1). The Conservatives (and the nation) were now paying the price for this failure, as public concern about Labour's 'constitutional vandalism' remained muted (1998b: 1). The question was therefore whether the Conservatives could, or should, accept the new settlement:

> Some Conservatives believe we will simply have to shrug our shoulders and accept whatever arrangements we inherit. But how can we accept constitutional arrangements which are unstable and undemocratic and with whose underlying principles we profoundly disagree? I do not believe we can or should just put up with them. (Hague, 1998b: 2)

The practical reality, however, was that undoing these measures would be impossible: the Conservatives could not hope to 'unscramble the omelette' (1998b: 11). The only realistic response, Hague claimed, was to develop a programme of further change aimed at correcting 'the dangerous imbalances and tensions which Labour's constitutional reforms will unleash'. The Conservatives must seek 'to construct a set of constitutional relationships which will preserve the key, overarching principles of our existing constitution: limited government, the rule of law, the unity of the kingdom and, above all, democratic accountability' (1998b: 3). This was a theme that Hague echoed in another speech to the Centre for Policy Studies the following year, in which he sought to explain how Conservatives could 'strengthen the Union after devolution' (1999b: 2). This debate centred in particular around the asymmetrical nature of the devolution and where this left England: the West Lothian Question.[3]

Hague claimed that devolution struck 'at the heart of the constitutional arrangement that has held our Union together for hundreds of years' (1998b: 11). As a response he suggested four possible options for the Conservatives to consider in what Harris labelled an exercise in constitutional 'damage limitation' (2005: 135). These were: the creation of an English parliament; English votes for English laws (EvfEl); a major cut in the number of Scottish MPs; and substantial devolution of power in England to local councils and other bodies such as hospital trusts (Hague, 1998b: 13–14; Harris, 2005: 135). Labour's proposal of English regional government was rejected as 'such assemblies assume that strong regional identities exist in England, which they do not' and 'an extra layer of politicians . . . would lack legitimacy in the eyes of the voters and would simply confuse accountability still further' (Hague, 1998b: 13). Lacking legislative powers, regional assemblies would also 'fail to ameliorate the West Lothian Question' (Harris, 2005: 135).

In 1998, Hague warned that the 'dark clouds of nationalism are gathering – not just Scottish and Welsh nationalism, but English nationalism too' and pledged that 'a patriotic Conservative Party will fight it wherever it seeks to gain support' (1998b: 12). By the following year, however, he was more confident that this 'flowering of English consciousness' could 'play an increasingly important part in our sense of British national identity' (1999b: 6). However, he also warned:

> Try to ignore this English consciousness, or bottle it up, and it could turn into a more dangerous English nationalism that could threaten the future of the United Kingdom. Recognise its value and it can actually strengthen our common British identity. I believe answering the English Question is vital to the future stability of the United Kingdom. Giving the voters of England a fair say is the way to strengthen the Union after devolution. (1999b: 6)

Hague announced in his speech of 15 July 1999 that the options of creating an English parliament or slashing the number of Scottish MPs (to the effect that Scots would be underrepresented at Westminster) had been rejected (Harris, 2005:

137–40). Elements of the localist proposal to devolve more powers to English councils were endorsed, but were not seen as an answer to the West Lothian Question as they did not rectify the imbalance of legislative devolution. The fourth option, of EvfEl, was consequently adopted as Conservative Party policy. This was not viewed as an ideal solution. Hague had noted in 1998 that each of the four proposals under consideration had drawbacks, but that the party was merely seeking 'the least damaging answer to the West Lothian Question' (1998b: 14). The adoption of EvfEl did, however, usher in a prolonged period of policy stability in this area, and effectively marginalised debate on the issue within the parliamentary party. EvfEl featured in the form outlined by Hague in both the 2001 and 2005 Conservative election manifestos, with little detailed elaboration. For example the 2005 manifesto pledged simply to 'ensure that English laws are decided by English votes' (Conservative Party, 2005: 22).

Harris asserts that under William Hague's leadership, the Conservatives 'remained a steadfastly unionist party' (2005: 143). For example she quotes Michael Ancram, who said: 'I believe that the Conservative Party is the unionist party and that we should never do anything that actually remotely is going to undermine the Union'; and Lord Strathclyde, who stated that English nationalism: 'is of no serious intellectual interest to Conservatives, who are a United Kingdom party' (interviewed in Harris, 2005: 142). As leader of the opposition David Cameron similarly sought to display his unionist credentials, claiming that the Conservatives are 'a party of the Union and as long as I lead it that is how it will stay', and pledging to 'carry out my duty to nurture and support the Union whatever my party's political standing in any of the Union's constituent parts' (2007: 1). However, the Hague proposals for EvfEl that Cameron inherited were widely criticised as potentially damaging to the Union, as they presented the possibility of intractable deadlock should a UK government be confronted with a majority of English MPs from other parties. Conscious of this charge, Cameron established a Democracy Taskforce chaired by Ken Clarke to investigate this issue. In July 2008 the Taskforce presented its recommendations, which amounted to a significantly watered-down version of EvfEl. Under these proposals MPs from outside of England would be excluded from debate and scrutiny of English-only legislation at the committee and report stages, but all MPs would retain a final say on whether all bills became law. The practical effect of this procedure would be to give English MPs and the UK government an effective veto on any measures they did not want to see enacted, effectively forcing both sides to compromise or face deadlock.

The 2010 Conservative election manifesto did not refer directly to the Democracy Taskforce proposals, but it did criticise Labour for failing to address the West Lothian Question, and pledged to 'introduce new rules so that legislation referring specifically to England, or to England and Wales, cannot be enacted without the consent of MPs representing constituencies of those countries' (Conservative Party, 2010: 84). It also reaffirmed both commitment to the Union and support for devolution. The coalition agreement with the Liberal Democrats signed in May 2010 committed the new government to establishing a commission to consider the West Lothian Question, suggesting that the two parties had agreed as part of their negotiations to despatch the issue to the long grass.

In thirteen years of opposition the PCP and leadership remained broadly unionist, and the variants of EvfEl it proposed emerged from this sentiment. This needs to be explained, as a number of contextual factors would suggest that the Conservatives could have profited from adopting a less unionist, and more English-orientated position. Most visibly, the Conservatives became an almost exclusively English party. In the 1997 landslide, they lost all 8 of their seats in Scotland and all 11 of their seats in Wales. In Scotland their share of the vote was just 17.5 per cent and in Wales 19.6 per cent, compared to 33.7 per cent in England (Butler and Kavanagh, 1997: 256). In 2001, they won just 1 seat in Scotland and none in Wales. By 2005 there had been little change to this picture. The Conservative vote in England was up to 35.7 per cent, marginally ahead of Labour on 35.5 per cent (although Labour won 92 more English seats). In Scotland, however, the Conservatives lan-guished in fourth place, with just 15.8 per cent of the vote (although this did deliver one seat to Westminster). In Wales they finished second in terms of vote-share (with 21.4 per cent) but fourth in terms of seats, winning only 3 (Kavanagh and Butler, 2005: 205). In the 2010 election the Conservatives gained 97 seats across the UK as a whole, but could still only win 1 in Scotland where a marginal increase in their vote share (to 16.7 per cent) still left them in fourth place. In Wales the pic-ture was brighter for the Conservatives with an increase in vote share to 26.1 per cent delivering 8 seats in total.

This disastrous performance in Scotland in particular is the culmination of longer-term trends (Figure 5.1). The Conservatives' share of the vote in England

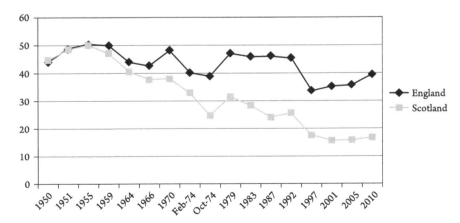

Figure 5.1 Conservative vote share at general elections, 1950–2010.
Source: Data from Seawright (2002) and http://news.bbc.co.uk.

and Scotland began to deviate in the 1950s, with a significant gap appearing in the 1970s. Since 1983, the party has performed approximately twice as well in England compared to Scotland in terms of vote share. Seawright attributes this to a divergence between mainstream Scottish public opinion, which moved to the left in the 1970s, and Conservative Party ideology, which simultaneously swung to the right: 'The laissez-faire discourse gained ground in the party at the very time when the Scottish indigenous industrial base was facing an acute crisis of survival and it is not surprising that the Scots should have developed a taste for economic intervention' (Seawright, 2002: 4). The Conservatives were aware of this disparity and the potential electoral danger it posed, and contrary to popular belief, sought to shield Scotland from the full force of Thatcherite policies (Gamble, 2006: 27). Alert to the threat of Scottish nationalism to the Union, under both Thatcher's and Major's public spending levels in Scotland and England did not converge: indeed, protection of this differential was one of the arguments they attempted to deploy *against* devolution (McLean and McMillan, 2003: 54). Clearly however, this strategy failed to placate the Scottish electorate, as despite a small upturn in 1992, the Conservative vote in Scotland almost halved between 1979 (31.4 per cent) and 1997 (17.5 per cent). One explanation for this, as Chapter 4 noted, is that the Conservatives under Thatcher developed a more overtly English nationalist discourse (Gamble, 1996: 35).

Combined with the electoral logic, another reason for the Conservatives to embrace English nationalism was that following the referendums in Scotland and Wales, the Conservatives could claim (as Hague did) that circumstances had fundamentally changed in such a way that they could not be reversed, and that the party should therefore adapt, perhaps radically, to the new situation. Indeed, the idea of an English parliament was championed by the Conservative backbencher Teresa Gorman, who in late 1997, supported by David Davis and Eric Forth, introduced a Private Member's Bill proposing a referendum on the creation of such a body, but garnered little support (Harris, 2005: 131–2).

Such a move could also be seen as a consistent development of the Powellite themes of Thatcher's national strategy. Although Powell himself was an ardent unionist, devolution changed the nature of the British state and meant that his vision of national unity based around the supreme authority of parliament could never be realised. For some Conservative followers of Powell, however, within England it still might. Powell's biographer and intellectual disciple, Simon Heffer, has been the most forceful exponent of a Conservative Englishness. Heffer's self-proclaimed 'Toryism' has, at its heart, a concern with the nation. It is perhaps therefore surprising that his most prominent contribution to British politics has been his advocacy of English independence, particularly as he acknowledges that 'for much of the last three centuries, belief in nation was synonymous with a belief in the Union' (2005: 200). This seemingly un-conservative policy was his response to the rise of separatism in Scotland, and the acquiescence of the New Labour government in legislating for devolution shortly after its election in 1997. His call to break the Union is presented as a pragmatic reaction to this new political reality. For Heffer, the union with Scotland has long since lost its strategic importance to England: the benefits (particularly financial), run purely in one direction. 'It is hard to see what the English have to fear from fragmentation of the Union', as the loss of Scotland 'would only be a marginal loss to England, and no loss at all in economic terms' (1999: 12).

This political Englishness was most clearly linked to the constitutional changes in Scotland and Wales, but a growing commitment to Englishness, at least in cultural terms, pre-dated this legislation. Indeed, 'a new mood of English nationalism was discernible as far back as the early 1990s, and was gathering momentum well before New Labour came to power in 1997' (Hayton, English and Kenny, 2007: 122). Aughey traced this to 1996, when the swathe of St George's flags that accompanied the hosting of the European football championships 'helped to dispel the myth of the English being reserved and reluctant to engage in collective celebration' (2007: 1). It could also be seen in the upsurge of interest in, and writings about the history, sociology and national character of the English.[4] This range of cultural reflections offered itself as a potential source of a new identity for Conservatives, particularly as their traditional appeal of a national ideal based on Empire, Union and anti-socialism appeared increasingly irrelevant. However, 'English historical understanding remains tied to a remarkably selective set of (largely mythical) stories and icons', particularly those associated with antagonism towards European rivals (Hayton, English and Kenny, 2007: 128). The nature of these dominant themes of English nationalism, which failed to adequately reflect the varied sources of the new Englishness, made the construction of a modern, inclusive, plural appeal based around it difficult for politicians of all parties. For the Conservatives, the only viable political Englishness available was the rather hard-edged nationalism promulgated by Heffer, which came with clear political risks. It is linked to a belligerent Euro-scepticism and comes perilously close to becoming a race-based argument. To have embraced it would have been to associate with what Cameron (2006b) labelled 'sour Little Englanders' – in party image terms an electorally foolish strategy.

Whilst they shied away from outright little-Englander populism, the Conservatives also struggled to articulate a convincing narrative of Britishness, or present themselves successfully as a party that embodied the British nation. The prevailing consensus in the party was effectively summarised by Michael Howard:

> I don't want to turn the clock back on devolution; but I do, however, believe there should be English votes for English laws. I think that members of Parliament from Scotland shouldn't be able to vote on matters that have been devolved to the Scottish Parliament. So I look at each issue on its merits. I don't think that the things that I've suggested are a recipe for an English party, which I wouldn't like to see. We have three members in Wales and one in Scotland, and I'd like to see more of them, and I'm confident that we will at the next election. (Private interview, 2006)

The view Howard expressed represented the mainstream Conservative position in the first decade of the twenty-first century. Wary of presenting themselves as an English party, the Conservatives instead preferred to claim they were addressing the English question pragmatically within a Unionist framework. Despite the grim electoral cartography after 1997, they continued to regard themselves as a UK-wide party. This identification was partly a negative one – lacking a sufficiently palatable English-based identity, the Conservatives attempted to maintain a British-based national appeal, even as the traditional Conservative understanding of Britishness appeared to be losing its relevance.

The new Englishness has implications beyond the constitutional question of the future of the Union and the nature of the relationship between England and Scotland. It also informs the broader issue of attitudes to English and British national identities. The Conservatives' uncertainties about what form these should take can be further revealed and explored through the examination of the politics of immigration and race.

Nationhood and the politics of immigration

I don't wish to have what they call a multicultural society. I hate these phrases. Multi-cultural society! A multicultural society will never be a united society. (Margaret Thatcher, 22 May 2001, quoted in Walters, 2001: 174)

A patriotic attachment to nation and empire was the cornerstone of British conservatism for much of the twentieth century and, as noted above, can be seen as one of the pillars of Conservative hegemony. However, the position of Britain as a great power was challenged by relative decline and the disintegration of empire, whilst the traditional view of Britishness was further brought into question by immigration from the New Commonwealth. As Lynch notes, 'The conservative nation is constructed around ideas of authority, patriotic allegiance, national character and the organic evolution of institutions, which sit uneasily with a plural society' (1999: 152). Immigration and race thus form an important part of the politics of nationhood, and have been at the heart of the debate about what the conservative nation should look like. However, the fervour of this debate in British politics has varied over time, in terms of both the level of public interest and the attention paid to it by politicians.

The bipartisan approach that had characterised immigration policy-making in the 1950s and 1960s was one of the victims of Thatcher's suspicion of consensus, and was abandoned in 1976 (Lynch, 1999: 134). Populist Powellite rhetoric was employed by Thatcher in the early years of her leadership. In an interview with Granada Television in 1978, she expressed people's fears that indigenous culture was being 'swamped' by immigration, 'echoing Powell's belief that such prejudices were legitimate and had to be addressed' (Lynch, 1999: 134). Here, the debate about the number of migrants was crucial. Thatcher argued that 'if you want good race relations, you have got to allay people's fears about immigration', and suggested the government 'must hold out the clear prospect of an end to immigration' (Thatcher, 1978).

The first Thatcher government did legislate to reduce immigration, introducing the British Nationality Act (1981) to tighten citizenship criteria. However, the Powellite rhetoric did not result in a full-blown Powellite policy, and some immigration continued. After playing a significant role in the first Thatcher administration the issues of race and immigration subsided, as the party leadership decided to play them down (Layton-Henry, 1986: 73, 95–7). The effect of Thatcher's first term was to depoliticise the issue, as 'there was nowhere else for ostensibly liberal politicians to go and little scope for the racist extreme right to make a breakthrough . . . Both the rhetorical and physical limits of control appeared to have been reached' (Geddes, 2003: 39–40). Thus, race questions were progressively marginalised, to the extent that in the 1987 general election, only 1 per cent of voters regarded them as amongst the most important (Rich, 1998: 100). This trend was continued under Major. Some further restrictions on entry to the United Kingdom were introduced, particularly with regard to asylum seekers, whose numbers had markedly increased (Lynch, 1999: 140). However, in terms of political debate within the party race and ethnicity faded into the background as other subjects, notably Europe, took centre stage (Rich, 1998: 103).

On becoming leader, Hague was keen to present himself as embodying a 'fresh start' for the Conservative Party (Chapter 3). One of his first (and most publicised) acts was to attend the Notting Hill Carnival, in a conscious effort to display his multicultural credentials (Nadler, 2000: 212). This visit symbolised the 'Fresh Conservatism' propounded by what Kelly labels 'Hague Mark I', and which was abandoned in favour of the more populist 'Common-sense Conservatism' by 'Hague Mark II' (Kelly, 2001: 197–203; Chapter 3). It also exposed the dilemma faced by the Conservatives between 1997 and 2010: whether to try to rebuild electoral support with strong messages on populist 'core-vote' issues, or whether to deliberately downplay such issues in an effort to demonstrate that the party had changed, and to allow space for a new narrative of conservatism to emerge. As Chapter 3 discussed, Hague sided firmly with the traditionalist 'rockers' in mid-1999, in the light of the reaction to Lilley's R. A. Butler Memorial Lecture and the European election results. Central to this shift was Hague's message on Europe and the single currency, but it also involved more emphasis on appearing tough on asylum and immigration.

Was this a strategic mistake? In 1998, Rich argued that 'by the early 1990s the electorate appeared only marginally interested in the immigration issue, and appeared far more concerned about Europe', and as such, 'the debate over nationhood in Britain has not lived up to predictions that it would connect up with issues of race' (1998: 106). However, there was some blurry amalgamation of the two issues, illustrated by the rhetoric of Hague's (2001) 'foreign land' speech, when he claimed that his policy was 'not bigotry' but 'plain common sense' and reflected the wishes of the people. Almost immediately this speech was attacked by Gurbux Singh, the chairman of the Campaign for Racial Equality, for undermining the fight against racial discrimination, but was 'spun' by party officials as an attack on the European Union (Walters, 2001: 147). The 2001 manifesto pledged to end the 'chaos' in the asylum system by interning all asylum seekers in reception centres, and blamed the government for giving Britain 'a reputation as a soft touch for bogus asylum seekers' (Conservative Party, 2001: 31). The Party Chairman at the 2001 election, Michael Ancram, also argued that the Conservative campaign agenda reflected public concerns. He recalled that immigration was an issue raised repeatedly by focus groups, hence the decision to include it as a theme in the Conservative campaign (private interview, 2007). Ancram also identified a wider problem at the 2001 election, namely that people were not interested in listening to Conservative messages on other issues, particularly public services. As he states:

> There was another problem, which was that the electorate were comfortable and simply didn't want to listen. The biggest expenditure I had as Chairman in the run-up to the 2001 election was a series of posters which said: 'You've paid your taxes, where are the nurses, you've paid your taxes, where are the police?' And those were not what you have just identified as the core issues, and we had them plastered all over the country for two months, and we didn't get a single move in the polls from that. So when it got to the election in a sense we were trying to find anything that was going to shift what was a very rigid political situation, not because people were determined not to move, but there was an inertia, they were comfortable, so anything that was going to make them sit up a bit. (Ancram, private interview, 2007)

This frank admission that the Conservatives were fumbling around in a rather desperate search for anything that would grab public attention encapsulates the inconsistent and incoherent nature of party strategy for much of this period, as well as the rather disjointed approach to the issue of immigration. Lacking a clear approach to the politics of nationhood, immigration policy and positioning under Hague was driven by short-term electoral strategies and calculations, which themselves were disputed in Conservative ranks.

The immigration issue was brought even more to the fore during the 2005 campaign, to the extent that it completely overshadowed European integration as the main focus of the politics of nationhood. It is therefore worth tracing its salience in order to discover to what extent this was a response to an upsurge in public interest and concern. In April 2008, MORI (2008b) conducted an opinion poll of attitudes towards race and immigration to mark the 40th anniversary of Enoch Powell's 'Rivers of Blood' speech. This found that 79 per cent of the population regard themselves as 'not prejudiced at all' against people from other races. However, 58 per cent of respondents agreed that 'parts of this country don't feel like Britain anymore because of immigration', and 59 per cent agreed that 'there are too many immigrants in Britain'. This figure has been relatively stable however, varying between 54 and 68 per cent between 1989 and 2008. The idea that government should encourage immigrants to return to their country of origin was supported by 49 per cent. Analysing data from the British social attitudes survey, Somerville suggests that 'the trend over the course of Labour's administration is one of rising resentment' as the proportion of the population believing the number of immigrants should be reduced has risen from approximately two-thirds to three-quarters (2007: 130). Polling evidence also shows that between 2000 and 2010 there was a clear upsurge in the proportion of the population who regarded immigration as one of the major issues facing the country (Figure 5.2).

Conservative policy and rhetoric on immigration can be contextualised by this increase. Making it a major campaign issue at the May 2005 election, when the importance of the issue to the public had averaged 29.5 per cent over the preceding two years, can be seen as a sound electoral calculation in response to public concern (by contrast, in the two years prior to the June 2001 election, the figure was 10.5 per cent). Indeed, Cowley and Green suggest that the Conservatives 'had little choice' but to focus heavily on immigration in 2005, as its salience had risen substantially whilst the Conservatives had maintained a clear lead over Labour as the best party on the issue (2005: 61). In April 2005, 52 per cent of voters named the Conservatives as the party with the best policies on asylum and immigration, whilst just 11 per cent selected Labour (MORI, 2008c). Consequently, 'by focussing on this issue the Conservatives' strategy was consistent with salience theory: to raise the salience of your own issue strengths and neutralise or downplay the strengths of

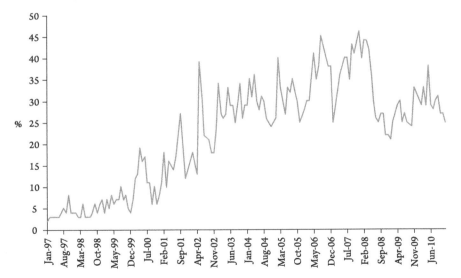

Figure 5.2 The salience of immigration to the British public, 1997–2010.
Questions: What would you say is the most important issue facing Britain today?
What do you see as other important issues facing Britain today? (Respondents are
unprompted, answers are combined). *Source*: IpsosMORI (2010).

your opponent' (Cowley and Green, 2005: 62). The Conservatives also hoped that their tough policies and rhetoric would prevent them being outflanked by UKIP, whose voters tended to be concerned about immigration (Cowley and Green, 2005: 62). In Bercow's view this was Howard's strategy: 'I think he thought he would try to neutralise our disadvantages on the public services and show that we were reasonable, and then get on to the "red meat" of taxation, crime and immigration'. He recalled how at a meeting of the 1922 committee about six months into his leadership, Howard 'said that he thought that he had addressed those issues and that the time had come "to move onto potentially fruitful territory for the Conservative Party" namely taxation, immigration and Europe. That was a mistake' (private interview, 2008).

As Bercow implies, the apparent logic of Howard's strategy has to be weighed against the wider implications of it, particularly the risk that it reinforced negative aspects of the party's image, the problem captured in Theresa May's comment that the Conservatives were seen as the 'nasty party'. Iain Duncan Smith noted how this could be a difficult issue to handle during elections, one which 'during an election campaign could probably bear two or three days, but you need to move on after that, because after that it just gets nasty' (private interview, 2006). Commenting on the 2005 election campaign, he noted: 'We got terribly bogged-down with asylum and immigration, which was a mistake' (private interview, 2006). He suggested that under his successor the party had handled the issue poorly and let it get out of control, and that this had damaged public perceptions of the Conservatives. This he contrasted with his own efforts to stop the Conservatives 'banging-on' about immigration, which were part of a more general strategy to challenge people's preconceptions about the party by downplaying subjects traditionally associated with the core-vote, and to move into new territory. He argued that voters: 'needed to understand that there was something wider about us, something bigger, so that's why we stayed off them' (private interview, 2006).

As Chapter 3 discussed, this strategy failed, due to his poor leadership skills and inability to manage the party and therefore present his agenda in a disciplined and coherent manner. Pursued successfully, however, Duncan Smith's approach may have avoided some of the pitfalls encountered by his successor. According to Peter Lilley, a particular problem faced by Michael Howard was that his policy on immigration, whilst popular, was viewed cynically by the electorate. Lilley explained: 'partly because he [Howard] was only there towards the end, there was a feeling that everything was opportunist. Immigration policy seemed to be opportunist, although about 70 per cent of the population agreed with it, about 20 per cent thought he would do it' (private interview, 2006).

For Ann Widdecombe, the way in which immigration came to dominate the 2005 campaign was symptomatic of a wider problem, as the public were no longer sure, beyond this issue, what the Conservatives actually stood for (private interview, 2007). This partly reflects the role of the media in setting the agenda, particularly during general election campaigns, but that is something that the party leadership must respond to:

> You cannot stop, in the end, the media homing in on whatever it wants to home in on. You can call a press conference on one thing, but if all they want to talk about is another, that is what will be reported. And I think Michael [Howard] was in that bind, William [Hague] was in that bind. (Widdecombe, private interview, 2007)

Michael Howard denied that it was a mistake for the Conservatives to campaign on immigration, and dismissed the characterisation of the 2005 campaign as one that concentrated almost exclusively on core-vote issues (particularly immigration). He did, however, acknowledge the role of the media in shaping which of the Conservatives' messages were communicated most forcefully to the electorate: 'It was only one of our five themes. I think the media gave it disproportionate attention, but I only devoted one press conference to immigration' (private interview, 2006). In this sense, Howard acknowledged the quandary Widdecombe highlighted: 'I didn't think that I had much alternative but to respond to questions that were put to me – it was part of our campaign, and I didn't want to pretend that it was not' (Howard, private interview, 2006).

The only way out of this difficulty, Widdecombe argues, is to forge a clearer alternative image of your party over a much longer period. If the 'nasty party' image could be dispelled, the Conservatives would be able to talk about issues such as immigration during election campaigns without reviving voters' negative preconceptions about the party. Widdecombe argued that the key to this was to set different 'mood music' over a number of years before a general election, which would allow 'tough policies' on issues such as immigration to be presented at election time without the accusation that the party lacked a wider agenda (private interview, 2007). This was a central element of David Cameron's strategy, as particularly in his first two years as leader of the opposition he tried to concentrate his messages on alternative issues such as the environment. Whilst the emphasis placed on immigration policy declined greatly under Cameron's stewardship (and the language and tone used to discuss the issue contrasted sharply with his predecessor's tenure) the substance of Conservative policy did not shift dramatically. The party went into the 2010 election promising to cap the number of non-EU migrants coming to Britain; tighten visa controls on foreign students; and 'take net migration back to the levels of the 1990s – tens of thousands a year, not hundreds of thousands' (Conservative Party, 2010: 21). The 2010 manifesto was careful however to present these policies as part of plan for the economy to encourage enterprise, rather than in the language of the 2005 document, which had proclaimed that 'it is not racist to impose limits on immigration' (Conservative Party, 2005: 18).

In contrast to Cameron who had over four years to define his approach before the 2010 election, Howard had just eighteen months as party leader before Tony Blair went to the country in 2005. This inevitably meant that Howard's opportunity to change the 'mood music' and set the agenda was more limited than that enjoyed by Cameron. He could have chosen to continue Duncan Smith's strategy (namely his focus on public services and social justice, and relative silence on 'core-vote' issues) that if implemented successfully may have altered the electorate's impression of the Conservatives. However, he saw his priorities as imposing discipline and making the party appear credible (Chapter 4), two things that had been lacking under his predecessor.

One source of indiscipline under Duncan Smith was that a large section of the party was unconvinced by his strategy. Therefore, for Howard, the easiest way to rapidly create the appearance of a united and disciplined party was to offer clear leadership on familiar Conservative themes. To do otherwise was to risk appearing implausible to both the public and his party: as he candidly admitted, he probably was not 'the best person to convince the country that the Conservative Party had changed' (Howard, interviewed in Portillo, 2008). Moreover, he was 'ambivalent' about modernisation, and in his own words conceded that: 'I didn't feel that I could really be true to myself and present an appeal to the country based on the fact that the Conservative Party had changed' (Howard, interviewed in Portillo, 2008). Howard thus calculated that to shun issues such as immigration would not only mean that the Conservatives were passing up the opportunity to capitalise on high-salience issues on which they had a clear lead over Labour, but would also breed public suspicion. As he commented: 'I was very reluctant not to talk about things which I thought were very important to people. I didn't stop talking about Europe or crime or immigration, and I think that if I had people would have realised I wasn't being true to myself' (Howard, interviewed in Portillo, 2008).

If the prominent role of immigration in the 2005 Conservative campaign can be understood as a strategic calculation consistent with salience theory, what can be said about 2010? As Figure 5.2 illustrates, immigration remained a highly salient issue during the 2005–10 parliament. In opinion polls conducted by IpsosMORI it never dropped out of the top five 'most important issues facing the country' and more often than not was one of the top two (Carey and Geddes, 2010: 853). This consistent high level of public concern was accompanied by public mistrust of Labour's ability to handle immigration competently: going into the campaign the Conservative opposition enjoyed a 25 per cent lead over the governing party on the issue (Carey and Geddes, 2010: 854). These high levels of salience and partisan advantage suggested that the Conservatives might seek to push the issue hard during the campaign. However, although it featured at key moments (notably the televised leadership debates and as a result of Gordon Brown's 'bigotgate' incident) the Conservatives sought to downplay the issue for fear of 'being seen as negative and extreme' (Carey and Geddes, 2010: 856). Cameron's retention of a relatively hardline policy nonetheless demonstrated an awareness in Conservative circles of the popularity of a tough line on immigration, even though they chose not to 'dog whistle' the electorate about it as they had in 2005.

The Cameron leadership and 2010 campaign once again demonstrated the dominance of electoral calculations in shaping policy in this area. As under his three predecessors, the Conservatives continued to lack an unambiguous approach to the politics of nationhood. The next section considers this identity question more broadly, and asks whether between 1997 and 2010 the Conservatives became a party of English (rather than British) nationalism, be that by accident or design.

An English party? The Conservatives and the politics of nationhood since 1997

On both the constitutional question of the future of the post-devolution Union, and the cultural question of immigration and national identity, the Conservatives' approach to the politics of nationhood between 1997 and 2010 was mixed. In respect of both issues, the party appeared unsure whether to seek to exploit them in the hope of gaining political advantage over their opponents, or to downplay them to reduce their political temperature and/or improve their party image. This reflected the absence of a dominant, coherent view of national identity in contemporary Conservative thought to provide clear answers to these policy questions.

The lack of such a perspective is perhaps unsurprising. The traditional Conservative view of Britishness and the state was brought into question by factors largely beyond their control, such as globalisation, increased immigration and a more multicultural society. Conservatives also unsuccessfully fought to defend the constitutional status quo against reform (notably devolution). The numerous reports of the death of Britain may have been exaggerated, but it is undoubtedly the case that a range of social, cultural, economic and political factors have undermined the traditions, values and beliefs associated with Britishness for much of the twentieth century.[5] Writing in 1995, Dodd saw British identity as 'in turmoil' (1995: 5). Five years later, Alibhai-Brown noted that: 'Over the latter half of the twentieth century there has been a considerable weakening of the most abiding myths which have created this sense of nationhood in Britain' (2000: 27). As both authors note, this occurred despite the efforts of Mrs Thatcher to resist this trend and hold on to the traditional pillars of the Conservative nation.

The Conservatives' conception of nationhood is important for their identity as a party, and has historically been a primary aspect of their electoral appeal. However, as the traditional view of Britishness weakened, so did the Conservative appeal built around it. As discussed in the context of devolution above, one distinctively Conservative narrative of nationhood offered itself as a potential response to these changed circumstances. However, to declare Britishness and the United Kingdom as defunct and embrace English nationalism in the way that Heffer (1999) has suggested would involve a number of pitfalls. It would provide a clear-cut conception of national identity across the issues of Europe, the Union, and immigration and race, but as Cameron (2006b) and other Conservatives recognised, carried with it the risk that it would have only a narrow appeal and damage the image of the party. This dilemma was neatly summarised by Lynch (1999: 168), and remained a decade later:

> Pragmatic moves towards a reforming, pro-European centre ground would have political benefits and mark a development of themes evident in an earlier Conservative national strategy: but it would erode the distinctiveness of the Conservative politics of nationhood. Alternatively, further moves in the direction of a nationalist strategy built around Euroscepticism and English nationalism would establish a clear Conservative vision of the nation-state and national identity, but would consign the party to a reactive and outdated view of the nation-state and might allow Labour to establish predominance in the politics of nationhood.

This latter approach would be consistent with the ideological trajectory set by Thatcherism, and the party has moved partway there by embedding a solidly Eurosceptic position (Chapter 4). However, it is an unfair caricature to suggest that the Conservatives have 'progressively ceased to be a Unionist Party of the whole of the United Kingdom and become instead largely a party of English nationalism' (Rich, 1998: 97). Ironically, Thatcher's vigorous nationalism, pursued in the name of Britain against 'threats' such as Europe, Argentina and devolution, actually helped to fertilise Scottish and Welsh nationalism, and took on an English nationalist character. It is also true that the reforming zeal of her administration and that of her successor radically reshaped the British state, and in the process 'massively undermined the principal remaining props of Britishness: the National Health Service, state education, trade unionism, British Rail, the Post Office, the BBC and the nationalized industries' (Kumar, 2003: 264). Further to this, in terms of its geographical representation the trend between 1997 and 2010 continued the drift towards becoming an overwhelmingly English party.

However, the analysis of both case-study areas in this chapter demonstrates the clear reluctance of the party to fully embrace the English nationalist position, although at times (perhaps out of desperation, and for want of better alternatives) the party has sought to exploit it. At the 2001 general election, for example, the 'race card' appeared opportunistically on the political scene (Saggar, 2001). As Clarke commented, 'When it became obvious we weren't going to win the election, they kind of panicked, and decided that we'd better start "blowing the dog whistles" and getting the core vote back' (interviewed in Portillo, 2008).

The Conservative approach to Englishness and Britishness became entangled with the wider debate over how to reinvigorate the party's electoral appeal. The message of 'change' that David Cameron sought to promote required a new identity for the party, which sat uneasily with the sectional appeal of English nationalism. This was recognised by the party leadership before Cameron: witness Hague's early attempts to embrace multiculturalism; Duncan Smith's attempt to move away from core-vote issues such as immigration; and the willingness of senior figures such as Michael

Portillo and Kenneth Clarke to question the electoral sense of the tone taken on asylum during the 2001 election campaign (Saggar, 2001: 767). As William Hague noted, the Conservatives needed a new identity to persuade the electorate that they had really changed, and the problem was presenting one convincingly:

> Clearly people found that this was not a believable thing about the Conservative Party. The leader who went to the Notting Hill Carnival wasn't believable. That the Conservative Party was open to ethnic minorities, and that we were genuinely young – there must be something phoney about this, some pretence. And so that did make it quite hard to carry on with a 'change' message. (Hague, interviewed in Portillo, 2008)

The difficulty of appearing credible whilst presenting a message of change was also recognised by Michael Howard (above), and used to justify his focus on more traditional Conservative messages at the 2005 election. This dilemma, and the awareness of it amongst the party leadership, illustrates why the party did not pursue one approach to the politics of nationhood consistently between 1997 and 2010, but offered contradictory messages at different times. David Cameron was more successful than his three predecessors in consistently pursuing a message of change and modernisation of the party, and presenting it credibly. His major advantage in this regard was that after three heavy election defeats both the parliamentary party and the wider membership was more easily persuadable of the importance of changing its image, messages and strategy. After all, by his own admission, Howard had 'tested the alternative theory to destruction in the 2005 election, and lost!' (interviewed in Portillo, 2008). As Michael Portillo dryly observed: 'maybe even the Conservative Party reacts after three defeats' (private interview, 2006). However, as he also noted, the 2005 leadership election did not demonstrate that even then the parliamentary party was wholly convinced of the need to radically alter course: 'I observe that more members of parliament voted against David Cameron than voted for him. There were two candidates who were no-change candidates and one candidate who was a change candidate – more people voted no-change than change, even in 2005' (private interview, 2006).

Cameron was able to sustain his modernising agenda and mute criticism from sceptics in his own party as under his leadership the Conservatives performed relatively well in the opinion polls and in local elections. Without these indicators of success, his project may well have foundered before the 2010 election. In terms of the politics of nationhood, the challenge for Cameron was to articulate a vision of national identity that supported his agenda of presenting the Conservative Party as modern, inclusive and best placed to solve contemporary social and economic problems. However, this mainly involved a change of language, tone and rhetoric, rather than any substantial policy shifts. Somewhat ironically, given the emphasis the modernisers placed on the need to adapt to contemporary society, it also involved a return to a traditional language of unionism more associated with the 'One Nation' tradition of conservatism than the neo-Thatcherite strand.

Cameron expressed his faith in the future of the Union not only as a constitutional arrangement, but 'as something much deeper' which embodies 'the bonds of kinship and the strength of our individual, and community, relationships which span the border' (Cameron, 2007b). In a practical demonstration of his unionism, in 2008 Cameron also negotiated an alliance with the Ulster Unionist Party in Northern Ireland (one that failed to pay off electorally in 2010 as the UUP lost its last remaining seat). Similarly, while retaining the principle established by William Hague that something should be done to tackle the perceived unfairness of the West Lothian Question, via his Democracy Taskforce Cameron also diluted Conservative commitment to EvfEl. The Taskforce chairman Ken Clarke acknowledged that the asymmetric nature of the current arrangements might lead to nationalistic English resentment towards Scotland, and that 'he would like to nip that in the bud by some sensible constitutional minor change . . . to finish the business of devolution' (HC 75, 2008). As such under Cameron Conservative discourse on the issue remained within unionist parameters – the problem was presented as a procedural 'niggle' rather than a more far-reaching question of identity.

On immigration, too, Cameron changed Conservative language, tone and presentation, but made no radical changes to the policy the party took into the 2005 election. The 2005 manifesto pledged to introduce 24-hour surveillance at ports and create a Border Police Force; implement a points-based system for work permits; withdraw from the 1951 Geneva Convention on refugees; and 'set an overall annual limit on the numbers coming to Britain' (Conservative Party, 2005: 19). With the exception of withdrawal from the Geneva Convention, essentially the same policies appeared in the 2010 manifesto. However, Cameron used more positive language than his predecessor when discussing immigration, emphasising its 'many benefits', and maintaining that 'Britain has so much to gain from being open to the world' (Cameron, 2007c). He also discussed the issue in relation to his broader professed concern with the 'general well-being' of society, meaning that consideration of 'the various social and environmental pressures that rapid population growth can bring' must underpin policy (Cameron, 2007c). As such, as leader of the opposition Cameron aimed to disassociate immigration from the identity debate and associate the Conservative Party with an inclusive national identity based on the Union.

Conclusion

Beneath the political debates, the broader cultural trend of the emergence of a stronger felt and more clearly defined sense of Englishness looks unlikely to abate (Hayton, English and Kenny, 2007). The challenge for the Conservatives in the early twenty-first century has been (and remains) to find a way to engage with this growing sense of English identity in a pluralistic and inclusive manner, which does not limit the party's electoral appeal by drawing on the exclusivist Powellite English nationalism that currently permeates much of this discourse on the right. Such a treatise need not be incompatible with unionism, or a form of Britishness shorn of its imperial past. However, the chapter has also highlighted the way in which the effect of the ideological legacy of Thatcherism is to pull conservatism in the Powellite direction, whereas statecraft favours a more moderate Britishness.

Examining this question in relation to two key policy areas, devolution and immigration, demonstrated how these ideological debates impact upon the formulation of party strategy. These two issues indicate that party leaders do not face simple choices between optimal electoral strategies and an 'ideological' path. Ideology is not crudely juxtaposed with electoral concerns, acting as an obstacle to moving towards the position of the median voter, but is an integral feature of the way in which actors understand their context and seek to develop strategies. The question of whether the Conservatives should reposition themselves as an overtly English party is a classic example of this. The party leadership demonstrated uncertainty and disagreement over whether this would be an electorally beneficial strategy, and consequently vacillated over its approach. However, this variance of opinion was not merely about electoral calculation, but also reflected ideological differences. For example, some of the most forceful exponents of the electoral benefits of fully embracing an English identity are clearly ideologically motivated. The Conservative response to devolution and the West Lothian Question – offering the prospect of some constitutional change in an effort to assuage perceived English concerns, but presented in a unionist discourse – surely reflects the history, ideology and tradition of the Conservative Party as a unionist party as much as electoral reckoning. As Wellings argued, English Conservatives are 'instinctively British' (2007: 398). Devolution, for them, is thus another reason to defend the British state, rather than to embrace English nationalism.

Ideology therefore plays an important role in the interpretation of the electoral context, and consequently in the strategies pursued. As a key site of ideological difference in contemporary conservatism, the national identity question demonstrates how the debate about such issues can impact on leadership strategies, illustrating their complexity, and the difficulties caused to the party by a lack of a coherent conception of nationhood.

Notes

1 There is a wealth of academic literature dedicated to discussing what constitutes 'national identity'. Here I adopt Anderson's (1991) definition of a nation as an 'imagined community'. Consequently, the key features of national identity are an historic territory, common myths and historical memories, a mass, public culture, a common economy and common legal rights and duties for all members (Smith, 1991: 14). For further discussion in relation to England and Britain see Aughey (2007), Kumar (2000, 2003) and Mandler (2006a, 2006b).

2 In Scotland, 1,775,045 voters (74.3 per cent) agreed that there should be a Scottish Parliament, whilst 614,400 (25.7 per cent) disagreed. 1,512,889 (63.5 per cent) agreed that it should have tax raising powers, with 870,263 (36.5 per cent) against. Turnout was 60.4 per cent. In Wales, 559,419 voters (50.3 per cent) agreed that there should be a Welsh Assembly, and 552,698 (49.7 per cent) disagreed, on a turnout of 50.1 per cent (BBC News, 1997).

3 The situation whereby Scottish MPs at Westminster were able to vote on legislation that only applied to England (or to England and Wales), whilst English and Welsh MPs enjoyed no such right over legislation that only applied to Scotland (as it had been devolved to the Scottish Parliament).

4 For example: Blunkett (2005); Bragg (2006); Heffer (1999); Hitchens (1999); Kumar (2003); Mandler (2006a); Marr (2000); Paxman (1998); Scruton (2000); Stapleton (2001); Weight (2002).

5 On the 'death', 'abolition' and/or 'break-up' of Britain, see Haseler (1996); Hitchens (1999); Marr (2000); Nairn (1981); Preston (1994); Redwood (1999); Scruton (2000); Weight (2002).

6

A new moral agenda?
Social liberalism and traditionalism

Just as I felt that the party was beginning to relax over the European issue it decided to have an explosive internal row about something else. (John Redwood MP, 2004: 143)

Introduction

A widely accepted and often repeated belief amongst both Conservatives and many of their critics, is that on the issue of the economy the Conservatives have been victorious in the 'battle of ideas'. The case for the free market over statist socialist planning was comprehensively demonstrated, they argue, by the failure of Keynesianism and the success of Thatcher's economic revolution, a success vindicated at the polls by four Conservative election victories and the emergence of New Labour. Whilst enjoying the taste of this triumph, some Conservatives saw it as the root cause of their electoral problems. They were the victims of their own success: by forcing Labour to accept their agenda, they created a new consensus and neutralised one of the most compelling reasons for voting Conservative. Indeed, after the collapse of the Conservatives' reputation for economic competence after 'Black Wednesday' in September 1992, Labour were able to argue that they were the party best able to manage the economy, and opinion polls demonstrate that until the credit crunch and subsequent recession the public believed this to be the case (Chapter 7). Shortly after becoming party leader, David Cameron (2006a) acknowledged this problem, claiming:

> We knew how to rescue Britain from Old Labour. We knew how to win the battle of ideas with Old Labour. We did not know how to deal with our own victory in that battle of ideas. That victory left us with an identity crisis. Having defined ourselves for many years as the anti-socialist Party, how were we to define ourselves once full-blooded socialism had disappeared from the political landscape?

The consequence of this difficulty, Cameron argued, was that 'as Labour moved towards the centre ground, the Conservative Party moved to the right. Instead of focusing on the areas where we now agreed with Labour on our aims . . . we ended up focusing on those areas where we didn't agree'. The Conservatives in opposition therefore emphasised taxation, immigration and Europe as areas of policy difference from Labour, but this left them lacking a clear message on the 'common ground' of British politics, namely Blair's agenda of 'social justice and economic efficiency' (Cameron, 2006a). As leader of the opposition, Cameron sought to reposition the Conservatives to compete with Labour on this territory, and to critique the government's record in these areas. To this end he repeatedly spoke of the need to mend Britain's 'broken society', citing problems such as poverty, drug abuse, debt, family breakdown and educational failure. Cameron also frequently emphasised the importance of supporting families and marriage (for example through the tax system) as a central part of his approach to tackling these issues. However, the Conservatives' capacity to forge a coherent narrative on social and moral issues between 1997 and 2010 was limited by significant divisions within the party over how they should be approached. This chapter examines Conservative policy and rhetoric on social and moral issues, particularly gay rights and family policy. It considers whether the key dividing line within the Conservative Party in the period of study was no longer between Eurosceptics and Europhiles, but between social liberals and traditionalists. How this division informed the strategies of Hague, Duncan Smith and Howard and the debate over modernisation is explored. The chapter ends with an assessment of Cameron's claim that under his leadership the Conservatives came to terms with this dilemma, and evaluates whether his efforts to appear socially liberal whilst also emphasising the centrality of family policy constituted a distinctively Conservative answer to it.[1]

Mods and rockers: Conservative divisions over social and moral issues

Social and moral issues have long been of concern to Conservatives, and form a distinctive aspect of conservatism. In the 1990s the notion that positioning on such issues marked an important divide for Conservatives became increasingly prevalent, linked to the need to develop a post-Thatcherite agenda. In an effort to map the ideological composition of contemporary conservatism and explain ideological discord within the Conservative Party a number of different typologies have been developed. These have highlighted divisions between 'wets' and 'dries' on economic policy and conflict between Europhiles and Eurosceptics. For Heppell and Hill, Europe and economic policy are 'the two most significant ideological policy divides' (2005: 347). However, Heppell's (2002) model also mapped the 'social, sexual and moral policy divide', distinguishing social liberals from social conservatives to create a three-dimensional typology (2002: 312). Such issues also came to form a more central feature of Conservative identity as self-identification as the anti-socialist party (as Cameron highlights above) diminished. At the same time, Conservative ideology failed to establish the degree of hegemony it enjoyed in the economic arena. As Pilbeam notes, 'modern Conservatism has signally failed to close down

contestation over moral issues in the same way that it has done over others'
(Pilbeam, 2005: 158).

In spite of these challenges, some Conservatives demonstrated an increasing
willingness to engage in social and cultural debates. For example in 2002 the Conservative MP John Hayes argued that politicians had come to see 'good politics'
and economic success as synonymous, and wrongly allowed material advance to
become the main driver of public policy. For him, this amounted to 'a reductionist
view of politics that ignores all those components necessary to a balanced quality
of life that do not relate to economic well being' (Hayes, 2002: 68). These senti-
ments were echoed by Cameron's call (albeit before the credit crunch) for politicians
to focus 'not just on GDP, but on GWB – General Well-Being' and his suggestion
that it was 'time we admitted that there's more to life than money' (Cameron,
2006b). For Hayes, the reluctance of most politicians to address such issues can be
explained by the fact that they have 'awkward associations with values and morals',
so 'it became convenient for politicians to retreat to the safer ground of managing
the public purse and advocacy of ever greater material consumption' (2002: 68).
In the case of the Conservatives this reluctance can partly be explained by the ill-
fated 'Back to Basics' campaign of 1993–94. This effort to re-launch John Major's
government sought to divert attention to social issues after the economic *débâcle*
of withdrawal from the ERM, but quickly unravelled in the face of allegations of
sleaze and immoral behaviour on the part of (mainly Conservative) parliamentarians. In Gary Streeter's words, it left a 'scar' on the party, and 'made people cautious
about those kind of value-laden statements and directions' (private interview, 2008).
Another Conservative MP, John Bercow, similarly agreed that memory of the 'very
damaging' Back to Basics campaign meant the post-1997 party 'was rather more
wary under successive leaders of sounding too shrill or judgemental on that whole
set of issues' (private interview, 2008).

For Streeter, re-engaging with social and moral issues was a necessary if daunting
task, on a scale 'similar to the economic battles that faced the incoming Conservative government of 1979' (2002: 4). David Willetts (1994) similarly argued that
Conservative politics should be about more than economics, and a vibrant civil
society is a central component of his vision of 'civic conservatism'. Likewise Oliver
Letwin (2003) called for Conservatives to foster a 'neighbourly society' in which
social duties and obligations have the same importance and recognition as the
pursuit of material gain.

Whilst Conservatives were increasingly keen to re-associate themselves with
social and moral issues, how to do so has been the cause of disagreement between
social liberals and social conservatives. In 1998, *The Times* argued that the key
dividing line in the Conservative Party was no longer over Europe or between Left
and Right, but that: 'the real division is between liberals and reactionaries, modernisers and traditionalists, those armed primarily with principle and those whose
first instinct is to take shelter in institutions'. Furthermore, for the Conservatives

to regain power, the 'liberals must first win the battle of ideas within their party' (*The Times*, 1998). The paper's leader went on:

> The more important argument the Conservative Party still needs to have is between those sensitive to changing times and those inclined to nostalgia. It is a battle, we believe, between Tory Mods and Rockers. In the Sixties the former were those comfortable with change, the latter those who followed old fads. It is the difference between those with a gaze fixed on new horizons and those either blinkered or still dreaming.

Regardless of their personal preferences, electoral necessity demanded that Conservatives recognise the changing society in which they had to operate. 'Wise Conservatives deal with the world as it is, not as it should be or once was. They respect the changing landscape and are sensitive to its contours.' The Conservatives could demonstrate this pragmatic attitude 'by showing a liberal face to the electorate and extending an emancipating hand to all voters', and by taking 'government out of the boardroom and the bedroom', contrasting themselves with an interventionist statist Labour Party (*The Times*, 1998).

The version of modernisation sponsored by *The Times* in 1998 bears a notable resemblance to that advanced by David Cameron during his time as leader of the opposition between 2005 and 2010. Modernisation implies disassociation with the recent past as continued association carries with it negative electoral consequences. To modernise is to attempt change the narrative and/or image of the party, through processes of change that can embrace the party leader, the policy agenda and/or the organisational structures of the party (Denham and O'Hara, 2007a). As this chapter explores, changes of policy and presentation on social and moral issues formed an important part of Cameron's modernisation project. However, significant disagreement over what constituted modernisation (and the place of social and moral issues within it) was an important feature of Conservative politics between 1997 and 2010.

After losing his seat in the 1997 election Michael Portillo became a leading 'mod' and argued that embracing social liberalism must be central to any modernisation strategy and offered the best hope for electoral recovery. For him, this route offered a clear and distinctive narrative with 'tremendous coherence' which would appeal to the centre-ground (private interview, 2006). Streeter, by contrast, did not see embracing social liberalism as the way onto this territory for Conservatives, or as a prerequisite for electoral success. For him, the agenda for helping the vulnerable 'is not about extending laissez-faire doctrines throughout society', but about representing 'the small platoons' against big business as well as against big government. As such, 'Conservatives must not stand for social liberalism, but social justice' (2002: 9). He also argued that the distinction *The Times* made between mods and rockers had lost its usefulness for understanding the Conservative Party, as 'the boundaries have become much more fluid' (private interview, 2008). For Bercow, too, whilst 'there is a dividing line between people who fall into those different categories' it is not a distinction that 'defines the party on a daily basis'. Nor was it, he suggested, the source of an 'unbridgeable and dangerous gulf' (private interview, 2008). Nonetheless, it was the arena for significant disagreement within the party in opposition, interlaced with the strategic question of how to broaden the Conservatives' appeal. This debate reflected the ideological legacy of Thatcherism in the Conservative Party, which continued to frame party positioning post-1997. For Heppell, 'Thatcherism constituted a self-conscious ideological strategy to redefine the Conservatives as a party of *economic liberalism, national independence* and *moral authoritarianism*' (2002: 302, original emphasises). By the end of the twentieth century the doctrines of economic liberalism and national independence (at least in terms of Euroscepticism) appeared to be firmly embedded in the party, but the case-study period demonstrates that moral authoritarianism did not have the same grip. However, as the following sections explore, it was a significant feature of the debate over gay rights and family policy between 1997 and 2010.

Hague: bandwagon politics?

There are millions of people in this country who are white, Anglo-Saxon and bigoted, and they need to be represented. (Eric Forth MP, 24 October 2000, quoted in Walters, 2001: 86)

During his leadership campaign and in the early part of his tenure William Hague was keen to present himself as embodying a fresh face for conservatism. As such, he recognised the need to present himself and his party as at ease with modern British society, including its non-traditional and multicultural aspects. Another element of this strategy was a more liberal approach and softer tone on sexual and moral issues such as gay rights. In this respect, Hague could point to his own record as having voted to equalise the age of consent at sixteen for homosexual and heterosexual acts. He also sent a message of support to a Gay Pride event and publicly rebuked members of the 'old guard' such as Norman Tebbit who criticised his stance on homosexual rights and multiculturalism. In his first conference speech as leader, Hague noted his wish to lead 'a new, united, inclusive, democratic, de-centralised, and open party'. He spoke of his desire to articulate 'an open conservatism, that is tolerant, that believes freedom is about much more than economics, that believes freedom doesn't stop at the shop counter' and argued that Conservatives are 'caring'. Compassion, he argued 'is not a bolt-on extra to conservatism' but is 'at its very core' (Hague, 1997).

However, this socially inclusive and liberal-minded conservatism, even if it reflected Hague's own personal preferences, was short-lived. The most obvious reason for this was that it did not reflect the opinion of the majority of Conservative MPs, and Hague failed to convince them to alter their approach. For example in the 1998 vote on reducing the age of consent for gay sex to sixteen, only sixteen

Conservative MPs voted in favour of equalisation (Dorey, 2003: 134). Although this vote was passed by the Commons, it was subsequently defeated by the votes of Conservative hereditary peers in the Lords (Waites, 2001: 496). The government reintroduced a similar measure during the next parliamentary session and it was again defeated in the second chamber. Sexual equality was finally achieved in November 2000, but only after the government had invoked the Parliament Act to overrule the House of Lords (Waites, 2001: 497).

Hague had avoided the appearance of party disunity over the age of consent by allowing a free vote on what he described as 'a matter of conscience' (Brogan, 2000). This liberal approach was abandoned, however, on the issue of Section 28. This clause in the Local Government Act (1988) was introduced by the Thatcher administration to forbid councils from promoting homosexuality or promoting its acceptability as a family relationship (Durham, 2005: 98). The Conservatives imposed a three-line whip against the government's proposal to abolish Section 28, and successfully prevented repeal in the upper house. For Bercow, this decision was a 'great mistake' as 'it made us look and sound very unattractive'. It was also, Bercow thought, driven by populism: whilst it may have reflected Hague's personal views 'I suspect he thought the government's position would be unpopular with large swathes of the population and that the Conservatives should capitalise on that' (private interview, 2008). Once again this Conservative victory was only possible with the votes of hereditary peers (Waites, 2001: 498), but on this occasion the government was unable to invoke the Parliament Act (which only covers legislation initiated in the Commons) as the Bill had initially been introduced in the House of Lords (Dorey, 2003: 135).

The retention of Section 28 was just one element in the panoply of populist positions adopted by Hague throughout 1999 and 2000, on issues such as asylum, Europe, and the Tony Martin case (Walters, 2001: 64). Theresa May, who as a member of the shadow cabinet supported the party line, candidly admitted that 'I think I was wrong on Section 28, and have changed my view on Section 28'. She also acknowledged that the stance taken on this issue, and on the strong defence of grammar schools, appealed to 'the traditional image of the party rather than to the more modern image of the party' (private interview, 2006). For Waites, these kind of issues were deliberately linked together by the Conservatives in an effort to define the party under Hague, and 'may be interpreted as including partially-coded appeals to certain racist and homophobic elements of the electorate, presenting Conservatives as defendants of the imagined British nation beloved of traditionalists, in contrast to the modernising multiculturalist Blairites' (Waites, 2001: 503). The language of fear and 'threats' was echoed in the party's 2001 election manifesto, which pledged to retain Section 28 and argued that 'the common sense wisdom of the mainstream majority, on crime, or on taxes, or the family, or on Europe, is under threat as never before' (Conservative Party, 2001: 2).

Hague's hard line on Section 28 led to the defections to Labour of MP Shaun Woodward, who had been sacked from the frontbench for refusing to support it; and Ivan Massow, the prominent Conservative businessman who had sought the party's nomination as candidate for Mayor of London. Massow lambasted the 'skinhead conservatism that has marked the "tabloidification" of the Conservatives' and claimed that on the issues of race and sex Hague had been manipulated against his better instincts by 'loony right-wingers' amongst the party membership, who 'set the tone of the party by their sheer dedication to "the cause"'. (Massow, 2000).

Populist appeal, as Waites suggests, was undoubtedly a factor in the Conservative leadership's decision to oppose the repeal of Section 28 during Labour's first term. Party pressures, as Massow argues, were also a factor, although the picture he presents of a leader powerless to resist the wider membership is overdone. A more telling factor on Hague's decision was opinion within his own shadow cabinet and parliamentary party, illustrated by the free votes on the age of consent. The position on Section 28 can also be seen as part of a wider move towards a more traditionally Conservative stance on family life and marriage, which quickly encroached upon Hague's early flirtation with a socially liberal agenda. By the time the government began its legislative attempts to repeal Section 28 in 1999, the Conservatives' traditional stance on family values was firmly embedded. Indeed, the first hints of this agenda were contained in Hague's 1997 conference speech, when he declared that: 'I personally believe that it is best for children to be brought up in a traditional family. That means their mother and their father in their home.' In this speech, he attempted to combine a pro-family stance with a liberal agenda. He noted that Conservatives should show 'understanding and tolerance of people making their own decisions about how they lead their lives' (the extension of liberalism on economics to social issues, as advocated by Portillo above), whilst also claiming 'that doesn't alter our unshakeable belief in the enduring value of traditional family life' (Hague, 1997).

The flagship policy adopted on the family under Hague was a commitment to introduce a new married couple's tax allowance, replacing that which had been finally abolished in the April 2000 budget. This would, the 2001 manifesto claimed, be worth £1,000 a year to married couples. In addition, Child Tax Credit for families with a child under five would be increased by £200 a year, and those with children under eleven and not using all or part of their personal tax allowance would be able to transfer it to their working spouse (Conservative Party, 2001: 3–4).

Hague's approach to social, moral and sexual politics was a consistent part of the core-vote strategy he adopted from the October 1998 conference onwards, initially under the 'British Way' label, and later as the 'Common Sense Revolution'. Like Duncan Smith and Cameron in subsequent years, Hague hoped to address the charge that the Conservatives were not interested in society, and were merely concerned with economics. In this respect, Hague was engaged with 'one of the most important imperatives of post-Thatcher conservatism', namely the attempt to balance the Thatcherite legacy with the construction of a Conservative politics that 'could escape the allegations of harshness and economic monomania' that had dogged Thatcherism (Durham, 2001: 471). The form that this took, however, illustrated the enduring hold of the traditional values promoted by Thatcher on the Conservative Party. For Waites, 'Thatcherism signalled the resilience of homophobia on the political right' (2001: 502), and Hague's stance on Section 28 was consistent with this. His populist line on this issue also signalled that he 'had effectively abandoned his earlier attempts to reposition the party' (Nadler, 2000: 284). This strategy was premised on the belief, expressed by Norman Tebbit, that substantial numbers of Conservative voters were 'out there' waiting to be persuaded back to the fold by more strident policies (private interview, 2007).

Hague's promises of tax cuts for families, support for marriage, retention of Section 28, a crackdown on 'bogus' asylum seekers, calls for tougher sentences for paedophiles, and his suggestion of a change in the law to protect homeowners defending their property (in response to the Tony Martin case) were designed to chime with this forgotten 'silent majority' and encourage them back to the polling station. Nadler claims that for Hague this phase was 'about more than shoring up his core vote' – it flowed from 'his own convictions', reflected his 'gut instincts' and in this sense represents the authentic voice of William Hague (Nadler, 2000: 288). One problem with it, however, was that it appeared inauthentic, contradicting his earlier attempts to paint himself as liberal-minded and socially inclusive. Hague thus found himself the target of criticism from both modernisers and traditionalists in his own party.

Hague's prescriptive stance on marriage and the desirability of 'traditional' families was in harmony with the socially authoritarian aspects of New Right thinking, and parallels can be drawn with the 'compassionate conservatism' of George W. Bush (Ashbee, 2003: 43–6). In this sense Hague's offering at the 2001 election – of economic liberalism, vigorous nationalism and traditional social values – was firmly within Thatcherite parameters. Indeed, for Portillo, this agenda was 'arguably to the right of Margaret Thatcher' (2008). Hague defended it on the grounds of practical necessity, claiming afterwards that for the Conservatives 'the 2001 result could have been worse, even worse, than it was' (Hague, interviewed in Portillo, 2008).

A final consequence of Hague's strategy was to increase division within the party on the social, sexual and moral policy divide, and to highlight the emerging rupture between mods and rockers. His initial dalliance with social liberalism gave credence to the modernising view that embracing societal change was essential for Conservative electoral revival, and his abandonment of it provided the modernisers with ammunition with which to attack his leadership. Intraparty discord over social, sexual and moral issues would intensify under his successor.

Duncan Smith and Howard: (mis)managing divisions

In the case of Iain Duncan Smith it is repeated slightly tragically, because he begins as an arch-conservative but ends up as a moderniser, but by then it's too late. (Michael Portillo, private interview, 2006)

Two factors were pivotal in Duncan Smith's election as leader of the Conservative Party. The first was that he was not Michael Portillo, the second that he was not Kenneth Clarke. In the final ballot of party members, Clarke was comprehensively defeated because of his pro-European views (Chapter 4; Redwood, 2004: 152). In the parliamentary contest, Duncan Smith was able to beat Portillo into third place (by one vote) because of unease amongst a substantial number of Conservative MPs about both Portillo personally and his plans to remodel the party. Unlike in 1997, when the right of the parliamentary party failed to coalesce behind a single candidate, once David Davis had been eliminated Duncan Smith became the standard bearer for traditionalists. Whilst Davis adopted a more reformist tone and promised 'a fundamental policy review', Duncan Smith rejected modernisation, opting for 'neoliberal generalisations such as the need for more choice in education and health' (Alderman and Carter, 2002: 577). In a direct challenge to Portillo's agenda, he explicitly rejected all-women shortlists or any possibility of relaxing the law on drugs. Portillo commented that: 'too many MPs disliked me, and/or my uncompromising agenda for modernisation. One offered me his vote if I'd water down my plans for change. I refused, and lost by one vote' (Portillo, 2008). For Streeter, this mix of personal and political factors explained the result: 'some people didn't like the message, and some people didn't like the messenger' (private interview, 2008). To understand the result, Bercow suggests, 'for Ken's Europhilia substitute Michael's socially liberal credentials'. For him, Portillo 'was clearly the modernising candidate in 2001' but the party 'wasn't ready for and wasn't signed-up to the idea that it needed fundamentally to change its approach' (private interview, 2008).

According to John Redwood, Portillo 'did not define a distinctively social liberal agenda which made any sense' (2004: 152). Michael Ancram echoed this sentiment: he felt unable to support Portillo because 'I had no idea where he intended to take the Conservative Party and I don't think he did either' (private interview, 2007). Portillo believed that 'the party needed to change radically, and accept the social changes it had resisted, especially sexual, racial and cultural equality' (Portillo, 2008). However, this modernising agenda had become intertwined with Portillo's own personality and life since losing his Enfield Southgate seat at the 1997 general election. Shortly before re-entering parliament at the Kensington and Chelsea by-election in November 1999, he admitted to having had gay experiences in his youth (Jones, 1999). He later described this admission as a 'big mistake' for his standing in the party, and it resurfaced in the leadership campaign (Portillo, 2008). One former member of the shadow cabinet commented that 'an element of homophobia' had counted against Portillo (private interview, 2007).

Ken Clarke also offered a prescription for change at the 2001 leadership election, but his was limited to addressing the issues of greatest public concern (public services) and a critique of Hague's focus on Europe and the Euro (Denham and O' Hara, 2008: 59). Clarke also made much of his ability to 'carry the fight to Labour' to win back lost voters (Alderman and Carter, 2002: 576). Portillo's message was much more wide-ranging, leaving him vulnerable to attack and unable to establish a hold on 'solid Tory ground' (Denham and O'Hara, 2008: 60). In spite of this, many of his shadow cabinet colleagues, he claimed, were also convinced of the need for a modernisation strategy by mid-2000 (Portillo, private interview, 2006) and at the launch of his 2001 leadership bid he received public endorsements from eleven, making him the clear frontrunner.[2] For Theresa May, the decision to back Portillo was straightforward: she supported him 'because he was the change candidate. I thought he was the one who understood the depth of change that was needed'. Portillo's failure to win the election is also relatively easily explained: 'the party didn't want change' (private interview, 2006). Lilley suggests that Duncan Smith's victory may have been partly accidental, and the result of a miscalculation by some MPs who wished to caution future-leader Portillo against an all-out modernisation strategy:

> There was a feeling that people were making a statement by voting for Iain Duncan Smith, but didn't really expect him to become leader as a result of it. It was more a way of saying to Portillo, 'remember, there are lots of us' . . . The Right wanted a choice between Iain Duncan Smith and Portillo, not Iain Duncan Smith and Ken Clarke. Their second choice of choices would have been Portillo versus Clarke. (Lilley, private interview, 2006)

Ultimately, however, the result of the final round of the parliamentary ballot (Clarke 59, Duncan Smith 54, Portillo 53) demonstrated that with less than one-third of them supporting him, Conservative MPs 'were not persuaded by Portillo' (Ancram, private interview, 2007). The debate between mods and rockers did not end there, however.

Duncan Smith attempted both to re-orientate the Conservatives' policy focus towards public services and social justice, and to downplay 'core-vote' campaign themes such as tax, Europe and immigration. However, he did not regard this as modernisation, preferring instead to highlight his agenda for 'change' (Hayton and Heppell, 2010). Duncan Smith's distaste for the concept of modernisation derived from its association with the form of social liberalism Portillo had championed, which contrasted with his own traditionalist leanings on social and moral issues. These came to the fore in 2002, when Duncan Smith opted to impose a three-line whip against government proposals to grant adoption rights to unmarried and gay couples on an equal basis with married couples. For the Conservatives this question went to the heart of the debate over the status of marriage that had featured heavily during the Hague years. Should they take a liberal view and accept these different forms of family life, or continue to advocate their preferred traditional model for raising children?

Duncan Smith's instinctive response was to seek to defend the traditional view of marriage, but he was unable to carry a significant element of his party with him. Thirty-five Conservatives absented themselves from the Commons, and eight MPs defied the whip and voted against the party line. The most high-profile rebel was John Bercow, who resigned from the shadow cabinet. Not entirely inaccurately, Duncan Smith interpreted this rebellion as a conspiracy designed to destabilise his position, leading him to make his desperate call for the party to 'unite or die' (Hayton and Heppell, 2010: 432–3).

Bercow resigned because he both felt strongly about the issue and was unhappy with the direction of the party under Duncan Smith's leadership. As he explained:

> I felt very strongly that the party was wrong to do what it did. It could of course be argued – and it was, by some – that I should have simply gone missing that night and abstained, rather than make a huge fuss about it, but I felt strongly that the party had got it completely wrong. And it was also the case that I was disillusioned on several other fronts: I felt that the party was not really making any great progress and I didn't want to be part of that frontbench team. I thought we weren't going anywhere as a party and I didn't want to be part of it, and this issue was the final straw. (Bercow, private interview, 2008)

Duncan Smith's leadership was badly damaged by his mishandling of what became known as the 'gay adoption' episode. It exposed both his ineptitude as a party leader and the problematic context he faced. The party was clearly divided, and a modernising leader would have faced similar (or perhaps even more acute) difficulties in terms of keeping the party together. However, the incident also exposed Duncan Smith's personal failings and the barely muffled murmurs of discontent with his leadership became thunderous. However, lessons were learned by both himself and his successors as leader, who from then on allowed free votes on subjects seen as a matters of conscience – for example, the repeal of Section 28, which was finally achieved in 2003. Keen to avoid a repeat of the rebellion over adoption, Duncan Smith and his party chairman, David Davis, devised a compromise on Section 28 whereby Conservative MPs were ordered to vote for a Conservative amendment to replace rather than abolish the Clause. By suggesting a middle way between abolition and retention the leadership hoped to garner support from both modernisers and traditionalists, thus presenting an image of unity to the electorate (Durham, 2005). However, another amendment to retain Section 28 was also tabled by the traditionalists Edward Leigh and Ann Widdecombe. On a free vote, 71 Conservatives supported this amendment (including Duncan Smith and Michael Howard) whilst just 23 voted against (although on this occasion the clause was finally scrapped). As such, the Conservatives clearly remained fundamentally divided on these issues, although the free-vote tactic helped defuse them in party management terms.

This pattern was repeated under Duncan Smith's successor, Michael Howard. Howard sought to restore party discipline and the image of public unity. Howard's strategy reveals an effort to downplay party divisions on a number of controversial social, sexual and moral questions by allowing free votes. Notably, he opted for free votes on the Civil Partnership Bill, which gave gay couples entering into a civil partnership the same rights as married couples; and on the Gender Recognition Bill, which gave transsexuals legal recognition and the right to marry in their adopted sex (Cowley and Stuart, 2004: 1–2). One effect of the free votes was that many Conservative MPs did not vote at all, but those that did vote revealed the depth of the split on such issues in the party. On the Gender Recognition Bill, a total of 36 Conservative MPs voted in favour of either Second or Third Reading (or both) and a total of 44 Conservative MPs voted against either Second or Third Reading (or both). Combining the votes on the Second and Third Readings of the Civil Partnership Bill reveals 'similarly stark splits', with a total of 74 voting in favour on at least one occasion, and 49 opposing it at least once (Cowley and Stuart, 2004: 2–3).

Howard's relatively brief tenure as leader of the Conservative Party can therefore be regarded as period of better party management tactics on the social, sexual and moral policy cleavage, but it was still characterised by significant internal division on such questions. Howard also lacked a clear strategy to improve the image of the party by moderating positions on such issues: whilst morality/individual behaviour has remained a low-salience issue in terms of having a direct impact on how people vote,[3] such issues may affect a party's image (Chapter 3). Quinn argued that the major problem the Conservatives faced in opposition was not that they had been too right-wing in their policy positions, but that they suffered from a severe image problem. In short, the Conservatives were seen as 'angry, stuck in the past, and socially intolerant' (Quinn, 2008: 179). Electoral revival, therefore, required them to revitalise their image rather than reinvent their policy programme. 'Shifting to the centre ground' could therefore be achieved by 'softening the Conservatives' image, toning down their language, and appearing more socially inclusive, rather than [by] the wholesale abandonment of policies that were not particularly different from those of Labour' (Quinn, 2008: 179). Under Howard, the party gave the impression that it was reluctantly conceding to social change, rather than welcoming and adapting to it enthusiastically.

The following section considers whether David Cameron has finally resolved this problem by forging a distinctive position on the social, sexual and moral policy divide. If Cameron has been able to resolve this question, it will mark an important conclusion to the ideological differences highlighted by this case study, and indicate strategic learning from past mistakes by the party leadership.

Cameron: the family man

I am unashamedly pro-family. For me it comes absolutely first. (David Cameron, quoted in Grice, 2007)

David Cameron repeatedly sought to emphasise his credentials as a 'family man'. As leader of the opposition he placed the family at the heart of his policy agenda and his public image, and stated on a number of occasions that his family is more important to him that his political ambitions (Sky News, 2006). In some key respects, Cameron's policy on the family represents a clear continuation of the direction set by Iain Duncan Smith, who he appointed Chairman of his Social Justice Policy Group. Cameron frequently claimed that his priority as Prime Minister would be to 'mend Britain's broken society' and argued that strengthening families would be central to this. Yet in contrast to Duncan Smith, Cameron also sought to portray himself as a social liberal, at ease with contemporary British society. The central message of his leadership campaign was that the party must 'change to win' (Cameron, 2005). He described himself as a 'liberal Conservative', deliberately went 'out of his way to strike a very different note about asylum seekers', and gave strong support to civil partnerships for same-sex couples (Rawnsley, 2005). This liberal element of Cameron's approach conformed to Quinn's strategy of changing party image by moving closer to groups not traditionally part of the Conservative support base, rather than necessarily through a wholesale policy shift. The question for Cameron was whether this socially liberal image could be successfully balanced (or maintained) with a strong family policy.

In June 2008 Cameron gave a speech entitled 'Stronger Families' to Relate, the family counselling service. In it, he echoed William Hague's comments of a decade earlier, when he noted that 'for too long, politicians here have been afraid of getting into this territory, for fear of looking old-fashioned or preachy' (Cameron, 2008). His message that he wished to see marriage once again as a 'positive social norm' was one that could have appeared in a speech by any of his three predecessors as leader of the opposition. The family, he observed, is the 'best institution' for raising children, and (again echoing policy under Hague) reiterated his commitment to delivering a tax break for married couples, a pledge he first made during his leadership campaign:

> Yes, I do think it's wrong that our benefits system gives couples with children more money if they live apart – and we will bring an end to the couple penalty. And yes, I do think it's wrong that we're the only country in the western world that doesn't properly recognise marriage in the tax system – and I will ensure that we do. So we will change tax and benefits to make them more family-friendly. (Cameron, 2008)

He also made clear, however, that any tax cuts for married couples would also apply equally to people in civil partnerships. This represented a significant shift in the Conservatives' attitude towards homosexuality, and fitted with Cameron's efforts to rebrand the party as more socially inclusive and tolerant. To this end, the Conservatives also actively recruited gay prospective parliamentary candidates and gave them priority in winnable seats (Woolf, 2006). The party also signed an agreement with Stonewall (the gay rights' pressure group) to become part of its 'Diversity Champions' programme of gay-friendly employers (Grimston, 2006).

In essence, however, Cameron's position remained fundamentally Conservative and consistent with that of his predecessors, in that he regarded marriage as the best model of family life and believed that the state should recognise and promote it in some way. For some modernisers, this was the cause of unease. John Bercow, whilst pleased with Cameron's broadly socially liberal disposition, saw 'some tension' between this and his family policy:

> He takes what I think would be regarded as a traditionalist view of marriage and the family. That is reflected in some of what he has said about wanting to reward marriage through the tax system, and I have grave reservations about that. But overall, he is very much more socially liberal than his predecessors. (Private interview, 2008)

Tim Yeo also questioned the fairness of weighting the tax system in favour of marriage, and warned that effectively discriminating against many families with single or unmarried parents 'would be seen as wrong' and would thus backfire on the Conservatives (Tory Diary, 2006). A report for the Centre for Policy Studies found that this apprehension amongst Conservative MPs was widespread, as many saw the electoral risk of being perceived as 'victimising single mothers'. This timidity, the report's author fears, meant that 'there is a serious danger that, in this area at least, the "modernising" of the party's image . . . could simply be a cover for political cowardice and a retreat from what elected politicians personally believe to be right for the well-being of society' (Daley, 2006: 3).

As under Iain Duncan Smith, supporting marriage was explicitly linked by Cameron to the issue of social justice and his stated aim to renew the societal fabric. Commenting on the publication of the Social Justice Policy Group's report *Breakthrough Britain* (SJPG, 2007), Cameron said: 'I welcome this report's emphasis on the family, and on marriage, as the basis for the social progress we all want to see' adding that: 'If we can get the family right, we can fix our broken society' (conservatives.com, 2007). The report itself argued, in effect, that unmarried couples damage society, as 'the ongoing rise in family breakdown affecting young children has been driven by the dissolution of cohabiting partnerships', the majority of which 'are less stable than marriage' (SJPG, 2007: 3). Family breakdown is correlated with crime, drug abuse, educational failure and anti-social behaviour. The state should therefore 'create a positive policy bias in support of marriage' and end the 'downgrading' of marriage in official discourse which fails to recognise the 'marked discrepancies in the stability of married and cohabiting couples' (SJPG, 2007: 5–6).

For Toynbee, this represented a return to traditionalist, socially authoritarian conservatism designed to appease the *Daily Mail*. She argued that: 'His marriage policy is their victory' and 'reactionary mood music' that risked alienating supporters attracted to the fold by Cameron's ostensibly liberal outlook (Toynbee, 2007). To portray Cameron as having sold out to the traditionalists was a little strong, however, as it represented only one element of his strategy, and was tempered by the broader approach. Cameron's modernisation strategy involved not only modifying the party's stance on moral and sexual issues such as gay rights and civil partnerships, but attempted a much more far-reaching transformation of the party's image. To the irritation of traditionalists such as Widdecombe, this involved attempting to change the public face of the party through priority selection of female, gay and ethnic minority candidates, but it also encompassed a major push on issues not traditionally associated with the Conservatives such as the environment and climate change. According to Dorey, central to Cameron's policy modernisation was 'an explicitly avowed departure from Thatcherism' on the grounds that however vital it was to solving the problems of the 1970s and 1980s, it was no longer the most appropriate tool for addressing contemporary challenges (Dorey, 2007: 142). This has been signalled in two ways: through a return to the centre ground via the assertion of a 'new mode of Conservatism' which is plural, tolerant and compassionate, and 'by openly disavowing particular policy stances adopted by the Thatcher Governments during the 1980s and acknowledging that these were, at least with the benefit of hindsight, unnecessary or unwise' (2007: 142–3).

Whereas Cameron's three predecessors had all, to varying degrees, experimented with elements of this approach, none were able to do so with his apparent conviction or authenticity, so tended to slip back onto more familiar territory when opinion poll ratings failed to improve (Dorey, 2007: 139). The fragility of Cameron's project was briefly exposed in the summer of 2007, when Gordon Brown's arrival in Downing Street substantially cut the Conservatives' opinion poll lead. Cameron's wide lead had 'kept the diehards quiet for a while' but as it faded away they began to argue more forcefully that his project was failing (Portillo, 2007). 'Lamentably', Portillo noted, 'the signs are that Cameron is now caving in to Tory pressure' (2007). Crucially for Cameron, Conservative fortunes revived in the autumn, when Brown failed to call a general election and was hit by a series of negative headlines. The maintenance of this poll lead was a key factor enabling Cameron to stick to a modernising agenda, and was a luxury not enjoyed by his predecessors.

Widdecombe argues that, in policy terms, Cameron did not represent a rejection of Conservative tradition, but can be better understood as a new application of core principles. To represent Cameron's agenda as a victory by modernisers over diametrically opposed traditionalists is therefore inaccurate, but (damagingly in her view) is an interpretation that has seduced many Conservatives and undermined party unity (private interview, 2007). Cameron offered some reassurance to Conservative traditionalists with his strong message on the importance of the family. This aspect of his policy programme remained compatible with the fundamental tenets of Thatcherism. Where he differed from his predecessors, however, was that his broader programme of modernisation allowed him to make marriage and the traditional family the centre of his social policy without appearing intolerant to other groups, and thus undermining the whole project. The formation of a coalition government with the Liberal Democrats offered Cameron the opportunity to further the modernisation of his party by emphasising its liberal aspects, with less hindrance from the Conservative right wing. Indeed, Cameron's liberalising modernisation strategy as leader of the opposition was an essential precursor to his alliance with Nick Clegg. It is impossible, for example, to imagine the two parties linking up in 2005 (had the election result made it a mathematical possibility).

However, the area of family policy could prove to be a cause of significant tension between the coalition partners. The coalition agreement published in May 2010 notes that the government: 'will bring forward plans to reduce the couple penalty in the tax credit system as we make savings from our welfare reform plans' (Cabinet Office, 2010: 19). This represents a watered-down version of the Conservative manifesto pledge to '*end* the couple penalty' and 'recognise marriage and civil partnerships in the tax system' (Conservative Party, 2010: 41, emphasis added) – a policy that was opposed by the Liberal Democrats. Nonetheless, the two parties found common ground by prioritising increasing the personal allowance for income tax over other tax cuts, and the large fiscal deficit provides Cameron with cover for not fulfilling his undertaking on a tax break for married couples.

Conclusion

Between 1997 and 2010 the most significant division in the Conservative Party was along the social, sexual and moral policy divide. Unlike in the economic sphere, the ideological ascendency of Thatcherism on these issues was far from complete, but socially authoritarian spokespeople for 'Victorian values' remained vocal on the party's backbenches. Cameron's rebranding of the Conservatives as more tolerant and inclusive could not disguise the fact that for much of this period in opposition issues such as Section 28, civil partnerships and gay adoption caused deep divisions within the party.

During these years of opposition the debate between modernisers and traditionalists on social issues also became inextricably intertwined with the wider question of how the party should seek to revive its electoral fortunes. A consensus quickly emerged in the party that a key factor in the electoral success of New Labour was the perception that Conservatives had no interest in, and were unable to offer solutions to, problems beyond the economic sphere. Conservatives did not agree, however, on how to address this difficulty. Should they seek to extend the economic liberalism of Thatcherism into the social sphere, or aim to 'remoralise' politics in a manner akin to American Republicans?

Hague, Duncan Smith and Howard all quickly abandoned initial tentative moves towards social liberalism when they failed to yield positive opinion poll results and came under fire from within the party. A renewed emphasis on the family did occur under Hague's leadership, although along strictly traditionalist Conservative lines, involving an implicit (and occasionally explicit) criticism of the Thatcher and Major governments for failing to do enough to support marriage, particularly through the tax system. Combined with his hard line on Section 28, this amounted to a populist appeal to the Conservative core vote. Under Duncan Smith, a significant broadening of the party's agenda on social issues occurred, particularly in terms of his efforts to position the party as concerned with poverty, social exclusion and 'championing the vulnerable'. If this strategy had been pursued for longer, it may have helped dispel the Conservatives' image as selfish and socially exclusive. However, in some ways the socially conservative approach taken on these issues (for example, the emphasis on marriage) may have actually reinforced public perception that the party was old-fashioned and stuck in the past, and risked alienating support amongst excluded groups such as single parents. Under Howard, the party attempted to downplay divisions on the social, sexual and moral policy divide, and although he did not solve them he was more successful in party management terms. Public disunity between mods and rockers subsided, and the party went into the 2005 election with the vague pledge to 'govern in the interests of everyone', whether they be 'black or white, young or old, straight or gay, rural or urban, rich or poor' (Conservative Party, 2005).

Cameron enjoyed a more favourable context than his three predecessors for the successful pursuit of a modernisation strategy. Most of New Labour's legislative programme for sexual equality was complete by the end of their second term, so he could reasonably argue that the Conservatives simply had to accept this new reality, as it would be very difficult to reverse it. Failure at three previous general elections also gave him more room for manoeuvre, as even the most intransigent Conservatives began to acknowledge the need for some sort of change. Most fundamentally, however, Cameron benefitted from a much more propitious electoral context – firstly with the final tired years of Blair's premiership, and latterly with the extraordinary implosion of Brown's. It was these auspicious circumstances and the accompanying Conservative poll leads that muted criticism from traditionalists and allowed Cameron to maintain his modernising course, and ultimately to form a civil partnership few had predicted: with Nick Clegg.

Notes

1 This chapter draws in substantial part on an article previously published in *Political Quarterly* (Hayton, 2010b) and expands on the argument made there.

2 The eleven were: Peter Ainsworth, Edward Garnier, David Heathcoat-Amory, Oliver Letwin, Andrew Mackay, Francis Maude, Theresa May, Archie Norman, Gary Streeter, David Willetts and Tim Yeo, (BBC News, 2001a).

3 Since 1997, morality/individual behaviour has never been regarded as one of the most important issues facing the country by more than 10 per cent of the electorate. It has averaged 4.6 per cent (MORI 2008a).

7

The political economy of twenty-first-century conservatism

Introduction

This chapter argues that the political economy of twenty-first-century conservatism has remained firmly within neo-liberal parameters. The endurance of neo-liberalism in the Conservative Party was illustrated by the response offered to the financial crisis of 2007–8 and the subsequent recession, which was characterised by an over-riding concern about the size of the fiscal deficit. However, the ideological hold of Thatcherism on Conservative economic thinking can be traced throughout the whole of the 1997–2010 period, shaping the Conservatives' response to the challenge presented by New Labour in the field of economic policy. Conservative politicians recognised the success of the governing party in building a reputation for sound economic management under the direction of Chancellor of the Ex-chequer Gordon Brown, and sought to respond in a number of ways in an effort to neutralise this relative weakness. However, the neo-Thatcherite ideals of a smaller state intervening less in the economy, lower taxes and a highly cautious fiscal policy, all retained significant influence in this area. This chapter argues that the electoral calculations made by the Conservative leadership and the political strategies they devised in pursuit of this objective were shaped and constrained by their Thatcherite ideological inheritance.

The argument of this chapter therefore builds directly on that advanced earlier in the book. Chapter 2 argued that three distinctive responses within conservatism to the post-Thatcher political settlement could be identified: anti-Thatcherite, neo-Thatcherite and post-Thatcherite. It also suggested that within the Conservative Party the neo-Thatcherite perspective dominated the debate about how the party should seek to respond to defeat in 1997, and that this dominance was reflected in the nature of different strategies for change pursued. This chapter unpacks this argument further in relation to economic policy. It demonstrates that the Conservatives struggled to formulate an effective critique of the Labour government's approach to economic management in part because key policy fundamentals were shared by both parties, which restricted the scope for the Conservatives to differen-tiate themselves. This reflected the ascendancy of neo-liberalism in Anglo-American economic policy-making, something which the New Labour project had reconciled itself with (Hay, 1997). It was also reinforced by the Conservatives' self-proclaimed victory in the battle of ideas on the economy, noted at the beginning of Chapter 6. However, while the 'Third Way' project embraced the capacity for markets to drive economic expansion and accepted the perceived 'realities' of globalisation, it retained a commitment to social justice. Consequently New Labour in office pursued a range of social policies which many neo-Thatcherite Conservatives opposed. Faced with the competing pressures of the public popularity of many of these measures and their own ideological unease, the Conservative leadership between 1997 and 2007 went through a stop–start process of policy accommodation in order to accept a number of them.

A more rigorous Conservative critique of New Labour's political economy, followed by significant policy divergence, began to emerge in the spring of 2007 (Lee, 2009: 62). This was characterised by Thatcherite fiscal conservatism. Although the Conservative Party had gone through a decade of policy accommodation, the key tenets of its economic outlook had not been challenged in opposition. As a result, on the economy the prevailing ideological outlook of the party remained largely unchanged, and reasserted itself when the opportunity provided by the financial crisis and subsequent recession presented itself.

Looking at each in turn, this chapter traces Conservative economic policy through the three parliaments of opposition between 1997 and 2010. Considering the development of policy over this period contextualises the debate which opened up on the economy during Labour's third term in office. It also reveals the entrenchment of neo-liberal thinking in the Conservative Party across the period, which helps us to better account for the way in which it responded to the financial crisis. The chapter concludes that with the return of the Conservatives to office, this has profound implications for the future role of the state in Britain.

'Prudence with a purpose': the Conservative response, 1997–2001

Chapter 6 suggested that on the spectrum of social liberalism versus social authoritarianism, Thatcherite ideals were vigorously contested within the Conservative Party in the 1990s – ideological supremacy had not been established. The same could not be said in the field of economic policy. The critique of neo-liberalism advanced by One Nation 'wets' such as Gilmour discussed in Chapter 2 had been totally marginalised by 1997. This reflected the dominant position of neo-liberalism (and the associated discourse of globalisation) in national and global politics more generally.[1] Given that Conservative administrations had been at the forefront of the neo-liberal revolution, it is hardly surprising that this outlook on economic policy-making achieved near-universal acceptance within the Conservative Party. The far-reaching intellectual critique warning of the self-undermining nature of neo-liberalism advanced by John Gray did not permeate mainstream intraparty debate. The acceptance by New Labour of the essence of Thatcherite economic strategy only served to reinforce this dominance. Electoral competition on the economy in 1997 thus centred on a debate over the respective ability of the parties to competently manage the economy, rather than competing approaches to doing so (Hay, 1997).

A central element of New Labour's political strategy was to establish a reputation for economic competence. This concern derived from recognition that the Conservatives' traditional lead in the economic management stakes had given them a significant electoral advantage, and a belief that Labour's approach to taxation and public spending had been a key reason for defeat at the 1992 general election. The opportunity to cultivate a higher public standing on this issue than their opponents was presented to Labour by the collapse in the Conservatives' reputation prompted by the ERM *débâcle* (Chapter 2). Over the following five years, Labour assiduously avoided any commitments which would allow the Conservatives to repeat their charge that a Labour government would drop a 'tax bombshell' on the electorate. Shadow Chancellor Gordon Brown even went as far as to commit himself to Conservative spending plans for his first two years in office, should Labour be elected. This was a pledge that he would indeed fulfil as Chancellor – in spite of the admission by his Conservative predecessor Ken Clarke (who had laid out the plans) that the figures were so tight he probably would not have stuck to them himself.

As well as promising to match the Conservative plans for public expenditure, the 1997 Labour manifesto also guaranteed that income tax rates would not be increased, and prioritised the control of inflation as the centrepiece of a sound economic policy. This commitment to low inflation was enshrined by Gordon Brown's first significant announcement as Chancellor of the Exchequer: granting the Bank of England operational independence over monetary policy. These measures were accompanied by repeated expressions of the importance of 'prudence' by the Chancellor, and together succeeded in establishing a clear lead for Labour over the Conservatives as the party best able to manage the economy. Within a year of coming to power, Labour had transformed a 7-point deficit on the issue into a 21-point lead over the Conservatives. They retained a lead over their opponents for the following decade, until the financial crisis of 2008 (Figure 7.1).

Brown's cautious approach in the first two years of Labour government made it difficult for the Conservatives to attack their handling of the economy. William Hague's charge that Brown's 1998 pre-budget report was a betrayal of 'the golden economic legacy' bequeathed by the Conservatives sounded hollow when inflation remained low, the economy was growing and the budget deficit was falling (BBC News, 1998). This poorly thought-through position reflected confusion and complacency amongst Conservatives, many of whom appeared to believe that it was only a matter of time before New Labour exposed their true socialist (and economically incompetent) colours 'at which point the electorate would come back home' (Bale, 2010: 73). However, rather than return to 'old Labour' policies of nationalisation and higher taxes, the first Blair government greatly extended the use of the Private Finance Initiative (PFI) and cut corporation tax (Dorey, 2003: 127).

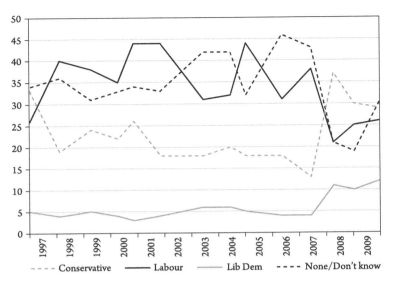

Figure 7.1 Best party at managing the economy, 1997–2010.
Source: Data from IpsosMORI, www.ipsos-mori.com.

In an effort to establish 'clear blue water' between the parties, Hague unveiled his 'tax guarantee' policy at the party conference in October 1999. In essence this policy promised that over the lifetime of the next parliament a Conservative government would reduce the proportion of national income taken in taxation, although it did not specify which taxes would be reduced, or by how much. This pledge was designed to be the centrepiece of Hague's 'Common Sense Revolution' (Chapter 3). Hague hoped that it would help re-establish Conservative credentials as the party of low taxation, a key element in his strategy to reconnect with the 'core vote'. However, critics were quick to question the commonsense of such a pledge, with Hague's predecessor John Major labelling it 'mad' (Grice, 2000). If the economy were to grow it might be relatively easily fulfilled, as a proportion of the benefits accruing to the public finances from economic expansion could be used to reduce taxation. However, in the event of a recession it could force a government to make massive cuts in public expenditure at the very time it would be expected to rise.

In an embarrassing U-turn for Hague the tax guarantee was abandoned the following summer. This *volte-face* was a victory for Michael Portillo, who (having returned to the Commons at a by-election in November 1999) replaced Francis Maude as Shadow Chancellor in February 2000. Portillo regarded the policy as lacking credibility and threatened to resign over it (Bale, 2010: 109). Soon after his appointment Portillo had moved quickly to accept key elements of New Labour's political economy: dropping Conservative opposition to the national minimum wage which had come into force in April 1999; endorsing the independence of the Bank of England; and accepting 'the pursuit of full employment as a policy objective' (Dorey, 2003: 128). Portillo thus played a key role in converging Conservative economic policy with Labour's (Lee, 2009: 66). However, Bale argues that these moves did not signal a more general convergence of Conservative policy onto 'centrist' ground, as they were not accompanied by a pledge to match Labour's spending plans for the public services (Bale, 2010: 109–10). Portillo also emphasised difference from Labour by stressing the importance to the Conservatives of keeping the pound, and by noting his preference for curbing public spending. As he noted in a major speech on economic policy: 'constraining the rate of growth of government spending – is necessary not only to restore Britain's competitiveness, but also because we should in any case assume that the tax base will be constrained' (Portillo, 2000b). Nonetheless, at the 2001 election the Conservatives did commit themselves Labour's spending plans on health, education, crime, transport and defence – amounting to 42 per cent of government spending (BBC News, 2001). They also pledged £8 billion of tax cuts, implying significant reductions in spending elsewhere, particularly on welfare.

At the 2001 election, the Conservatives were unable to compete effectively with Labour on the economy, who led by more than 20 per cent on the issue in the polls (Figure 7.1). During the campaign Labour also enjoyed a 13-point lead over the Conservatives as the party most trusted on taxation (Dorey, 2003: 130). This was unsurprising given the mixed messages emanating from the shadow cabinet on the scale of proposed cuts: a suggestion by Oliver Letwin that they could amount to £20 billion gifted Labour the opportunity to attack the 'black hole' in Conservative figures (Dorey, 2003: 130). Whilst the hint of bigger tax cuts to come might have pleased some elements of the core Conservative support base, Labour effectively exploited these ambiguous figures to sustain their campaign theme of 'Labour investment' (in public services) versus 'Tory cuts' (Snowdon, 2010: 73).

The Conservative approach to economic policy between 1997 and 2001 betrayed confusion over whether to pursue a more radical Thatcherite agenda to distinguish themselves from Labour, particularly through a far-reaching plan for tax cuts, or to accommodate themselves to a consensual position aping the government's approach. In the end they did neither effectively – attempting to present themselves as a party of lower taxes whilst also grudgingly accepting some key elements of Labour policy. As such, as in other areas in the field of economic policy, this four-year period was largely wasted by the Conservatives. Fuelled by Thatcherite conviction that they had 'won' the economic battle of ideas and therefore had no need to rethink their approach, they missed the opportunity to engage in any kind of serious policy appraisal. Worse still, this Thatcherite economic stance acted as an obstacle to modernisation more generally as it was at the heart of the core-vote approach to opposition strategy. As Chapter 3 discussed, the one serious attempt to overcome this made by Peter Lilley in his 1999 R. A. Butler lecture – in which he sought to open a debate about how a greater focus on public services could sit alongside a fundamentally Thatcherite economic policy – quickly died a death as the party (from the leader downwards) did not yet have the stomach for its possible implications.

2001–5: neo-Thatcherism continued

Iain Duncan Smith's tenure as leader of the Conservative Party is an important (and underanalysed) phase in this thirteen-year period of opposition, as it saw a more determined effort to begin the process of policy renewal and strategic reorientation. As noted in Chapter 3, some important steps were taken in this regard, although these were ultimately overshadowed by Duncan Smith's leadership failings. In particular, Duncan Smith prioritised a focus on the public services – echoing the call made by Lilley two years earlier. Secondly, he sought to bring about a more far-reaching change in both the image and priorities of the Conservative Party by pledging to 'champion the vulnerable' (Chapter 3). However, Duncan Smith did not seek to challenge the core assumptions of Thatcherite economic thinking, to which he remained firmly committed. This limited his ability to forge a new Conservative narrative centred on public services and social justice, and was reflected in his professed idea to pursue an agenda of 'change' rather than modernisation.

Duncan Smith made a concerted effort to concentrate a greater proportion of the Conservatives' campaigning and policy renewal on the public services. He hoped that by doing so he would demonstrate to the electorate that the Conservatives were in touch with their concerns. However, the endurance of a fundamentally Thatcherite framework guiding this process was illustrated by the approach Duncan Smith took: the emphasis on the public services did not automatically translate into a shift in the way that such issues were approached. Much of the campaigning focus had a negative tone. For example, from almost the very beginning of his leadership Duncan Smith repeatedly claimed that the public services were 'in crisis'. In his response to the Queen's Speech in November 2002, he used the same adjective in relation to pensions, transport, criminal justice, health and education (Duncan Smith, 2002f). This gloomy picture of a nation on the brink of a catastrophic failure of state provision sounded more like scaremongering than a hard-headed evidence-based analysis. It was also always going to be a difficult sell for Duncan Smith against the backdrop of the substantial real-terms expenditure increases across most of the state sector that were taking place at the time. While higher spending might not have bettered the public services as much or as quickly as the electorate would have liked, tangible evidence of improvement (for example on National Health Service (NHS) waiting times) was seeping through. Furthermore, the decision in summer 2002 to drop the commitment made before the previous election to match the government's spending plans on education and health (Dorey, 2004:

373) meant that Labour had an easy retort to the Conservatives' attacks: that cutting spending would make services worse, not better.

The policy proposals put forward on the public services between 2001 and 2005 also reflected a neo-Thatcherite approach. The notions of competition and consumer choice were at the heart of Conservative proposals for 'patient passports' in the NHS and a voucher system in education (Dorey, 2004: 374–5). For his critics, these proposals signalled the marketisation (and possibly privatisation) of public services. As Bale commented, this suggested that 'Duncan Smith represented not a transcendence of Thatcherism but a desire to resume where it had left off' (Bale, 2010: 147). However, having abandoned the pledge to match Labour's spending, Shadow Chancellor Michael Howard announced in November 2002 that a future Conservative government could not promise to offer any immediate tax cuts – a move intended to signal Conservative commitment to the public services (*Guardian*, 20 November 2002).

As noted in Chapter 3, elements of the policy agenda developed under Duncan Smith were continued under the leadership of Michael Howard. However, discussing issues such as the public services did little to dispel the Conservatives' image as anti-state and by implication not to be trusted with the public services. As under Duncan Smith, the Conservatives continued to pursue the idea of patient passports in the NHS and education vouchers for schools, both of which could be used to purchase from private as well as state providers. These policies continued to provoke the charge that they amounted to privatisation by the backdoor, and also looked very much like a state-funded subsidy towards the cost of private services bought by the wealthy. So the shift in policy focus prompted by Duncan Smith did not cause a move towards a more centrist or 'One Nation' approach to these policy questions. As Bale argued: 'talking about the issues voters were most interested in was not the same thing as fighting the government on the centre ground'. For him the hindrance to this 'was ideological', as 'Thatcherite views were deeply held by the leader and the majority of his parliamentary party' (Bale, 2010: 219).

Whilst the Conservatives attempted to critique Labour's approach to public services, they deliberately emphasised the consensus between the major parties on economic policy more broadly. This represented another step in the convergence process begun in the previous parliament. As Shadow Chancellor, Michael Howard built on the steps taken by his predecessor Michael Portillo by enthusiastically praising the government's monetary policy. In a speech to the left-leaning think-tank the Institute for Public Policy Research, Howard (2002) commented on 'how well the current monetary framework is performing', and reaffirmed Conservative commitment to it. Independence of the Bank of England 'was clearly a major step forward and one for which the present chancellor deserves great credit'. Howard went on: 'It particularly behoves those of us who were opposed to this step at the time to be unstinting in our praise . . . I fully recognise the enhancement in the credibility of monetary policy which this change ensures' (2002). This lavish endorsement was moderated only by the claim that this new framework was based largely on the reforms introduced by the Conservative government following the 1992 exit from the ERM. Howard's argument was essentially that advanced by Cameron four years later: that the Conservatives had 'won' the argument about the economy on Thatcherite terms, and that the Labour government's macroeconomic policy reflected this victory. Howard thus sought (as Shadow Chancellor and then as party leader) to attack Labour's ability to pursue these policies competently, and to target fiscal policy as an area to attack the government (for 'wasteful' spending and higher taxes). However, a debate about competence was always going to be difficult for the Conservatives given the damage done to their reputation by the ERM *débâcle*. It became impossible for them to win as Labour established a record of economic growth, coupled with relatively low inflation, unemployment and interest rates between 1997 and 2005. Having conceded Labour's supremacy on monetary policy the Conservatives were left trying to critique fiscal policy and *how* the proceeds of growth were being spent, and Labour's emphasis on investment in the public services continued to attract a sizable proportion of the electorate.

Under Howard's leadership the Conservatives eventually went into the 2005 election offering £4 billion of tax cuts. This compromise position of a relatively modest offering reflected the oscillating nature of the Conservatives' approach to tax and spend since the 2001 election (Dorey, 2004: 373). By the time of the 2005 general election, the Conservatives had changed their position on public spending back to promising to match Labour's spending in key areas (schools, the NHS, transport and international development) and claiming that they would spend 'more than Labour on police, defence and pensions' (Conservative Party, 2005: 3). However they also claimed they would save £12 billion from cuts elsewhere, using £4 billion to fund the promised tax cuts and £8 billion to reduce debt. The emphasis on debt reduction was a precursor to the fiscal conservatism that would come to dominate the party's approach after the 2008 financial crisis. The critique of Labour's 'big state' was a prominent feature of the 2005 manifesto, which argued that: 'government is spending too much, wasting too much and taxing too much . . . If we are to secure our future prosperity, government must once again start to live within its means' (Conservative Party, 2005: 3).

As under Hague between 1997 and 2001, during Labour's second term in office the Conservative leadership did not challenge the predominance of neo-Thatcherite economic thinking in their party. They remained utterly convinced of a neo-Thatcherite approach to economic management, evidenced by the apparent success of the government's monetary policy which they co-opted. This philosophy also inspired their fiscally conservative attacks on Labour's increases in public spending in this parliament. As in 2001, this was ultimately reflected in 2005 in a core-vote-orientated election campaign that promised tax cuts and lacked a coherent narrative built around public service reform. During this second term of opposition the Conservatives spent more time talking about issues of greatest concern to swing voters than they had during the first. However, their overarching neo-Thatcherite economic policy had a limiting effect on their ability to devise and communicate convincing solutions to the key policy problems they identified. Ultimately, having discounted the possibility of repudiating any of the key elements of their neo-Thatcherite approach, the Conservatives did not find a persuasive narrative about how they would seek to apply them to a new environment.

2005–10: economic policy under David Cameron

As with the other key issue areas explored in this book, the preceding eight years in opposition provide important context for understanding the development of Conservative economic policy under David Cameron. The Cameron leadership, particularly its first couple of years, is typically presented as representing a significant departure from that of his three predecessors as leader of the opposition. Indeed, a key feature of his modernisation strategy was to repeatedly emphasise the notion of change and to distance himself from his party's immediate past. However, this chapter argues that there was neither significant modernisation of the party's economic policy nor any attempt to challenge the core assumptions of the party's thinking in this area. Indeed, the economic policy review documents produced between 2005 and 2010 reveal a continued adherence to the core tenets of neo-Thatcherism, even during the 'modernising' phase of Cameron's leadership. Stephen Evans has similarly argued that there are notable areas of continuity between Cameron's leadership and that of Margaret Thatcher. For him, the financial crisis and subsequent recession provided Cameron with the opportunity to be more overtly Thatcherite in his language, 'but he has always tried to follow in at least some of her footsteps' (2010: 325). Tracing these continuities in the field of economic policy across the entire 1997–2010 period of opposition helps us to better appreciate how embedded they remained throughout it.

In a compelling analysis, Simon Lee (2009) argued that under David Cameron's leadership Conservative economic policy went through three distinct phases: an initial convergence towards New Labour's political economy; an increasingly strident critique of this in the light of the 2008 financial crisis; and divergence to a policy of neo-liberal austerity premised on a far-reaching critique of the role of the state itself. However, as Lee acknowledges, all of this took place within neo-Thatcherite parameters (2009: 78).

As discussed above, by the time of David Cameron's election as party leader the Conservatives had already moved to embrace a new macroeconomic consensus with Labour, and had fought the 2005 election promising to match government spending on key public services. As such, significant convergence had already occurred. The early years of Cameron's leadership saw a continuation of these positions and this trend. Cameron and his Shadow Chancellor George Osborne reaffirmed Conservative commitment to match Labour's spending on health and education, but sought to present these commitments as part of a broader commitment to social justice and as a break with Thatcherism. Osborne was particularly cautious on taxation, arguing that economic stability and improved public services would have to come before any tax cuts.

Although Osborne was careful not to make specific pledges on taxation, the longer-term aim of lower taxes remained in the formula of words he and other Conservatives stuck to. In one of his first major speeches as Shadow Chancellor, he accused Gordon Brown of creating a 'tax ratchet', as he 'uses the entire proceeds of economic growth (and more) to pay for his uncontrolled spending'. By contrast, Osborne promised that: 'as the economy grows, we will share the proceeds of that growth between spending on public services and reducing taxes.' However, in a foreshadowing of what was to come when the Conservatives eventually returned to office, he noted that 'if the public finances are in a mess then sorting them out will have to take priority over promises of tax cuts' (Osborne, 2006).

Continuation of trends established under Iain Duncan Smith could also be observed in Cameron's emphasis on social justice and the public services. However, these twin areas were pursued by Cameron and his fellow modernisers with an apparent conviction that Duncan Smith had been incapable of rendering. The key to this presentational shift was the apparent disavowal of key elements of Thatcherism in a way that Duncan Smith was either unwilling or unable to pull off. Cameron sought to distance himself from Thatcher on both economic and social policy, and declined the opportunity to describe himself in a BBC interview as a 'Thatcherite'. Part of this 'post-Thatcherite cross-dressing' was Cameron's call (noted in Chapter 6) for the Conservatives to focus on general well-being as well as economic growth (Kerr, 2007: 49). The other key feature was his retort to probably the most famous quote attributed to Mrs Thatcher, when he claimed during his leadership campaign that Conservatives 'do think there's such a thing as society, we just don't think it's the same thing as the state' (quoted in Kerr, 2007: 49). As Chapter 6 discussed, this theme was developed with input from Duncan Smith into a critique of Britain's 'broken society', and later still into Cameron's agenda for a 'big society'.

A further element in Cameron's strategy to disassociate the party from its past was the initiation of a wide-ranging policy review process, which also came with the added benefit of delaying the need to announce detailed policy proposals. Six policy review groups were established, each with a separate (albeit sometimes overlapping) remit. The groups and their chairs were: Social Justice (Iain Duncan Smith); Globalisation and Global Poverty (Peter Lilley); Public Services (Stephen Dorrell); Quality of Life (Zac Goldsmith and John Gummer); National Security (Pauline Neville-Jones); and Economic Competitiveness (ECPG) (John Redwood and Simon Wolfson). While the last two of these reflected what might be described as traditional Conservative concerns, the other four were all designed to reinforce the message that the party was changing and concerning itself with issue areas not typically regarded as Thatcherite priorities.

The appointment of arch-Thatcherite John Redwood to co-chair the Economic Competitiveness policy review group in December 2005 was an early indication that Cameron and Osborne had no intention of taking Conservative economic policy in a radical new direction. His co-chair Simon Wolfson (the son of a Conservative peer) was Chief Executive of the clothes retailer Next plc. The submission to the shadow cabinet published in August 2007 confirms that the review group had approached its task from a firmly Thatcherite perspective. Redwood's foreword to the report critiqued the record of the Labour government for relying on 'favourable trends' in the world economy to sustain growth, and argued that the United Kingdom was falling behind other states in terms of economic competiveness and productivity (ECPG, 2007: 3). Consequently the report argued for a radical attack on regulation, including a 'Deregulation Act' to cut restrictions on business. The centrepiece of this would be the repeal of European Working Time Regulations and key elements of data protection legislation (ECPG, 2007: 58). It claimed that 'UK tax is currently high, relative both to history and to our international peers', and warned that this would 'destroy enterprise' (ECPG, 2007: 78). The report recommended cutting corporation tax; abolishing inheritance tax; cutting capital gains tax; and cutting stamp duty (ECPG, 2007: 78–82).

As well as recommending substantial tax cuts and deregulation of business activity, a key theme of the report was a critical appraisal of the size and role of the state sector in Britain. 'The Government's Burgeoning Waste Line' was attacked not only on the grounds that it delivered poor value for taxpayers, but as a deadweight stifling the economy as a whole (ECPG, 2007: 70). Tellingly, the photograph chosen for the front page of the report is a shot of the Canary Wharf development in the London Docklands, which is looked on with pride by many Conservatives as story of successful economic regeneration in the 1980s. This picture featured the Canary Wharf tower, as well as the HSBC and Citigroup headquarters which stand close by. The report argued that 'the success of London and the financial services sector shows it is possible to be world class from a UK base' (ECPG, 2007: 83) – a sentence clearly written before the sector brought the global financial system close to collapse.

A companion report was also produced by a separate commission established with the narrower remit of examining taxation. Another prominent disciple of Thatcherite economics, Michael Forsyth, was appointed by Cameron to chair this body. In October 2006 the Tax Reform Commission (TRC) came forward with a package of proposed measures costed at £21 billion, including cuts to income tax, capital gains tax, inheritance tax and corporation tax. It also recommended simplification of the system, through the reform or abolition of a range of rates, reliefs and allowances (TRC, 2006: 7–10). A further illustration of the neo-liberal philosophy underpinning this report is found in its defence of the idea of a flat tax, which was deemed theoretically attractive, but reluctantly ruled it out on practical grounds (TRC, 2006: 113). The ECPG endorsed these findings, noting that 'the

Forsyth Report remains the most authoritative and wide-ranging treatment of the issue of tax reform written in recent years in this country, and we broadly welcome its findings' (ECPG, 2007, 80–1). The degree of consensus between the ECPG and TRC not only in terms of philosophical outlook but also in terms of practical recommendations is striking, and serves to illustrate the location of Conservative thinking on the economy during this period, even as the leadership sought to project a modernising image.

The basis of the critique of Labour's record of economic management that the Conservative leadership began to articulate much more forcefully from mid 2007 can also be found in these reports. The ECPG attacked Gordon Brown for imprudent handling of the public finances from 2000 onwards, claiming he had broken his own 'golden rules' for sound fiscal management (ECPG, 2007: 14–15). This assessment received official endorsement from Cameron and Osborne in the official Conservative policy document *Reconstruction: Plan for a Strong Economy*, published in September 2008. This report argued that:

> Britain faces today's economic crisis less well prepared than any of our major competitors. A decade long experiment in tax and spending on the back of a debt-fuelled boom has left us uniquely exposed. The Brown bubble has burst . . . It is the failure of an entire economic approach. (Conservative Party, 2008: 1)

This broadside begged the question of what was the Conservative response. As the financial crisis took hold from late 2007 onwards the Conservatives struggled to articulate a compelling alternative to the government's strategy of increasingly drastic interventions in an effort to stabilise the banking sector. As Dorey notes, the incoherence of Conservative attacks on Labour's effort to contain the crisis were illustrated by their response to the decision in early 2008 to finally nationalise the floundering Northern Rock bank: 'Having berated ministers for dithering and procrastination over the preceding months, senior Conservatives then lined up to condemn the Brown government for resorting to public ownership too hastily' (2009: 264). As the financial crisis worsened partial nationalisation of several more banks was accompanied by a neo-Keynesian economic stimulus, as the government cut taxes and increased public spending (and debt) in an effort to ameliorate the worst effects of the recession. Labour politicians became increasingly confident in their approach, and denounced their Conservative opponents as the 'do nothing' party.

Led by the Shadow Chancellor George Osborne, the Conservatives stuck to their neo-liberal guns, denouncing the 'comprehensively discredited' Keynesian approach adopted by the government (Osborne, 2008). Brown and his Chancellor Alistair Darling were attacked for taking irresponsible and unsustainable short-term measures which the country could ill afford (Lee, 2009: 68–71). The *Plan for a Strong Economy* that the Conservatives offered as an alternative stuck firmly to this neo-liberal orthodoxy, and was dedicated in large part to outlining measures which it claimed would prevent such a crisis reoccurring. The centrepiece of this would be an independent Office for Budget Responsibility (OBR), charged with monitoring the stability of the government's finances. Under this plan, the Chancellor of the Exchequer would be forced to report to parliament should his plans differ from recommendations produced by the OBR based on its 'independent' forecasts. The OBR would be mandated to pursue twin targets of a balanced budget (over an economic cycle) and a declining total public debt, as a proportion of gross domestic product (GDP) (Conservative Party, 2008: 11). To counter the problem of over-indebtedness in the economy more widely, a new 'Debt Responsibility Mechanism', overseen by the Bank of England would also be instituted, to manage credit in the financial system (Lee, 2009: 70–1).

As well as these preventative measures, the Conservative plan also pronounced the need for 'a more balanced economy' and economic growth built on a more sustainable footing. It pointed out that over the previous ten years the British economy had become almost entirely dependent on 'a narrow group of sectors – in particular financial services, housing and public spending', which together had accounted for over four-fifths of growth (Conservative Party, 2008: 34). An unfavourable contrast was made with Germany, where 24 per cent of growth was attributed to manufacturing, compared to the United Kingdom where the contribution from the same sector was *minus* 1 per cent. Further to this, the loss of one million jobs in manufacturing was highlighted (Conservative Party, 2008: 35). This was a curious line of attack for the Conservatives to take given that the relative shrinkage of the UK manufacturing sector was attributed by many economists to the neo-liberal policies they had introduced in the 1980s. However, anyone hoping to find a new industrial strategy in the Conservative policy document would have been sorely disappointed: although it declared that 'laissez-faire economics is not enough', it had very little to say about how a restructuring of the economy might be brought about.

The third phase in economic policy under Cameron identified by Lee – policy divergence – built on this critique. From 2009 onwards the key focus of disagreement was the deficit and how this should be dealt with. The decline in tax revenues resulting from the recession and the cost of government stimulus measures caused the deficit to balloon to £96.8 billion (6.7 per cent of GDP) during the financial year 2008/9 and £159.8 billion (11.4 per cent of GDP) in 2009/10 (ONS, 2010). In late 2008 the Conservatives announced that they were dropping their previous pledge to match Labour's spending plans from 2010/11 onwards, and condemned as irresponsible the Chancellor's decision to temporarily reduce VAT to 15 per cent for one year (Hutton, 2008).

The argument over the pace and magnitude of deficit reduction came to dominate the 2010 election campaign, as the Conservatives promised immediate action to reduce government spending, while Labour and the Liberal Democrats warned that to cut too soon would endanger the recovery. However, this was something of a phoney war as debate centred on the issue of the £6 billion of spending cuts suggested by the Conservatives for the financial year 2010/11, rather than the much bigger question of how to eliminate the bulk of the deficit over the medium term. The Conservative manifesto promised 'an emergency Budget within 50 days of taking office to set out a credible plan for eliminating the bulk of the structural current budget deficit over a Parliament' but gave little indication as to which areas of spending might be cut to achieve this ambitious target (Conservative Party, 2010: 7). The manifesto also promised to increase health spending every year, and to increase spending on overseas aid (as planned by Labour) to meet the target of 0.7 per cent of GDP. Other areas of public spending, notably on the police and education, were not similarly ring-fenced.

The Conservative manifesto also retained commitments to reducing taxation, particularly on business, which owed their lineage to the ECPG. It pledged to cancel the rise in employers' National Insurance pencilled in by Labour for April 2011, and to cut corporation tax, with the objective of creating 'the most competitive tax system in the G20 within five years' (Conservative Party, 2010: 19). It also retained the pledge first made by George Osborne at the 2007 party conference to raise the inheritance tax threshold to £1 million. This announcement had originally been made as the parties geared up for the 'election that never was' shortly after Gordon Brown became Prime Minister, and after some agonising decided not to go to the country in the autumn of that year. Again echoing the ECPG, the manifesto pledged to reduce red tape, although few details were provided about precisely which regulations would be scrapped.

The focus during the 2010 campaign on whether or not public spending cuts should begin in the current financial year or the next effectively muted any in-depth debate about the impact of the cuts in the longer term on the size and functioning of the state sector. Given that all the major parties were committed to substantially reducing the deficit, this general unwillingness to discuss in detail the likely effect on public services was hardly surprising. However, the election campaign did highlight the divergence of ideological approach between Labour and the Conservatives that stemmed from the recession. As noted above, the Labour government rediscovered a taste for Keynesian economic management, attempting to stimulate the economy during the recession through tax cuts and public spending. This was also accompanied by a renewed state-led industrial activism, particularly associated with Peter Mandelson's tenure as Business Secretary between October 2008 and May 2010. Emblematic of this approach was the decision by Mandelson shortly before the election to grant a loan of £80 million to fund expansion at the Sheffield Forgemaster's steelworks. This was controversially withdrawn by the coalition government within weeks of coming to office, on the grounds that it was unaffordable. Although only a tiny fraction of government spending, the issue illustrated the divergent ideological approach of the Conservatives and Labour and the way this could translate through to policy decisions. As the ECPG highlighted, the

Conservatives might have shared the desire to rebalance the economy, but 'they did so on the basis of market mechanisms and private financing rather than Labour's state-led industrial policy' (Smith, 2010: 831).

Remarkably, given the length and depth of the recession the economy had experienced, Labour were only 3 percentage points behind the Conservatives as the party best able to manage the economy in the months before the 2010 general election (Figure 7.1, p. 122). This reflected a continued lack of confidence in the Conservatives' abilities in this respect, rather than any substantial recovery in Labour's standing on the issue. So, while the 2010 general election saw the economy return to the centre stage of political debate, the inconclusive result did not indicate a groundswell of public approval for the neo-Thatcherite prescription offered by the Conservative Party. However, an about turn on the economy by the Liberal Democrats led by Nick Clegg, and the successful negotiation of a coalition agreement between the two parties, would give Cameron and Osborne the opportunity to dispense it in office.

Conclusion: neo-Thatcherism and Conservative politics

This chapter has argued that throughout the thirteen years of opposition under analysis the political economy of twenty-first-century conservatism remained firmly within the bounds of neo-liberalism. Given the dominance of neo-liberal ideology and political economy not only in the United Kingdom but across the world during this period, it is unsurprising that this orthodoxy was not subject to significant challenge within the Conservative Party. The Conservatives had, after all, played the leading role in establishing the ascendency of neo-liberal economic thinking in British policy-making in the 1980s, and had then witnessed their Labour opponents accommodate their own position to this.

However, what this analysis has highlighted is the grip of neo-Thatcherism on Conservative economic thinking throughout this period. While the political economy of New Labour also fell within the broad parameters of neo-liberalism (and consequently met with Conservative approval in some parts), it was still subject to significant neo-Thatcherite critique within the Conservative Party. More specifically, this analysis has revealed the intensity of Conservative commitment to the neo-Thatcherite ideals of a smaller state, intervening less in the economy; lower taxes; and a highly cautious fiscal policy. These beliefs repeatedly manifested themselves between 1997 and 2010, but became particularly acute as the party attempted to formulate a response to the financial crisis from 2008 onwards. The key thrust of the Conservatives' attack on the Labour government was that it had been fiscally profligate in the 'boom years' which meant that the public finances were less able to cope with the downturn than they might otherwise have been, and that the neo-Keynesian response to the recession was a reckless gamble the country could ill afford.

During the 2010 election the Conservatives consequently focused their attacks on the 'crisis' in the public finances, and the need to reduce the deficit as rapidly as possible. On their return to office, George Osborne's emergency budget of June 2010 confirmed that the new government aimed to eliminate the structural deficit by 2014–15. To do this, the Chancellor announced a fiscal tightening of £40 billion per year by 2014–15, on top of the plan inherited from Labour worth £113 billion per year by the same date. The additional £40 billion squeeze would be made up of £8 billion of net tax increases (most dramatically a rise in value added tax (VAT) to 20 per cent) and a further £32 billion per year of spending reductions (HC 61, 2010: 1–2). To meet these plans would require cuts in public expenditure far deeper even than those made by the Thatcher government. The Comprehensive Spending Review (published in October 2010) outlined how the Conservative-led coalition planned to achieve these reductions, with government departments facing an average real-terms budget cut of 19 per cent over four years (*Guardian*, 20 October 2010).

Perhaps what is most remarkable is the certainty with which the Conservatives stuck to their neo-Thatcherite economic positioning throughout this period, even as it limited their capacity to renew their electoral appeal, and (from 2007) was increasingly brought into question by the global financial crisis. Under the leadership of William Hague, the Conservatives did not make a serious or concerted attempt to revaluate their ideological or policy positioning in response to the 1997 election defeat. After the second landslide defeat in 2001, a more substantial effort at strategic reorientation took place. However, the unwillingness to challenge the core tenets of neo-Thatcherite economic thinking meant that the emphasis Duncan Smith sought to place on improving the public services and delivering social justice looked unconvincing. During Labour's second term the Conservatives also began to articulate a more forceful critique of the government's spending, and went in to the 2005 election promising to reduce borrowing if elected.

The financial crisis provided the opportunity for both the Conservatives and Labour to recast their economic policies. After some initial hesitancy the Labour government responded with an ambitious bailout of stricken banks and a Keynesian stimulus to combat the downturn that followed. The economic policies of the two major parties thus diverged, as the Conservatives attacked the government for profligate spending and argued that the deficit needed to be reduced as quickly as possible to aid a private sector-led economic recovery. Allied to this neo-Thatcherite appraisal Cameron pushed the ill-defined notion of the 'big society' as the alternative to Labour's 'big state'. Although on the surface Cameron's rhetoric of the big society had communitarian overtones, critics argued that in reality it was a mask for public spending cuts (Kisby, 2010). Even if it had not initially been intended as such, by the time of the 2010 election, constrained by the overriding concern with deficit reduction, the big society agenda had become a fig leaf for the withdrawal of state support from significant areas of civil society. In this sense, underpinned by the same neo-Thatcherite economic philosophy, upon returning to power in May 2010 the Conservatives under Cameron appeared keen to continue and extend the Thatcherite revolution. As such, the vaunted modernisation of the Conservative Party in opposition had consequently been considerably limited in terms of ideological renewal, giving credence to the charge that it represented a refashioning of style rather than a transformation of substance.

Note

1 This phenomenon has been widely discussed. See for example, Gamble (2001, 2009a, 2009b); Hay (1997, 2002b).

Part III

Conclusions

8

Reconstructed conservatism?
'Cameronism' in context

This book has focused on the Conservative Party leadership in opposition, between 1997 and 2010. The aim was to comprehend and explain the strategies employed by elite party actors in this period, in order to develop a better understanding of the Conservatives' electoral performance. The question underlying this study was a simple one: why did it take the Conservatives so long to recover power? The answer is rather more complex, but the book has argued that the ideological legacy of Thatcherism played a central role in framing and shaping the strategic debates that took place in the party during these thirteen years, and is an important feature of the explanation.

Part II of the book examined four key areas of ideological tension in contemporary conservatism, and how the party sought to reconcile these into viable political strategies. The analysis of the European question (Chapter 4) highlighted the apparent victory of neo-Thatcherite Euroscepticism in the contemporary Conservative Party, and also noted how this had been fully endorsed by Hague, Duncan Smith, Howard and Cameron. This settling of the Europe issue within the party reflected the near-universal hostility to European integration amongst Conservative parliamentarians and, indeed, the wider membership. It also delivered party management benefits to the leadership, which did not face the divisions that had racked the Conservatives under John Major. However, this attachment to neo-Thatcherite Euroscepticism also had detrimental effects, precluding Clarke from the party leadership in 1997 and 2001 (in spite of evidence to suggest that he offered greater electoral appeal than his rivals) and forming a key element of the 'core-vote' strategy the party repeatedly fell back on between 1997 and 2005.

The analysis of the politics of nationhood in relation to devolution and immigration (Chapter 5) also drew attention to the ways in which ideological debates impact upon the formulation of party strategy. Competing interpretations of conservatism suggested different responses to the changing nature of the British state and the development of a more multicultural society. One potential route was for the Conservative Party to present itself as an overtly English party – a path advocated by some on both electoral and ideological grounds. However, a traditional sense of attachment to the Union meant that this idea had only limited support within the party. Analysis of leadership strategy revealed an inconsistent approach to the politics of nationhood, as on the one hand elements were incorporated into the core-vote strategy (particularly in relation to immigration), and on the other efforts were made to present a modern and inclusive brand of conservatism.

The debate over social liberalism and traditionalism (Chapter 6) revealed a key ideological fault line in contemporary conservatism, which once again had an important bearing on the intraparty debate about modernisation and electoral strategy. Emphasising that the Conservatives had moved on from socially authoritarian Thatcherite values became a key feature of Cameron's effort to modernise his party. However, analysis of social, sexual and moral debates between 1997 and 2010 confirmed the depth of disagreement between those in the party who stuck firmly to a traditionalist approach, and those who regarded a more liberal outlook on social issues as the logical extension of economic liberalism.

In the field of economic policy (Chapter 7), neo-Thatcherite thinking was shown to have retained a virtually unchallenged dominance throughout the entire period of opposition under analysis. This is of great importance as it demonstrates not only the way in which Conservative political strategy was shaped by the Thatcherite ideological inheritance, but also the limits of Cameron's modernisation programme. Indeed, the modernisers themselves subscribed to a neo-Thatcherite outlook on economic policy so did not see any need for the party to significantly alter its approach in this area.

Conservatism under David Cameron

Given the book's central argument about the significance of the Thatcherite ideological inheritance over this period in opposition, what does this allow us to conclude about conservatism under David Cameron upon the party's return to government in 2010? To help place his leadership in context, let us briefly review the record of his three predecessors before examining contemporary conservatism more closely.

Hague, Duncan Smith and Howard all failed to develop an effective statecraft. The 'art of winning elections' eluded them, denying them the opportunity to try their hand at the premier objective identified by Bulpitt, namely 'achieving a necessary degree of governing competence in office' (1986: 19). Between 1997 and 2005, the Conservatives were unable to present themselves as a credible and competent alternative governing force to Labour, and their leaders were unable to present themselves as serious and viable alternatives to Blair as Prime Minister. In spite of several attempts, they failed to articulate a new or convincing narrative of conservatism. In short, the party lacked a clear understanding of its rationale in the post-Thatcherite era, and was consequently unable to fulfil the basic requirements of opposition.

As Chapter 3 demonstrated, Hague, Duncan Smith and Howard all made some initial efforts to devise a narrative of conservatism to widen the party's electoral appeal. To differing extents, they each signalled their desire to 'reach out' to voters disillusioned by the Conservatives in 1997. However, in all three cases these endeavours were abandoned in favour of more traditional messages designed to appeal to the core vote. Under Hague and Howard, these were inchoate efforts, which were rapidly ditched. Duncan Smith's more sustained effort to develop the themes of renewing the public services and helping the vulnerable also came under pressure as the party's poll ratings failed to improve. Had he won the vote of confidence in his leadership and stayed on until the 2005 election, the turn towards the core vote signalled shortly before his departure may have become much more deeply embedded, to the extent that a Conservative campaign under Duncan Smith might have been little different to that which was eventually fought by Howard.

All three leaders exhibited signs of strategic thinking, but ultimately failed to stick to the course of action that this implied. What has been referred to as 'core-vote' strategy throughout this book, namely policies and rhetoric designed to appeal to the mainstay of Conservative Party support, has therefore been revealed as the Conservatives' default position. In this sense, a 'core-vote strategy' is not a strategy at all, but what the party reverts to when it lacks a clear direction or purpose, or when the party's leaders fail to convince it of the merits of an alternative strategic direction.

The default core-vote position therefore illustrates the influence of Thatcherism on the party in opposition. Its central components are firmly Thatcherite, based around a strong but limited state and economic liberalism (most commonly illustrated in policy terms by calls for the party to promise tax cuts), and social authoritarianism. The perceived need to defend national sovereignty (against encroachment from the European Union) and address social and moral decline also draw directly from the party's Thatcherite heritage. The continuing hold of Thatcher's aura on the party was illustrated by the significance of her endorsements in the 1997 and 2001 leadership elections, and her expression of displeasure with Lilley's R. A. Butler lecture in 1999. The importance of the manner of Thatcher's eviction from office cannot be understated: it left a scar on the Conservatives' collective psyche, and ironically reinforced the ideological hold of Thatcherism on the party. As Kenneth Clarke commented:

> I think the Conservative Party's problems really stem from the fall of Margaret Thatcher and the circumstances of it . . . That's what destroyed the equilibrium of the party. Of course, the disputes became about other things, but we never came to terms with that. The wound was quite dreadful, it caused bitterness on all sides. (Clarke, interviewed in Portillo, 2008).

As Michael Portillo graphically stated, some Thatcherites 'feel that a murder was committed, and I think that has made them cling all the more dearly to this very literal and unreconstructed idea of Thatcherism' (private interview, 2006). David Cameron was the first of Thatcher's successors not to receive her public endorsement during his leadership campaign. He was probably happier without it, as it would have called into question his claim to be the candidate for change. Cameron's election, over the more ideologically pure David Davis, was also viewed by some analysts as evidence that the Conservatives were 'ending their self-destructive obsession with ideology' (Heppell, 2008a: 206). However, as discussed below, the degree of policy change wrought by Cameron should not be overstated.

The prevalence of core-vote tendencies in Conservative opposition strategy also tells us something about the nature of contemporary conservatism and how Conservative politicians both understood their role and viewed their support. The essence of contemporary conservatism, when not being purposefully led elsewhere, is pungently Eurosceptic, socially illiberal and narrowly nationalistic. Between 1997 and 2005 in policy terms, this translated into opposition to the single currency and any moves towards further European integration; calls for significantly tighter controls on asylum and immigration; and a defence of traditional social values such as marriage against liberalising tendencies. Under Cameron's leadership between 2005 and 2010, the Conservatives continued to favour reducing immigration, but sought to downplay the sensitivity of the issue by focusing on economic migrants rather than asylum seekers. The opposition to European integration was also impervious to modernisation: Cameron even fulfilled his pledge to withdraw Conservative Members of the European Parliament (MEPs) from the EPP. Cameron did noticeably change Conservative rhetoric in a socially liberal direction, but he was also keen to accompany this with an emphasis on the importance of family to his political beliefs. When placed alongside the endurance of a neo-liberal economic outlook, these policy parallels serve to demonstrate the continuities between Cameron's conservatism and that of Hague, Duncan Smith and Howard.

So what did Cameron's modernisation strategy amount to? At its heart was an effort to 'detoxify' the Conservative brand so that the electorate would once again give the party serious consideration as a party of government. By emphasising policies and issues not traditionally associated with the Conservatives Cameron hoped to demonstrate that he was qualitatively different to his predecessors and that he was impressing change on his party. One of the most distinctive aspects of Cameron's conservatism in this respect was its focus on the environment and climate change, which he encapsulated in his call for people to 'vote blue, go green'. The environment was also implicit in the new logo the Conservatives adopted under Cameron: a scribbled green and blue tree. This decontamination strategy was premised on the belief that the Conservatives' problem since 1997 had been one of image rather than policy or ideology, and this was backed by research which seemed to indicate that polices were more unpopular when people were told that they were Conservative proposals, when in fact they were often similar to their opponents positions (Quinn, 2008). Consequently, rather than undergo a radical policy repositioning, to compete effectively on the centre-ground the Conservative Party needed to follow Cameron's lead in combating the view that it was backward-looking, out of touch and illiberal. A further aspect of this strategy was to change the composition of the parliamentary party so that it better reflected contemporary society, especially in terms of female and ethnic minority representatives (Dorey, 2007: 153). Cameron enjoyed only partial success in this regard, but his chosen mechanism (a priority candidates list) did help ensure that the Conservatives returned by far their highest ever number of female MPs (48) to Westminster in 2010.

The other key aspect of Cameron's modernisation strategy was his repeated effort to demonstrate both his connection with contemporary society and his concern with social issues. As chapter 6 noted, this agenda owned much to work done by his predecessor Iain Duncan Smith, and like the environment was used by Cameron to try and create distance from Thatcherism. Although Cameron had some success in liberalising the party line on moral issues, beyond this he struggled to articulate a convincing account of what he envisaged the 'big society' would really look like. As Chapter 7 discussed, after the 2008 financial crash and the reassertion of fiscal conservatism in economic policy, although Cameron continued to talk about the big society critics increasingly attacked this as cover for the Thatcherite economic medicine the Conservatives were planning to prescribe. In sum, Cameron's modernisation strategy was never intended to vanquish Thatcherism from the Conservative Party – hence its lack of a defining 'Clause IV' moment. It was instead an attempt to repackage and reconstitute it in an electorally agreeable manner, and as such it enjoyed some success at the 2010 election.

Back to power: the 2010 election[1]

The 2010 general election took place in the aftermath of the parliamentary expenses scandal, and as the United Kingdom was emerging from the deepest recession it had suffered since the Second World War. The issue of MPs' expenses afflicted all major parties, but was particularly damaging for Labour, who as the governing party were perceived as having greater responsibility for the structure of the system and had greater difficulty distancing themselves from it, and as Gordon Brown had been attacked for being slow to respond. More generally, Brown was an unpopular Prime Minister who had struggled to connect effectively with the public, while after thirteen years in office Labour was most definitely no longer 'New'. Under Brown's leadership Labour had suffered its lowest-ever approval ratings whilst in office: in mid-2008 things were even worse than during the 1976 IMF crisis, and Brown's personal approval ratings hit a low of minus 58 per cent (*Independent*, 3 July 2008). Labour consequently exhibited the key 'degenerative tendencies of long-serving governments' which tend to presage electoral defeat (Heppell, 2008b: 580), bringing into question the likelihood that the party would be able to hold onto power. These signs suggested that the Conservatives under Cameron might reasonably have expected to be quietly confident of victory. Yet as the election drew near it was widely anticipated it would be the closest for many years, and there was much speculation about the possibility of a hung parliament. In part this reflected a modest recovery by Labour in the opinion polls since late 2009, but it also signalled that in spite of the widespread feeling that it might be time for a change of government, the Conservatives under Cameron had failed to 'seal the deal' with the electorate.

The most striking feature of the campaign itself was the extraordinary surge in support for the Liberal Democrats, triggered by the stellar performance of Nick Clegg in the first of the three televised debates between the party leaders. Opinion polls were unanimous in reporting that the public regarded Clegg as the clear winner of the debate by a considerable margin (*Daily Telegraph*, 16 April 2010), and this was soon reflected in backing for his party. Before the first debate on 15 April, support for the Liberal Democrats had been hovering around 20 per cent. Afterwards it jumped to around 30 per cent, with several polls even giving the party a small lead over the Conservatives, with Labour in third place. This increase came at the expense of both the major parties, threatening Labour with the humiliation of finishing third on polling day (in terms of votes if not seats), and ominously for David Cameron suggesting that the Conservatives would fail to win an overall majority. Elements of the right-wing press seized the opportunity to criticise the Conservative leader, firstly as he was regarded as having performed below expectations in the first debate, and secondly as it had been persistent public pressure from Cameron that had been instrumental in forcing Gordon Brown to concede to the televised debates in the first place. Keen to exploit his telegenic advantage over the Prime Minister, Cameron had seemingly failed to anticipate the risk of providing an unprecedented platform for the leader of the third party.

Much of the praise heaped on Clegg's performance appeared to centre on the fact that (unlike Brown and Cameron) he spent much of the first debate looking straight at the camera, addressing the audience watching on television rather than the relatively small number of people in the studio itself. Cameron in particular took this lesson to heart, gazing intently into the nation's living rooms during the second and third debates. Both he and Brown raised their game, and the public verdict on the final two debates was much more divided, and roughly reflected the strength of each party's support. The Conservatives and Labour also attempted to turn the tide on the Liberal Democrats by warning of the 'danger' of a hung parliament. The Conservatives even went as far as to issue a spoof manifesto and party election broadcast on behalf of 'the hung parliament party', which variously suggested that such an outcome would lead to 'behind closed door politics . . . indecision, inaction and half measures', spook the markets and 'paralyse the economy' (conservatives.com, 2010). In spite of these attacks most opinion polls continued to suggest that the Liberal Democrats were maintaining their increased support as the election approached. Nick Clegg appeared to have cornered a gap in the market, offering a 'vote for change' (the Conservatives' slogan) without the need to support

Cameron's party. Beyond the televised debates the election struggled to capture the public imagination, despite the prospect of a close result. In part this reflected cynicism towards the pledges by all parties to 'clean up politics' in the light of the expenses scandal, but it also stemmed from a deeper malaise affecting British politics, namely the rise of disenchantment with the political system itself (see Stoker, 2006).

Although Cameron proved unable to lead his party to an outright victory, the Conservatives were the clear winners on election night as both Labour and the Liberal Democrats lost seats. On a respectable swing from Labour of 5 per cent the Conservatives gained 97 seats, their biggest advance since 1931 (see Chapter 2). This still left the party 19 short of the 326 required for an overall victory, and Cameron swiftly moved to open discussions with the Liberal Democrats about a possible coalition. This was a brazen move by the Conservative leader, who had to make significant concessions on electoral reform and taxation policy in order to secure the agreement of Clegg's party. The prospect of governing in coalition caused unease amongst backbenchers in both parties, although publicly at least things were more strained amongst the Liberal Democrats, most of whom regarded Labour as their more natural bedfellows. Dissent on the Conservative side was surprisingly limited, kept in check by the tantalising prospect of power. When the coalition was formed some right-wing commentators immediately condemned the 'betrayal' of the Conservative Party by its leadership (Heffer, 2010) but those sharing such reservations in the parliamentary party largely kept them out of the newspapers. After thirteen long years in opposition Cameron had finally delivered what his party yearned for – a Conservative Prime Minister in Downing Street. The final section offers some concluding thoughts on the future of Conservative politics, and the lessons the party might draw from this study of opposition.

Conclusion: reconstructed conservatism?

After the fall of Thatcher, the Conservatives increasingly struggled to articulate a convincing answer to the question 'what is contemporary conservatism for?' The sense of purpose Thatcherism had given the party in the 1980s dissipated as the social, economic and political circumstances moved on, but the Conservatives' prevailing ideological outlook did not. However, as Chapter 1 noted, historical precedent suggested that the Conservatives would readapt their ideology, reposition their party and refresh their policy programme in order to rebuild their support. The failure of Conservative statecraft after the 1992 election is surprising not because it occurred, but because it took so long for the party to take significant steps to reverse it.

One interpretation of David Cameron's success in this regard might be to see him as a return to a form of elitist Conservative statecraft, redolent of the party leaders who emerged from the so-called 'magic circle' of party grandees in the days before the leader was elected, and more commonly associated with the One Nation tradition. Cameron's willingness to go into coalition with the Liberal Democrats might also been seen as evidence of his inclination for pragmatic high politics. Both Cameron and Clegg justified the formation of the coalition as being in the national interest, and have been keen to claim the mantle of pragmatic, sensible political leadership. Leading a coalition government has thus allowed Cameron to reinforce his message that the Conservatives have changed. Indeed, it is difficult to imagine that Hague, Duncan Smith or Howard would have been able to negotiate a coalition with the Liberal Democrats had the electoral mathematics made it a possibility. In this degree Cameron's modernisation agenda was successful: the party was perceived to have changed sufficiently for the Liberal Democrats to countenance such a deal, and had changed sufficiently for Cameron to persuade his MPs of the merits of the agreement.

To this extent, as leader of the opposition Cameron successfully reconstructed conservatism. As this book has shown, this reconstruction has been a long and difficult process of gradual rather than revolutionary change. However, it was also fundamentally limited in scope. Although Cameron has sometimes been described as a One Nation Conservative, and even heralded as the 'heir to Disraeli' by one of his MPs (*Daily Telegraph*, 28 December 2006), there is little to link his conservatism with the anti-Thatcherite One Nation tradition discussed in Chapter 2. As under his three predecessors, Cameron's tenure as leader of the opposition saw the Conservatives remain firmly within neo-Thatcherite parameters. The anti-Thatcherite position associated with Ian Gilmour and other 'wets' has not recovered from its marginalisation from the mainstream of the party in the 1980s. The thoughtful post-Thatcherite critique advanced by John Gray has also largely failed to penetrate intraparty debate. Downplaying ideological motives and policy justifications was a sensible tactical decision by Cameron, but should not be mistaken for a fundamental change of approach.

Whilst Cameron enjoyed much more favourable circumstances, his record is an indictment of his predecessors. The fact that Cameron steered his party within rather than against Thatcherism's wake suggests that greater progress in reconstructing conservatism could have been made between 1997 and 2005. Under Hague, the Conservatives were not constrained to core-vote themes and rhetoric simply by ideology, but by a lack of commitment to change by Hague and other members of the shadow cabinet, who failed to clearly articulate an alternative approach. Duncan Smith showed a greater degree of personal commitment to his own vision of how the Conservatives needed to change, but failed to communicate it effectively and persuade others of his case. Howard enjoyed much more authority than his predecessors, making his failure in this respect greater. Rather than challenge his party to change, he chose a core-vote electoral strategy which reinforced the negative preconceptions many voters held about the Conservatives.

The 1997–2005 period was not one of absolute leadership failure. William Hague succeeded in holding the party together as a single entity, a status which was far from guaranteed. We shall never know whether, as many Conservative MPs believe, the party would have split under the leadership of the Europhile Kenneth Clarke. But by choosing instead the candidate closest to the party's centre they may have avoided this fate. Iain Duncan Smith began the policy renewal and process in earnest, and began to forge a new statement of conservatism. Michael Howard restored party discipline and some sense of unity and professionalism. These were all essential prerequisites for an electoral revival, but it is remarkable that it took three different leaders and eight years to achieve such relatively modest steps.

Since Thatcher, the Conservatives have taken the long road to renewal. After thirteen years in opposition only a limited reconstruction of conservatism had been achieved. In 1997 the party found itself in an unfavourable strategic terrain, but this alone does not account for the failures that followed. Successive Conservative leaders grappled ineffectively with the challenge of reconstructing their party's ideology, policy agenda and electoral appeal. Cameron succeeded in presenting a fresh face of modern conservatism, but this was in large part a case of rebranding and repackaging a neo-Thatcherite product, rather than re-orientating the ideological trajectory of his party. Whether Cameron can rebuild Conservative hegemony on anything like the scale of Thatcherism is yet to be seen. The answer will depend on the effectiveness of his neo-Thatcherite statecraft, and the ability of his opponents to renew their own political narrative. The hope for the left must be that the limited extent of Conservative ideological revival will be exposed by the trials of office, while the danger is that coalition will provide the dynamic for renewal the Conservatives lacked in opposition. For both left and right, what defines them over the coming decades will be how they respond to the turmoil in the global economy and the political, social and economic challenges presented both in the United Kingdom and more widely. The stakes could not be higher.

Note

1 This section draws in substantial part on Hayton (2012).

Bibliography

Addison, P. (1999) 'The British Conservative Party from Churchill to Heath: Doctrine or Men?', *Contemporary European History*, 8(2): 289–98.

Alderman, K. (1998) 'The Conservative Party Leadership Election of 1997', *Parliamentary Affairs*, 51(1): 1–16.

Alderman, K. and Carter, N. (2002) 'The Conservative Party Leadership Election of 2001', *Parliamentary Affairs*, 55(3): 569–85.

Alibhai-Brown, Y. (2000) 'Muddled Leaders and the Future of the British National Identity', *Political Quarterly*, 71(1): 26–30.

Ancram, M. (2007) *Still a Conservative: Conservative Beliefs and Principles for the Twenty-first Century*, London.

Anderson, B. (1991) *Imagined Communities: Reflections on the Origin and Spread of Nationalism*, London: Verso.

Ashbee, E. (2003) 'The US Republicans: Lessons for the Conservatives', in M. Garnett and P. Lynch (eds.), *The Conservatives in Crisis*, Manchester: Manchester University Press: 9–48.

Ashcroft, M. (2005) *Smell the Coffee: A Wake-up Call for the Conservative Party*, London: MAA Publishing.

Aughey, A. (2007) *The Politics of Englishness*, Manchester: Manchester University Press.

Baker, D., Gamble, A. and Seawright, D. (2002) 'Sovereign Nations and Global Markets: Modern British Conservatism and Hyperglobalism', *British Journal of Politics and International Relations*, 4(3): 399–428.

Bale, T. (2006) 'Between a Soft and a Hard Place? The Conservative Party, Valence Politics and the Need for a New "Eurorealism"', *Parliamentary Affairs*, 59(3): 385–400.

Bale, T. (2008) '"A Bit Less Bunny-Hugging and a Bit More Bunny-Boiling"? Qualifying Conservative Party Change under David Cameron', *British Politics*, 3(3): 270–99.

Bale, T. (2009) 'Take your Pick', *Parliamentary Affairs*, 62(2): 364–9.

Bale, T. (2010) *The Conservative Party: From Thatcher to Cameron*, Cambridge: Polity.

Ball, S. (1998) *The Conservative Party since 1945*, Manchester: Manchester University Press.

Ball, S. (2005) 'Factors in Opposition Performance: The Conservative Experience since 1867', in S. Ball and A. Seldon (eds.), *Recovering Power: The Conservatives in Opposition since 1867*, Basingstoke: Palgrave Macmillan: 1–27.

Ball, S. and Seldon, A. (eds.) (2005) *Recovering Power: The Conservatives in Opposition since 1867*, Basingstoke: Palgrave Macmillan.

Barnes, J. (1994) 'Ideology and Factions', in A. Seldon and S. Ball (eds.), *Conservative Century*, Oxford: Oxford University Press: 315–47.

Bauman, Z. (2007) 'Britain after Blair, or Thatcherism Consolidated', in G. Hassan (ed.), *After Blair: Politics after the New Labour Decade*, London: Lawrence & Wishart: 60–74.

BBC News (1997) 'Devolution Results', www.bbc.co.uk/politics97/devolution/.

BBC News (1998) 'Gordon, Prudence and the other Woman', 3 November, http://news.bbc.co.uk/1/hi/events/budget_99/budget_briefing/201932.stm.

BBC News (1999) 'Tories Celebrate Euro Poll Success', 14 June, http://news.bbc.co.uk/1/hi/events/euros_99/news/368508.stm.

BBC News (2001) 'Do Tory Spending Plans Add Up?', 15 May, http://news.bbc.co.uk/news/vote2001/hi/english/newsid_1323000/1323374.stm.

Bevir, M. and Rhodes, R. A. W. (1998) 'Narratives of Thatcherism', *West European Politics*, 21(1): 97–119.

Blake, R. (1970) *The Conservative Party from Peel to Churchill*, London: Eyre & Spottiswoode.

Blake, R. (1998) *The Conservative Party from Peel to Major*, London: Arrow Books.

Blunkett, D. (2005) 'A New England: An English Identity within Britain', speech to the Institute for Public Policy Research (IPPR), 14 March 2005.

Booker, C. and North, R. (1997) *The Castle of Lies: Why Britain Must Get Out of Europe*, London: Gerald Duckworth.

Bragg, B. (2006) *The Progressive Patriot: A Search for Belonging*, London: Black Swan.

Brogan, B. (2000) 'Party Welcomes Gays, says Hague', *Daily Telegraph*, 19 November.

Buller, J. (2000) *National Statecraft and European Integration: The Conservative Government and the European Union, 1979–97*, London: Pinter.

Bulpitt, J. (1986) 'The Discipline of the New Democracy: Mrs Thatcher's Domestic Statecraft', *Political Studies*, 34(1): 19–39.

Butler, D. (1996) 'Review of *SDP: The Birth, Life and Death of the Social Democratic Party*, by Ivor Crewe and Anthony King', *American Political Science Review*, 90(4): 934–5.

Butler, D. and Kavanagh, D. (1997) *The British General Election of 1997*, Basingstoke: Macmillan.

Butler, D. and Kavanagh, D. (2002) *The British General Election of 2001*, Basingstoke: Palgrave.

Cabinet Office (2010) *The Coalition: Our Programme for Government*, London: H.M. Government.

Cameron, D. (2005) 'Change to Win', speech at the Conservative Party Conference, 4 October, www.conservatives.com/tile.do?def=news.story.page&obj_id =125400&speeches=1.

Cameron, D. (2006a) 'Modern Conservatism', speech at Demos, 30 January, www.conservatives.com/tile.do?def=news.story.page&obj_id=127560&speeches=1#.

Cameron, D. (2006b) 'I Will never Take Scotland for Granted', speech in Glasgow, 15 September, www.conservatives.com/tile.do?def=news.story.page&obj_id=132019&speeches=1#.

Cameron, D. (2006c) 'Improving Society's Sense of Well Being is Challenge of our Times', speech to Google Zeitgeist Europe, 22 May, www.conservatives.com/tile.do?def=news.story.page&obj_id=129957.

Cameron, D. (2007a) 'Stronger Together', speech in Edinburgh, 10 December, www.conservatives.com/tile.do?def=news.story.page&obj_id=141137&speeches=1.

Cameron, D. (2007b) 'Scots and English Flourish in the Union', *Daily Telegraph*, 11 April, www.conservatives.com/tile.do?def=news.show.article.page&obj_id=137258.

Cameron, D. (2007c) 'The Challenges of a Growing Population', speech, 29 October, www. conservatives.com/tile.do?def=news.story.page&obj_id=139990.

Cameron, D. (2008) 'Stronger Families', speech to Relate, 9 June, www.conservatives.com/ tile.do?def=news.story.page&obj_id=145186&speeches=1.

Carey. S. and Geddes, A. (2010) 'Less is More: Immigration and European Integration at the 2010 General Election', *Parliamentary Affairs*, 63(4): 849–65.

Carswell, D. (2006) Speech to Bruges Group, Conservative Party Conference Fringe Meeting, October 2006, www.brugesgroup.com/mediacentre/speeches.live?article=13624.

Carter, N. (2009) 'Vote Blue, Go Green? Cameron's Conservatives and the Environment', *Political Quarterly*, 80(2): 233–42.

Carter, N. and Alderman, K. (2002) 'The Conservative Party Leadership Election of 2001', *Parliamentary Affairs*, 55(3): 569–85.

Charmley, J. (1996) *A History of Conservative Politics, 1900–1996*, Basingstoke: Macmillan.

Clark, A. (1998) *The Tories: Conservatives and the Nation State, 1922–1997*, London: Weidenfeld & Nicolson.

Coetzee, F. (2005) 'Factions and Failure: 1905–1910', in S. Ball and A. Seldon (eds.), *Recovering Power: The Conservatives in Opposition since 1867*, Basingstoke: Palgrave Macmillan: 92–112.

Collings, D. and Seldon, A. (2001) 'Conservatives in Opposition', *Parliamentary Affairs*, 54(4): 624–37.

Colls, R. (1998) 'Ethics Man: John Gray's New Moral World', *Political Quarterly*, 68(1): 59–71.

Conservative Party (1998) 'Kitchen Table Conservatives: A Strategy Proposal', internal Conservative Party document (unpublished).

Conservative Party (1999) *In Europe, not Run by Europe* (Conservative Party European Elections Manifesto), London: Conservative Party.

Conservative Party (2000) *The Common Sense Revolution*, London: Conservative Party.

Conservative Party (2001) *Time for Common Sense* (2001 Election Manifesto), London: Conservative Party.

Conservative Party (2004) *Timetable for Action*, London: Conservative Party.

Conservative Party (2005) *It's Time for Action* (2005 Election Manifesto), London: Conservative Party.

Conservative Party (2007) *Scottish Conservative Manifesto*, Edinburgh: Conservative Party, www.scottishconservatives.com/news_press/manifesto.aspx.

Conservative Party (2008) *Reconstruction: Plan for a Strong Economy*, London: Conservative Party.

Conservative Party (2010) *Invitation to Join the Government of Britain: The Conservative Manifesto 2010*, London: Conservative Party.

conservatives.com (2007) 'Fixing our Broken Society' [news story], 10 July, www. conservatives.com/tile.do?def=news.story.page&obj_id=137513.

conservatives.com (2010) 'An Election Broadcast from the Hung Parliament Party', 26 April, www.conservatives.com/Video/Conservatives_TV.aspx?id=5fab8efd-8b85-497b-8fc9-cbd168b2384a.

Cooper, A. (2001) 'The Conservative Campaign', in J. Bartle, S. Atkinson and R. Mortimer (eds.), *Political Communications: The General Election Campaign of 2001*, London: Frank Cass: 98–108.

Cowley, P. (1997) 'The Conservative Party: Decline and Fall', in A. Geddes and J. Tonge (eds.), *Labour's Landslide*, Manchester: Manchester University Press: 37–52.

Cowley, P. and Green, J. (2005) 'New Leaders, Same Problems: The Conservatives', in A. Geddes and J. Tonge, *Britain Decides: The UK General Election 2005*, Basingstoke, Palgrave Macmillan: 46–69.

Cowley, P. and Stuart, M. (2004) 'Mapping Conservative Divisions under Howard', www. revolts.co.uk/cat_briefing_papers.html.

Crewe, I. (1993) 'The Thatcher Legacy', in A. King (ed.), *Britain at the Polls, 1992*, Chatham, NJ: Chatham House Publishers.

Crewe, I. and King, A. (1994) 'Did Major Win? Did Kinnock Lose? Leadership Effects in the 1992 General Election', in A. Heath, R. Jowell and J. Curtice (eds.), *Labour's Last Chance? The 1992 Election and Beyond*, Aldershot: Dartmouth.

Daley, J. (2006) 'What Does Modernisation Mean?', London: Centre for Policy Studies.

Davies, A. J. (1996) *We, The Nation: The Conservative Party and the Pursuit of Power*, London: Abacus.

Denham, A. and Garnett, M. (2002) 'Sir Keith Joseph and the Undoing of British Conservatism', *Journal of Political Ideologies*, 7(1): 57–75.

Denham, A. and O'Hara, K. (2007a) 'The Three Mantras: Modernisation and the Conservative Party', *British Politics*, 2(2): 167–90.

Denham, A. and O'Hara, K. (2007b) 'Cameron's "Mandate": Democracy, Legitimacy and Conservative Leadership', *Parliamentary Affairs*, 60(3): 409–23.

Denham, A. and O'Hara, K. (2008) *Democratising Conservative Leadership Selection: From Grey Suits to Grassroots*, Manchester: Manchester University Press.

Direct Democracy (2005) *Direct Democracy: An Agenda for a New Model Party*, London: direct-democracy.co.uk.

Dodd, P. (1995) *The Battle Over Britain*, London: Demos.

Dorey, P. (2003) 'Conservative Policy under Hague', in M. Garnett and P. Lynch (eds.), *The Conservatives in Crisis*, Manchester: Manchester University Press: 125–45.

Dorey, P. (2004) 'Attention to Detail: The Conservative Policy Agenda', *Political Quarterly*, 75(4): 373–7.

Dorey, P. (2007) 'A New Direction or Another False Dawn? David Cameron and the Crisis of British Conservatism', *British Politics*, 2(2): 137–66.

Dorey, P. (2009) 'Sharing the Proceeds of Growth: Conservative Economic Policy under Cameron', *Political Quarterly*, 80(2): 259–69.

Dorey, P. (2011) *British Conservatism: The Politics and Philosophy of Inequality*, London: I. B. Tauris.

Dorey, P., Garnett, M. and Denham, A. (2011) *From Crisis to Coalition*, Basingstoke: Palgrave Macmillan.

Duncan Smith, I. (2001) 'Public Services are our Greatest Mission', speech to the Conservative Party Conference, 10 October 2001.

Duncan Smith, I. (2002a) 'Community Government', speech to the Conservative Local Government Conference, 5 March.

Duncan Smith, I. (2002b) 'We Will Champion the Vulnerable', speech to the Conservative Spring Forum, 24 March.

Duncan Smith, I. (2002c) 'It's not Racist to Debate Immigration', *The Sun*, 8 May.

Duncan Smith, I. (2002d) 'Defeating the Five Giants', first anniversary speech, 23 September.

Duncan Smith, I. (2002e) 'The Necessary and Sometimes Painful Process of Modernisation', 5 November, www.iainduncansmith.org/article.aspx?id+10&ref=91.

Duncan Smith, I. (2002f) 'Response to the Queen's Speech', 13 November, http://news.bbc.co.uk/1/hi/uk_politics/2465007.stm.

Duncan Smith, I. (2003a) 'Labour Think they have a Monopoly on Compassion', speech to the 2003 Compassionate Conservatism Conference, 15 September.

Duncan Smith, I. (2003b) 'Speech to the Conservative Party Conference', 9 October.

Durham, M. (2001) 'The Conservative Party, New Labour and the Politics of the Family', *Parliamentary Affairs*, 54(3): 459–74.

Durham, M. (2005) 'Abortion, Gay Rights and Politics in Britain and America: A Comparison', *Parliamentary Affairs*, 58(1): 89–103.

Eccleshall, R. (2000a) 'The Doing of Conservatism', *Journal of Political Ideologies*, 5(3): 275–87.

Eccleshall, R. (2000b) 'Party Ideology and National Decline', in R. English and M. Kenny (eds.), *Rethinking British Decline*, Basingstoke: Macmillan.

Economic Competitiveness Policy Group (ECPG) (2007) *Freeing Britain to Compete: Equipping the UK for Globalisation (Submission to the Shadow Cabinet)*, London: Economic Competitiveness Policy Group.

English, R., Hayton, R. and Kenny, M. (2009) 'Englishness and the Union in Contemporary Conservative Thought', *Government and Opposition*, 44(4): 343–65.

English, R. and Kenny, M. (eds.) (2000) *Rethinking British Decline*, Basingstoke: Macmillan.

Evans, B. and Taylor, A. (1996) *From Salisbury to Major: Continuity and Change in Conservative Politics*, Manchester: Manchester University Press.

Evans, G. (1998) 'Euroscepticism and Conservative Electoral Support: How an Asset Became a Liability', *British Journal of Political Science*, 28(4): 573–90.

Evans, S. (2010) 'Mother's Boy: David Cameron and Margaret Thatcher', *British Journal of Politics and International Relations*, 12(3): 325–43.

Flinders, M. (2009) 'Conserving the Constitution? The Conservative Party and Democratic Renewal', *Political Quarterly*, 80(2): 248–58.

Fullbrook, E. (2007) 'Economics and Neo-liberalism', in G. Hassan (ed.), *After Blair: Politics after the New Labour Decade*, London: Lawrence & Wishart: 160–72.

Gamble, A. (1974) *The Conservative Nation*, London: Routledge & Kegan Paul.

Gamble, A. (1993) 'The Entrails of Thatcherism', *New Left Review*, I/198: 117–28.

Gamble, A. (1994a) *The Free Economy and the Strong State*, 2nd edition, Basingstoke: Macmillan.

Gamble, A. (1994b) *Britain in Decline: Economic Policy, Political Strategy and the British State*, 4th edition, Basingstoke: Macmillan.

Gamble, A. (1995) 'The Crisis of Conservatism', *New Left Review*, 214: 3–25.

Gamble, A. (1996) 'An Ideological Party', in S. Ludlam and M. J. Smith (eds.), *Contemporary British Conservatism*, Basingstoke: Macmillan.

Gamble, A. (1999) 'The Last Utopia', *New Left Review* I/236: 117–27.

Gamble, A. (2000a) *Politics and Fate*, Oxford: Blackwell.

Gamble, A. (2000b) 'Theories and Explanations of British Decline', in R. English and M. Kenny (eds.), *Rethinking British Decline*, Basingstoke, Macmillan: 1–22.

Gamble, A. (2001) 'Neo-liberalism', *Capital and Class*, 25(3): 127–34.

Gamble, A. (2003) *Between Europe and America: The Future of British Politics*, Basingstoke: Palgrave Macmillan.

Gamble, A. (2006) 'The Constitutional Revolution in the United Kingdom', *Publius: The Journal of Federalism*, 36(1): 19–35.

Gamble, A. (2009a) *The Spectre at the Feast*, Basingstoke: Palgrave Macmillan.

Gamble, A. (2009b) 'The Western Ideology', *Government and Opposition*, 44(1): 1–19.

Garnett, M. (2003) 'A Question of Definition? Ideology and the Conservative Party, 1997–2001', in M. Garnett and P. Lynch (eds.), *The Conservatives in Crisis*, Manchester: Manchester University Press: 107–24.

Garnett, M. (2004) 'The Free Economy and the Schizophrenic State: Ideology and the Conservatives', *Political Quarterly*, 75(4): 367–72.

Garnett, M. and Gilmour, I. (1998) 'The Lessons of Defeat', *Political Quarterly*, 69(2): 126–32.

Garnett, M. and Lynch, P. (eds.) (2003a) *The Conservatives in Crisis*, Manchester: Manchester University Press.

Garnett, M. and Lynch, P. (2003b) 'The Tribulations of a Quiet Man: Iain Duncan Smith and the Conservative Party', paper presented to the 53rd Annual Political Studies Association Conference, University of Leicester, 15–17 April.

Garrett, G. (1994) 'Popular Capitalism: The Electoral Legacy of Thatcherism', in A. Heath, R. Jowell and J. Curtice (eds.), *Labour's Last Chance? The 1992 Election and Beyond*, Aldershot: Dartmouth: 107–23.

Geddes, A. (2003) *The Politics of Migration and Immigration in Europe*, London: Sage.

Geddes, A. (2004) *The European Union and British Politics*, Basingstoke: Palgrave Macmillan.

Geddes, A. (2005a) 'Nationalism: Immigration and European Integration at the 2005 General Election', in A. Geddes and J. Tonge (eds.), *Britain Decides: The UK General Election 2005*, Basingstoke: Palgrave Macmillan.

Geddes, A. (2005b) 'Europe', in K. Hickson (ed.), *The Political Thought of the Conservative Party since 1945*, Basingstoke: Palgrave Macmillan: 113–32.

Geddes, A. and Tonge, J. (eds.) (2001) *Labour's Second Landslide: The British General Election 2001*, Manchester: Manchester University Press.

George, S. and Sowemimo, M. (1996) 'Conservative Foreign Policy towards the European Union', in S. Ludlam and M. J. Smith (eds.), *Contemporary British Conservatism*, Basingstoke: Macmillan.

Gilmour, I. (1978) *Inside Right*, London: Quartet Books.

Gilmour, I. (1983) 'Tories, Social Democracy and the Centre', *Political Quarterly*, 54(3): 257–67.

Gilmour, I. (1992) *Dancing with Dogma: Britain under Thatcherism*, London: Simon & Schuster.

Gilmour, I. (2001) 'Little Mercians', *London Review of Books*, 23(13), 5 July.

Gilmour, I. (2002) 'The Other Side have Got One', *London Review of Books*, 24(11), 6 June.

Gilmour, I. (2005) 'Vote for the Beast!', *London Review of Books*, 27(20), 20 October.

Gilmour, I. and Garnett, M. (1997) *Whatever Happened to the Tories? The Conservatives since 1945*, London: Fourth Estate.

Gould, P. (1999) *The Unfinished Revolution*, London: Abacus.

Gray, J. (1993) *Beyond the New Right*, London: Routledge.

Gray, J. (1994) *The Undoing of Conservatism*, London: Social Market Foundation.

Gray, J. (1997) *Endgames: Questions in Late Modern Political Thought*, Cambridge: Polity Press.

Gray, J. (1998) *False Dawn: The Delusions of Global Capitalism*, London: Granta.

Gray, J. (2003) *Al Qaeda and What it Means to be Modern*, London: Faber & Faber.

Green, D. (2000) Macmillan Lecture to the Tory Reform Group, 14 March.

Green, D. (2001) 'Conservatives will defend teachers, not criticise', speech to the Conservative Party Conference, 9 October, www.conservatives.com/tile.do?def =news.story.page&obj_id=18035&speeches=1.

Green, E. H. H. (2004) *Ideologies of Conservatism*, Oxford: Oxford University Press.

Green, J. (2010) 'Strategic Recovery? The Conservatives Under David Cameron', *Parliamentary Affairs*, 63(4): 667–88.

Grice, A. (2000) 'Portillo Allies Hail Tory U-turn on Tax Guarantee as a Triumph', *The Independent*, 12 July, www.independent.co.uk/news/uk/politics/portillo-allies-hail-tory-uturn-on-tax-guarantee-as-a-triumph-707331.html.

Grice, A. (2007) 'Cameron's Family Tax Breaks Will Leave Unmarried Couples Paying More', *The Independent*, 31 August, www.independent.co.uk/news/uk/politics/camerons-family-tax-breaks-will-leave-unmarried-couples-paying-more-463670.html.

Grimston, J. (2006) 'Pink Tories Learn the Art of being Gay Friendly', *The Times*, 15 October, www.timesonline.co.uk/tol/news/uk/article601104.ece.

Guardian, The (2003) 'Duncan Smith Defends Stance on Section 28', 16 January, www.guardian.co.uk/politics/2003/jan/16/immigrationpolicy.gayrights.

Guardian, The (2005) 'Conservative Party Members Retain Leadership Vote', 22 September, www.guardian.co.uk/politics/2005/sep/27/toryleadership2005.conservatives1.

Guardian, The (2008) 'Economic Fears Drive Labour to 24-year Low', 18 March, www.guardian.co.uk/politics/2008/mar/18/labour.conservatives.

Hague, W. (1997) 'Speech to the Conservative Party Conference', 10 October.

Hague, W. (1998a) 'Speech to the Conservative Party Conference', 8 October.

Hague, W. (1998b) 'Change and Tradition: Thinking Creatively about the Constitution', speech to the Centre for Policy Studies, 24 February.

Hague, W. (1998c) 'Freedom and the Family', speech to the Social Market Foundation, 29 January.

Hague, W. (1999a) 'Speech to the Conservative Party Conference', 7 October.

Hague, W. (1999b) 'Strengthening the Union After Devolution', speech to the Centre for Policy Studies, 15 July.

Hague, W. (2001) 'Speech to Conservative Spring Forum', 4 March 2001.

Hall, S. (1983) 'The Great Moving Right Show', in S. Hall and M. Jacques (eds.), *The Politics of Thatcherism*, London: Lawrence & Wishart, in association with *Marxism Today*.

Hall, S. (1998) 'The Great Moving Nowhere Show', in *Wrong: Marxism Today Special Issue*, London: *Marxism Today*.

Hall, S. (2007) 'Will Life after Blair be Different?', *British Politics*, 2(1): 118–22.

Hall, S. and Jacques, M. (eds.) (1983) *The Politics of Thatcherism*, London: Lawrence & Wishart, in association with *Marxism Today*.

Harris, C. (2005) 'Conservative Party Strategy, 1997–2001: Nation and National Identity', unpublished PhD thesis, Sheffield: University of Sheffield.

Haseler, S. (1996) *The English Tribe: Identity, Nation and Europe*, Basingstoke: Palgrave Macmillan.

Hay, C. (1997) 'Blaijorism: Towards a One-vision Polity?', *Political Quarterly*, 68(4): 372–8.

Hay, C. (2002a) *Political Analysis: A Critical Introduction*, Basingstoke: Palgrave.

Hay, C. (2002b) 'New Labour and "Third Way" Political Economy: Paving the European Road to Washington?', in M. Bevir and F. Trentmann (eds.), *Critiques of Capital in Modern Britain and America*, Basingstoke: Palgrave Macmillan.

Hay, C. (2006) 'What's Globalization Got to Do with It? Economic Interdependence and the Future of European Welfare States', *Government and Opposition*, 41(1): 1–22.

Hay, C. (2007) 'Whatever Happened to Thatcherism?', *Political Studies Review*, 5(2): 183–201.

Hay, C. (2009) 'On Times, Tides And Heresthetics: Or King Canute and the "Problem" of Structure And Agency', *Political Studies*, 57(2): 260–79.

Hay, C. and Wincott, D. (1998) 'Structure, Agency and Historical Institutionalism', *Political Studies*, 46(5): 951–7.

Hayes, J. (2002) 'Politics on a Human Scale', in G. Streeter (ed.), *There is such a Thing as Society*, London: Methuen: 68–78.

Hayton, R. (2010a) 'Towards the Mainstream? UKIP and the 2009 Elections to the European Parliament', *Politics*, 30(1): 26–35.

Hayton, R. (2010b) 'Conservative Party Modernisation and David Cameron's Politics of the Family', *Political Quarterly*, 81(4): 492–500.

Hayton, R. (2012) 'The Path to (Sharing) Power: The Conservatives', in G. Baldini and J. Hopkin (eds.), *Cameron's Britain: UK Politics and the 2010 Election*, Manchester: Manchester University Press.

Hayton, R., English, R. and Kenny, M. (2007) 'Englishness in Contemporary British Politics', *Political Quarterly* (Special Edition on Britishness), 78(s1): 122–35.

Hayton, R. and Heppell, T. (2010) 'The Quiet Man of British Politics: The Rise, Fall and Significance of Iain Duncan Smith', *Parliamentary Affairs*, 63(3): 425–45.

Hayton, R. and Kenny, M. (2008) 'The English Question', *The Guardian*, 17 March, http://commentisfree.guardian.co.uk/richard_hayton_and_michael_kenny/2008/03/the_english_question.html.

HC 61 (2010) *Budget 2010*, London: Stationery Office.

HC 75 (2008) *Devolution: A Decade On*, Minutes of Evidence, Justice Committee, Session 2007/08, London: Stationery Office, www.publications.parliament.uk/pa/cm200708/cmselect/cmjust/uc75-iii/uc7502.htm.

Heath, A., Jowell, R. and Curtice, J. (eds.) (1994) *Labour's Last Chance? The 1992 Election and Beyond*, Aldershot: Dartmouth.

Heffer, Simon (1998) *Like the Roman: The Life of Enoch Powell*, London: Weidenfeld & Nicolson.

Heffer, Simon (1999) *Nor Shall My Sword: Reinvention of England*, London: Weidenfeld & Nicolson.

Heffer, Simon (2005) 'Traditional Toryism', in K. Hickson (ed.), *The Political Thought of the Conservative Party since 1945*, Basingstoke: Palgrave Macmillan: 197–201.

Heffer, Simon (2010) 'David Cameron will Rue the Day He Betrayed the Conservatives', *Daily Telegraph*, 21 May.

Heffernan, R. (2000) *New Labour and Thatcherism: Political Change in Britain*, Basingstoke: Macmillan.

Heppell, T. (2002) 'The Ideological Composition of the Parliamentary Conservative Party 1992–97', *British Journal of Politics and International Relations*, 4(2): 299–324.

Heppell, T. (2008a) *Choosing the Tory Leader: Conservative Party Leadership Elections from Heath to Cameron*, London: I. B. Tauris.

Heppell, T. (2008b) 'The Degenerative Tendencies of Long-Serving Governments . . . 1963 . . . 1996 . . . 2008?', *Parliamentary Affairs*, 61(4): 578–96.

Heppell, T. and Hill, M. (2005) 'Ideological Typologies of Contemporary British Conservatism', *Political Studies Review*, 3(3): 335–55.

Heppell, T. and Hill, M. (2008) 'The Conservative Party Leadership Election of 1997: An Analysis of the Voting Motivations of Conservative Parliamentarians', *British Politics*, 3(1): 63–91.

Heppell, T. and Hill, M. (2009) 'Transcending Thatcherism? Ideology and the Conservative Party Leadership Mandate of David Cameron', *Political Quarterly*, 80(3): 388–99.

Heppell, T. and Hill, M. (2010) 'The Voting Motivations of Conservative Parliamentarians in the Conservative Party Leadership Election of 2001', *Politics*, 30(1): 36–51.

Hickson, K. (ed.) (2005) *The Political Thought of the Conservative Party since 1945*, Basingstoke: Palgrave Macmillan.

Hitchens, Peter (1999) *The Abolition of Britain*, London: Quartet Books.

Howard, M. (2002) 'Speech to the Institute for Public Policy Research', 11 March.

Howard, M. (2003) 'We Must Look Forward, Not Back', speech announcing his candidature for the Conservative Party leadership at the Saatchi Gallery, London, 31 October.

Howard, M. (2004) *The British Dream*, speech to Policy Exchange, 9 February, London: Policy Exchange.

Howard, M. (2005) 'It's Time to Take a Stand', speech in Hastings, 23 April.

Hutton, W. (2008) 'Spend or Save? Free-marketeers and the Keynesians Row over the Road to Salvation', *The Observer*, 14 December.

ICM (2001) 'Business for Sterling/ICM Research European Survey January 2001', www.icmresearch.co.uk/pdfs/2001_january_business_for_sterling_euro_poll.pdf#search=%22euro%22.

IpsosMORI (2010) 'Issues Index: The Most Important Issues Facing Britain Today', accessed 7 January 2011, http://www.ipsos-mori.com/researchpublications/researcharchive/poll.aspx?oItemID=56&view=wide.

Jenkins, P. (1989) *Mrs. Thatcher's Revolution*, London: Pan Books.

Jessop, B. (2007) 'New Labour or The Normalization of Neo-liberalism?', *British Politics*, 2(2): 282–8.

Jessop, B., Bonnett, K., Bromley, S. and Ling, T. (1988) *Thatcherism: A Tale of Two Nations*, Cambridge: Polity Press.

Jones, G. (1997) '72 hours to save Union, says Major', *Daily Telegraph*, 29 April 1997, www.telegraph.co.uk/htmlContent.jhtml?html=/archive/1997/04/29/ne29.html.

Jones, G. (1999) 'Portillo: I was Gay in my Youth', *Daily Telegraph*, 9 September, www.telegraph.co.uk/htmlContent.jhtml?html=/archive/1999/09/09/nclrk409.html.

Jones, G. (2001) 'Two Weeks to Save the Pound, says Hague', *Daily Telegraph*, 22 June, www.telegraph.co.uk/news/main.jhtml?xml=/news/2001/05/26/neuro226.xml.

Joseph, K. (1976a) *Monetarism is not Enough*, London: Centre for Policy Studies.

Joseph, K. (1976b) *Stranded on the Middle Ground*, London: Centre for Policy Studies.

Joseph, K. (1979) *Solving the Union Problem is the Key to Britain's Recovery*, London: Centre for Policy Studies.

Kavanagh, D. (1997) *The Reordering of British Politics: Politics After Thatcher*, Oxford: Oxford University Press.

Kavanagh, D. and Butler, D. (2005) *The British General Election of 2005*, Basingstoke: Palgrave Macmillan.

Kavanagh, D. and Cowley, P. (2010) *The British General Election of 2010*, Basingstoke: Palgrave Macmillan.

Kelly, R. (2001) 'Conservatism under Hague: The Fatal Dilemma', *Political Quarterly*, 72(2): 197–203.

Kelly, R. (2002) 'The Party Didn't Work: Conservative Reorganisation and Electoral Failure', *Political Quarterly*, 73(1): 38–43.

Kelly, R. (2003) 'Organisational Reform and the Extra-parliamentary Party', in M. Garnett and P. Lynch (eds.), *The Conservatives in Crisis*, Manchester: Manchester University Press: 82–106.

Kenny, M. (1998) 'Review of *False Dawn* by John Gray', *Renewal*, 6(3): 84–8.

Kenny, M., English, R. and Hayton, R. (2008) *Beyond the Constitution: Englishness in a Post-devolved Britain*, London: Institute for Public Policy Research.

Kerr, P. (2007) 'Cameron Chameleon and the Current State of Britain's Consensus', *Parliamentary Affairs*, 60(1): 46–65.

King, A. (1975) 'Overload: Problems of Governing in the 1970s', *Political Studies*, 23(2): 284–96.

King, A. (1993) 'The Implications of One-party Government', in A. King (ed.), *Britain at the Polls, 1992*, Chatham, NJ: Chatham House Publishers: 223–48.

Kirby, J. (2009) 'From Broken Families to the Broken Society', *Political Quarterly*, 80(2): 243–7.

Kisby, B. (2010) 'The Big Society: Power to the People?', *Political Quarterly*, 81(4): 484–91.

Krieger, J. (1986) *Reagan, Thatcher and the Politics of Decline*, Cambridge: Polity.

Kruger, D. (2006) 'The Right Dialectic', *Prospect*, 126, September 2006: 32–7.

Kumar, K. (2000) 'Nation and Empire: English and British National Identity in Comparative Perspective', *Theory and Society*, 29: 575–608.

Kumar, K. (2003) *The Making of English National Identity*, Cambridge: Cambridge University Press.

Lamont, N. (1999) *In Office*, London: Little, Brown & Co.

Lansley, A. (2001) 'Conservative Party Strategy', in J. Bartle, S. Atkinson and R. Mortimer (eds.), *Political Communications: The General Election Campaign of 2001*, London: Frank Cass: 69–74.

Lansley, A. (2003) 'From Values to Policy: The Conservative Challenge', in M. Garnett and P. Lynch (eds.), *The Conservatives in Crisis*, Manchester: Manchester University Press: 221–8.

Layton-Henry, Z. (1986) 'Race and the Thatcher Government', in Z. Layton-Henry and P. B. Rich (eds.), *Race, Government and Politics in Britain*, Basingstoke: Macmillan: 73–99.

Leach, R. (2002) *Political Ideology in Britain*, Basingstoke: Palgrave.

Lee, S. (2009) 'Convergence, Critique and Divergence: The Development of Economic Policy under David Cameron', in S. Lee and M. Beech (eds.), *The Conservatives under David Cameron: Built to Last?*, Basingstoke: Palgrave Macmillan: 60–79.

Lee, S. and Beech, M. (eds.) (2009) *The Conservatives under David Cameron: Built to Last?*, Basingstoke: Palgrave Macmillan.

Lees-Marshment, J. (2001) *Political Marketing and British Political Parties: The Party's Just Begun*, Manchester: Manchester University Press.

Lees-Marshment, J. and Quayle, S. (2001) 'Empowering the Members or Marketing the Party? The Conservative Reforms of 1998', *Political Quarterly*, 72(2): 204–12.

Letwin, O. (2003) *The Neighbourly Society: Collected Speeches, 2001–3*, London, Centre for Policy Studies.

Letwin, S. (1992) *The Anatomy of Thatcherism*, London: Transaction Publishers.

Letwin, S. (1996) 'British Conservatism in the 1990s', in K. Minogue (ed.), *Conservative Realism: New Essays in Conservatism*, London: HarperCollins: 173–80.

Lilley, P. (1999) 'R. A. Butler Memorial Lecture', speech at the Carlton Club, London, 20 April, www.peterlilley.co.uk/speeches.php?action=show&id=16.

Lynch, P. (1999) *The Politics of Nationhood: Sovereignty, Britishness and Conservative Politics*, Basingstoke: Macmillan.

Lynch, P. (2009) 'The Conservatives and the European Union: The Lull before the Storm?', in S. Lee and M. Beech (eds.) *The Conservatives under David Cameron: Built to Last?*, Palgrave Macmillan: 187–207.

Lynch, P. and Whitaker, R. (2008), 'A Loveless Marriage: The Conservatives and the European People's Party', *Parliamentary Affairs* 61(1): 31–51.

Mandelson, P. (2007) 'The EU, Britain and Globalisation', speech at Hull University, 7 September, http://ec.europa.eu/commission_barroso/mandelson/speeches_articles/sppm166_en.htm.

McLean, I. and McMillan, A. (2003) 'The Distribution of Public Spending across the UK Regions', *Fiscal Studies*, 24(1): 45–71.

Mandler, P. (2006a) *The English National Character: The History of an Idea from Edmund Burke to Tony Blair*, New Haven and London: Yale University Press.

Mandler, P. (2006b) 'What is "National Identity"? Definitions and Applications in Modern British Historiography', *Modern Intellectual History*, 3(2): 271–97.

Marks, G. and Wilson, C. J. (2000) 'The Past in the Present: A Cleavage Theory of Party Response to European Integration', *British Journal of Political Science*, 30(3): 433–59.

Marquand, D. (1991) 'The Meaning of Major', in G. Smyth (ed.), *Can the Tories Lose?*, London: Lawrence & Wishart.

Marr, A. (2000) *The Day Britain Died*, London: Profile Books.

Marsh, D. (1995) 'Explaining "Thatcherite" Policies: Beyond Uni-dimensional Explanation', *Political Studies*, 43(4): 595–613.

Massow, I. (2000) 'Nightmare on Downing Street', *New Statesman*, 2 October, http://www.newstatesman.com/200010020010.

Montgomerie, T. (2007) 'Right on Tax', 17 August, www.guardian.co.uk/commentisfree/2007/aug/17/rightontax.

Morgan, K. (2001) *Britain since 1945: The Peoples' Peace*, Oxford: Oxford University Press.

MORI (2006b) 'Conservative Party Image', www.ipsos-mori.com/content/conservative-party-image.ashx.

MORI (2006c) 'Voting Intentions in Great Britain: 1979–present (all adults naming a party)', www.ipsos-mori.com/polls/trends/voting-all-trends.shtml.

MORI (2008a) 'Ipsos Mori Political Monitor: Long Term Trends: The Most Important Issues Facing Britain Today', www.ipsos-mori.com/content/turnout/the-most-important-issues-facing-britain-today.ashx.

MORI (2008b) 'Rivers of Blood Survey', 13 April, http://www.ipsos-mori.com/content/rivers-of-blood-survey.ashx.

MORI (2008c) 'Best Party on Key Issues – Asylum', http://www.ipsos-mori.com/content/turnout/best-party-on-key-issues-asylum.ashx.

MORI (2008d) 'Best Party on Key Issues – Crime/Law and Order', www.ipsos-mori.com/content/turnout/best-party-on-key-issues-law-and-order.ashx.

MORI (2008e) 'Best Party on Key Issues – Education', www.ipsos-mori.com/content/turnout/best-party-on-key-issues-education.ashx.

MORI (2008f) 'Best Party on Key Issues – Europe', www.ipsos-mori.com/content/turnout/best-party-on-key-issues-europe.ashx.

MORI (2008g) 'Best Party on Key Issues – Health Care', www.ipsos-mori.com/content/turnout/best-party-on-key-issues-health-care.ashx.

MORI (2008h) 'Best Party on Key Issues – Managing the Economy', www.ipsos-mori.com/content/turnout/best-party-on-key-issues-managing-the-economy.ashx.

Murphy, J. (2002) ' "Surprised and Delighted" Clarke Praises Duncan Smith', *Daily Telegraph*, 7 April, www.telegraph.co.uk/news/uknews/1390052/'Surprised-and-delighted'-Clarke-praises-Duncan-Smith.html.

Nadler, J. (2000) *William Hague: In His Own Right*, London: Politicos.

Nairn, T. (1981) *The Break-up of Britain*, London: New Left Books.

Norris, P. and Lovenduski, J. (2004) 'Why Parties Fail to Learn: Electoral Defeat, Selective Perception and British Party Politics', *Party Politics*, 10(1): 85–104.

Office for National Statistics (ONS) (2008) 'International Migration: Citizenship, Population Trends 131' (dataset), London: Office for National Statistics, www.statistics.gov.uk/STATBASE/ssdataset.asp?vlnk=9549.

Office for National Statistics (ONS) (2010) *Statistical Bulletin: Government Deficit and Debt under the Maastricht Treaty*, London: Office for National Statistics, 31 March.

O'Hara, K. (2005) *After Blair: Conservatism Beyond Thatcher*, Cambridge: Icon.

Oppermann, K. (2008) 'The Blair Government and Europe: The Policy of Containing the Salience of European Integration', *British Politics*, 3(2): 156–82.

Osborne, G. (2006) 'Stability before Tax Cuts', speech, 23 January.

Osborne, G. (2008) 'Recovery through Fiscal Responsibility', speech, 31 October.

Parkinson, Lord (2003) 'The Reform of the Conservative Party', in M. Garnett and P. Lynch (eds.), *The Conservatives in Crisis*, Manchester: Manchester University Press: 217–20.

Paxman, J. (1998) *The English: A Portrait of a People*, London: Michael Joseph.

Pilbeam, B. (2005) 'Social Morality', in K. Hickson (ed.), *The Political Thought of the Conservative Party since 1945*, Basingstoke: Palgrave Macmillan: 158–77.

Portillo, M. (1998) *Democratic Values and the Currency*, London: IEA.

Portillo, M. (2000a) 'Michael Portillo's Address to Conservative Conference 2000', www. michaelportillo.co.uk/speeches/speeches_shad/speech23p.htm.

Portillo, M. (2000b) 'Five Disciplines for Macro-economic Policy', 11 December, www. michaelportillo.co.uk/speeches/speeches_shad/speech26p.htm.

Portillo, M. (2005) 'Cameron Mania could be an Election too Soon', *Sunday Times*, 9 October.

Portillo, M. (2006) 'A Cunning Euro plot that could Bolster Cameron', *Sunday Times*, 11 June.

Portillo, M. (2007) 'Cameron's White Flag', *Sunday Times*, 24 June.

Portillo, M. (2008) 'The Lady's Not for Spurning', documentary programme, first broadcast 25 February, BBC4 television.

Preston, Paul W. (1994) 'The Dissolution of Britain?', *Political Quarterly*, 65(2): 191–202.

Quinn, T. (2008) 'The Conservative Party and the "Centre Ground" of British Politics', *Journal of Elections, Public Opinion and Parties*, 18(2): 179–99.

Ramsden, J. (1995) *The Age of Churchill and Eden 1940–1957*, London: Longman.

Ramsden, J. (1996) *The Winds of Change: Macmillan to Heath 1957–1975*, London: Longman.

Ramsden, J. (1998) *An Appetite for Power: The History of the Conservative Party*, London: HarperCollins.

Rawnsley, A. (2005) 'Focus: David Cameron Interview', *The Observer*, 18 December, www. guardian.co.uk/politics/2005/dec/18/conservatives.interviews.

Redwood, J. (1999) *The Death of Britain?*, Basingstoke: Macmillan.

Redwood, J. (2004) *Singing the Blues: The Once and Future Conservatives*, London: Politicos.

Redwood, J. and Wolfson, S. (2007) *Freeing Britain to Compete: Equipping the UK for Globalisation*, Submission to the Shadow Cabinet by the Economic Competitiveness Policy Group, London: Conservative Party.

Reeves, R. (2008) 'This is David Cameron', *Public Policy Research*, 15(2): 63–7.

Rich, P. B. (1998) 'Ethnic Politics and the Conservatives in the Post-Thatcher Era', in S. Saggar (ed.), *Race and British Electoral Politics*, London, Routledge: 96–116.

Ridley, N. (1992) *My Style of Government: The Thatcher Years*, London: Fontana.

Saggar, S. (2001) 'The Race Card, Again', *Parliamentary Affairs*, 54(4): 759–74.

Sanders, D., Clarke, H., Stewart, M. and Whiteley, P. (2001) 'The Economy and Voting', *Parliamentary Affairs*, 54: 789–802.

Scruton, R. (2000) *England: An Elegy*, London: Chatto & Windus.

Seawright, D. (2002) 'The Scottish Conservative and Unionist Party: The Lesser Spotted Tory?', paper presented to the 52nd Annual Political Studies Association Conference, University of Aberdeen, 5–7 April.

Seldon, A. (ed.) (1996) *How Tory Governments Fall*, London: Fontana.

Seldon, A. (2005) 'The Only Way To Win Now', *The Guardian*, 11 September, www. guardian.co.uk/politics/2005/sep/11/conservatives.toryleadership2005.

Seldon, A. and Ball, S. (eds.) (1994) *Conservative Century: The Conservative Party since 1900*, Oxford: Oxford University Press.

Seldon, A. and Snowdon, P. (2001) *A New Conservative Century?*, London: Centre for Policy Studies.

Seldon, A. and Snowdon, P. (2005a) 'The Conservative Party', in A. Seldon and D. Kavanagh (eds.), *The Blair Effect: 2001–5*, Cambridge: Cambridge University Press: 131–56.

Seldon, A. and Snowdon, P. (2005b) 'The Barren Years: 1997–2005', in S. Ball and A. Seldon (eds.), *Recovering Power: The Conservatives in Opposition since 1867*, Basingstoke: Palgrave Macmillan.

Seldon, A. and Snowdon, P. (2005c) 'The Conservative Campaign', *Parliamentary Affairs*, 58(4): 725–42.

Sky News (2006) 'Tory Leader's a Family Guy', 18 June, http://news.sky.com/skynews/article/0,,70131-13528800,00.html.

Smith, A. (1991) *National Identity*, London: Penguin.

Smith, M. J. (1999) *The Core Executive in Britain*, Basingstoke: Macmillan.

Smith, M. J. (1994) 'Understanding the "Politics of Catch-up": The Modernization of the Labour Party', *Political Studies*, 42(4): 708–15.

Smith, M. J. (2010) 'From Big Government to Big Society: Changing the State–Society Balance', *Parliamentary Affairs*, 63(4): 818–33.

Smyth, G. (ed.) (1991) *Can the Tories Lose?*, London: Lawrence & Wishart.

Snowdon, P. (2010) *Back from the Brink: The Inside Story of The Tory Resurrection*, London: Harper Press.

Social Justice Policy Group (SJPG) (2007) *Breakthrough Britain (Volume 1): Family Breakdown*, London: Social Justice Policy Group.

Somerville, W. (2007) *Immigration Under New Labour*, Bristol: Policy Press.

Stapleton, J. (2001) *Political Identities and Public Intellectuals in Britain since 1850*, Manchester: Manchester University Press.

Stoker, G. (2006) *Why Politics Matters: Making Democracy Work*, Basingstoke: Palgrave Macmillan.

Streeter, G. (ed.) (2002) *There is Such a Thing as Society*, London: Methuen.

Tax Reform Commission (TRC) (2006) *Tax Matters: Reforming the Tax System*, London: Tax Reform Commission (chaired by Lord Forsyth).

Taylor, A. J. (2005) 'Economic Statecraft', in K. Hickson (ed.), *The Political Thought of the Conservative Party since 1945*, Basingstoke: Palgrave Macmillan: 133–57.

Taylor, A. J. (2008) 'Preface', in T. Heppell, *Choosing the Tory Leader: Conservative Party Leadership Elections from Heath to Cameron*, London: I. B. Tauris.

Taylor, I. (2003) 'The Conservatives, 1997–2001: A Party in Crisis?', in M. Garnett and P. Lynch (eds.), *The Conservatives in Crisis*, Manchester: Manchester University Press: 229–47.

Tebbit, N. (2005) 'On the Inner Culture of the Tories', in S. Roy and J. Clarke (eds.), *Margaret Thatcher's Revolution: How it Happened and what it Meant*, London: Continuum: 12–24.

Tempest, M. (2003) 'Tory Member Ballot Scrapped', *The Guardian*, 6 November, www.guardian.co.uk/politics/2003/nov/06/conservatives.uk4.

Thatcher, M. (1978) 'TV Interview for Granada *World in Action* ("rather swamped")', 27 January, www.margaretthatcher.org/speeches/displaydocument.asp?docid=103485.

Thatcher, M. (1988) 'Speech to the College of Europe (The Bruges Speech)', 20 September, www.margaretthatcher.org/speeches/displaydocument.asp?docid=107332.

Thatcher, M. (1993) *The Downing Street Years*, London: HarperCollins.

Thatcher, M. (2002) *Statecraft: Strategies for a Changing World*, London: HarperCollins.

The Times (1998) 'Mods and Rockers', 6 July.

Thompson, H. (1996) *The British Conservative Government and the European Exchange Rate Mechanism, 1979–1994*, London: Pinter.

Tomlinson, J. (2000) *The Politics of Decline: Understanding Post-war Britain*. Harlow: Pearson Education.

Tory Diary (2006) 'Tim Yeo Questions David Cameron's Marriage Policy', 5 February, http://conservativehome.blogs.com/torydiary/2006/02/tim_yeo_questio.html.

Toynbee, P. (2007) 'This Broken Society Rhetoric Leaves Cameron Marooned', *The Guardian*, 10 July, www.guardian.co.uk/commentisfree/2007/jul/10/comment.politics.

Turner, J. (1999) 'The British Conservative Party in the Twentieth Century: From Beginning to End?', *Contemporary European History*, 8(2): 275–87.

Tyrie, A. (2001) *Back from the Brink*, London: Parliamentary Mainstream.

Waites, M. (2001) 'Regulation of Sexuality: Age of Consent, Section 28 and Sex Education', *Parliamentary Affairs*, 54(3): 495–508.

Walters, S. (2001) *Tory Wars: Conservatives in Crisis*, London: Politicos.

Weight, R. (2002) *Patriots: National Identity in Britain 1940–2000*, Basingstoke: Macmillan.

Wellings, B. (2007) 'Rump Britain: Englishness and Britishness, 1992–2001', *National Identities*, 9(4): 395–412.

Wheatcroft, G. (2005) *The Strange Death of Tory England*, London: Allen Lane.

Willetts, D. (1992) *Modern Conservatism*, London: Penguin.

Willetts, D. (1994) *Civic Conservatism*, London: Social Market Foundation.

Willetts, D. (1996) 'The Free Market and Civic Conservatism', in K. Minogue (ed.), *Conservative Realism: New Essays in Conservatism*, London: HarperCollins: 80–97.

Willetts, D. (1997) 'Conservatism Now', *Prospect*, 23 (October), www.prospect-magazine.co.uk/article_details.php?id=4466.

Willetts, D. (1998a) 'Conservative Renewal', *Political Quarterly*, 69(2): 110–17.

Willetts, D. (1998b) *Who Do We Think We Are?*, London: Centre for Policy Studies.

Willetts, D. (1999) 'Reviving Civic Conservatism', in R. Skidelsky (ed.), *The Social Market and the State*, London: Social Market Foundation.

Willetts, D. (2002) 'The New Contours of British Politics', in G. Streeter (ed.), *There is Such a Thing as Society*, London: Methuen: 52–67.

Willetts, D. (2005a) 'A New Conservatism for a New Century', speech to the Social Market Foundation, 2 June, www.davidwilletts.org.uk/record.jsp?type=speech&ID=53&sectionID=3.

Willetts, D. (2005b) 'A Tory Community', *Prospect*, 115 (October): 73–4.

Willetts, D. and Forsdyke, R. (1999) *After the Landslide: Learning the Lessons of 1906 and 1945*, London: Centre for Policy Studies.

Wilson, J. and Macaulay, M. (2007) 'Britain and Blair: The Ideological Legacy?', paper presented to the American Political Science Association annual meeting, 29 August.

Woolf, M. (2006) 'Cameron's gAy List', *The Independent on Sunday*, 5 February, www.independent.co.uk/news/uk/politics/camerons-gay-list-465633.html.

YouGov (2008) 'YouGov/Daily Telegraph Survey Results', 25 July 2008, www.yougov.com/uk/archives/pdf/DT080725%20full%20topline.pdf.

Young, H. (2002) 'Where America has Elected to go, No one will Follow', *The Guardian*, 7 November, www.guardian.co.uk/world/2002/nov/07/usa.comment.

Index

Note: 'n' after a page reference indicates the number of a note on that page

Lightning Source UK Ltd.
Milton Keynes UK
UKOW06f1958090616

275945UK00008B/57/P

9 781784 993894